Information Coordination

BCS Practitioner Series

Series editor: Ray Welland

Information Coordination

The Management of Information Models, Systems and Organizations

Richard Veryard

MA MSc MBA MBCS CEng

Prentice Hall

New York London Toronto Sydney Tokyo Singapore

First published 1994 by
Prentice Hall International (UK) Limited
Campus 400, Maylands Avenue
Hemel Hempstead,
Hertfordshire, HP2 7EZ
A division of
Simon & Schuster International Group

Typeset in 10/12pt Times
by Pentacor PLC

Printed and bound in Great Britain by
Redwood Books Ltd, Trowbridge, Wiltshire

Library of Congress Cataloging-in-Publication Data

Veryard, R. (Richard)
  Information coordination : the management of information models,
  systems, and organizations / Richard Veryard
      p.   cm. —— (BCS practitioner series)
  Includes bibliographical references and index.
  ISBN 0–13–099243–7
  1. Management information systems. 2. System design. I. Title.
  II. Series
  T58.6.V478 1994
  658.4'038'011—dc20   93–8848
                                                          CIP

British Library Cataloguing in Publication Data

A catalogue record for this book is available from
the British Library

ISBN 0–13–099243–7 (pbk)

---

1   2   3   4   5   98   97   96   95   94

Contents

Editorial preface

The aim of the BCS Practitioner Series is to produce books that are relevant for practising computer professionals across the whole spectrum of Information Technology activities. We want to encourage practitioners to share their practical experience of methods and applications with fellow professionals. We also seek to disseminate information in a form that is suitable for the practitioner who often has only limited time to read widely within a new subject area or to assimilate research findings.

The role of the BCS is to provide advice on the suitability of books for the Series, via the Editorial Panel, and to provide a pool of potential authors upon which we can draw. Our objective is that this Series will reinforce the drive within the BCS to increase professional standards in IT. The other partners in this venture, Prentice Hall, provide the publishing expertise and international marketing capabilities of a leading publisher in the computing field.

The response when we set up the Series was extremely encouraging. However, the success of the Series depends on there being practitioners who want to learn as well as those who feel they have something to offer! The Series is under continual development and we are always looking for ideas for new topics and feedback on how to further improve the usefulness of the Series. If you are interested in writing for the Series then please contact us.

Maximizing the value of corporate data depends upon being able to manage information models both within and between businesses. A centralized information model is not appropriate for many organizations. Therefore, this book takes the approach that multiple information models exist, and the differences and links between them have to be managed. Richard Veryard has already produced a comprehensive book on the production of information models and this book moves on to discuss and illustrate the uses of information models.

Ray Welland
Computing Science Department, University of Glasgow

Editorial Panel Members
Frank Bott (UCW, Aberystwyth), Dermot Browne (KPMG Management Consulting), Nic Holt (ICL), Trevor King (Praxis Systems Plc), Tom Lake (GLOSSA), Kathy Spurr (Analysis and Design Consultants), Mario Wolczko (University of Manchester)

Author's preface

Why read this book? Why is coordination a fit topic for study and thought by students, practitioners and managers of information engineering and software engineering?

During the 1970s, the problems of piecemeal information systems started to become apparent, and the notion of corporate data-sharing became increasingly attractive. Since then, concepts of business organization and strategy have advanced considerably, and the technological opportunities have moved even further, yet many information specialists seem to be still battling with the agenda of the 1970s, still trying to implement corporate data-sharing through centralized hierarchical control of both logical information structures and physical technology. This book challenges the old visions, and offers some alternative approaches to coordination, at the same time more pragmatic than the old certainties, and better geared to the business pressures of the 1990s (as breathlessly documented by such management gurus as Tom Peters).

At the technical level, this book should be regarded as a sequel to my *Information Modelling: Practical Guidance* (Hemel Hempstead: Prentice Hall, 1992). It contains a practical approach to the management of information models, excluded from the previous book for reasons of space and time. This will be of particular interest to users of Computer-Aided Software Engineering (CASE) tools, although the principles can, if necesssary, also be adopted without the automated support provided by such tools. In order to explain what to do with information models, it is necessary to discuss issues of integration and coordination, information strategy and planning, etc. This topic is often referred to as Development Coordination, but it is in fact much broader than systems development, and covers all aspects of information management.

Since the approach will be new to most readers, and surprising to many, I have wherever possible included evidence of how it works in practice, both from the direct experience of myself and my colleagues at JMA and Texas Instruments, and also from the published literature. I have included arguments and analogies from other fields, including town planning and architecture, from which I believe information engineers have much to learn. I have also included many examples of the things that can go wrong. Readers without much commercial or industrial experience may find some of these examples hard to believe. On the other hand, readers who work within large organizations may think they recognize their own projects. When I described a coordination failure to a database expert recently, he was delighted that he had (as he thought) seen through the anonymity of my case study. Aha, he said, I know which company you are talking about. He named his company, a large American-owned multinational. He was wrong.

Coordination is currently an area both of intensive theoretical speculation and of practical research and development. The book attempts to distil and explain practical guidelines for information management, both from this ongoing research and from recent field experience with CASE tools and methods. The solutions are therefore provisional, and may well be bettered by future tools and methods. However, the practitioner faced with today's problems cannot wait for future solutions. This is not a research thesis, with perfect solutions to yesterday's problems. In the future, more theoretical treatments of coordination will be required, but this will be for others to provide. My book is offered as a snapshot of the state-of-the-art, a practical approach to achieving enterprise coordination through planning and managing information models. The primary purpose of the book is to guide, and to provoke ideas.

London   Richard Veryard
Easter 1993

Acknowledgements

Many of the ideas in this book have come from discussions with countless colleagues at JMA Information Engineering and Texas Instruments over the past couple of years. I must particularly mention Alan Biddlecombe, Charles Passmore, Clive Mabey, Kala Patel, Liz Pearcey, Michael Mills and Paul St Clair Terry.

My experience with development coordination has been gained with several IEF user organizations. Many thanks to my friends in Bracknell, Brighton, Basingstoke, Bilbao and elsewhere.

Especial thanks to Charles Passmore, Dip Ganguli, Garry Taylor, James Macfarlane, Liz Pearcey, Phil Voke, Ray Welland and Richard Gilyead for their detailed and valuable comments on earlier drafts of the manuscript.

For the editorial and production work, thanks to Viki Williams, Jill Birch and their colleagues at Prentice Hall.

1 Introduction

1.1 Introduction

This book is about coordination at three levels: the enterprise or organization, the computerized information systems that support the enterprise, and (in between) the information models of the enterprise. As we shall see, these models both belong to the enterprise and also represent the enterprise (or parts of it). Furthermore, when they have been used to plan and design computerized information systems, they represent the structure of these systems.

The structure of the book is as follows: after this introductory chapter, Chapter 2 describes some basic concepts of coordination, both at the enterprise level and at the technical level. Chapters 3 and 4 analyse how the various models of coordination influence the way we plan and scope systems development projects. Chapter 5 looks at the coordination of these projects once under way, while Chapter 6 looks at the coordination of the developed systems themselves. Chapter 7 provides some technical considerations for model management within a CASE environment. Finally, Chapter 8 examines the management of coordination.

The structure of this chapter is as follows: after informally considering some of the issues of enterprise-level coordination, we look at Business Process Reengineering, which is a formal approach to coordinating total business processes. Then we introduce some of the difficulties of information systems development, particularly within large organizations, to set the scene for the remainder of the book.

1.2 Tension and information systems

1.2.1 Introduction

Let us first consider coordination between organizations and within a single organization, as it affects and is affected by the information systems (both formal and informal) used by the organization(s).

Tight, taut, tense – these are ambivalent words. Individuals and organizations can experience tension, either permanently or temporarily. According to Pugh:[1]

> Organizations are coalitions of interest groups in tension. Management vs workers, productions vs sales, accounting vs R&D, Union A vs Union B, head office vs production location. . . . The resultant organization is a particular balance of forces which has been hammered out over a period of time and which is continually subject to minor modifications through hierarchically initiated adjustments and cross-group negotiations.

Tension can be a valuable component of the **learning organization**.[2] This section is about the beneficial role of tension in the modern corporation, and shows how information systems can help or hinder this role, sometimes affecting tension in useful ways, sometimes in less useful ways.[3]

1.2.2 Conflict and tension

- 'If only we could knock some sense into the X department . . .'
- 'The Y department is always messing up whatever we do . . .'
- 'How can we stop those idiots from the Z department from . . .'

Conflict is endemic in all organizations, large and small. It manifests itself in two ways. Either in personal clashes between staff and managers of the respective departments, whose communications become formal, strained, unfriendly, even openly hostile. Or in political feuding, in which departments manoeuvre to take resources and power from one another. In some organizations, breakdowns in communication and/or political wars between departments divert significant amounts of time and energy from the real mission, from the corporate bottom line. Such an organization is unhealthy.

However, conflict does not always need to be unhealthy. Healthy conflict and tension within an organization can be a stimulant, working for creativity and against stagnation. John Dewey wrote:

> Conflict is the gadfly of thought. It stirs us to observation and memory. It instigates to invention. It shocks us out of sheeplike passivity, and sets us at noting and contriving. . . . Conflict is a *sine qua non* of reflection and ingenuity.[4]

Many organizations thrive on tension, which may have evolved naturally or may have been deliberately fostered by past or present management. The concern here is not with competition between parallel departments, such as regional sales offices vying to outperform each other, but with situations where two or more departments must work together, with conflicting objectives. For example, one department may provide a service for another department, or two departments may need to collaborate in some decision-making process. Often the departments involved will have different performance measures, so that a gain to one department will often equate to a loss to another department, regardless of the effect on the whole company. It may be both necessary and sufficient, for a department to achieve its targets, to obtain or retain advantages from other departments. This tempts staff and managers to focus their attention on the rival departments, rather than on the competitive socio-political environment in which the organization operates.

There are a number of examples. Many, perhaps most, manufacturing companies have conflict between sales and marketing, and production. In simplistic terms, sales tends to make more promises to the customers than production can keep up with. Perhaps production wants to manufacture as small a range of products as possible, to keep costs down, while sales wants to offer a wider range of products, to increase revenue. This tension, if kept within reasonable limits, is normal and healthy. It ensures that the company is focused on producing the goods and services that its customers want, at an economic price.

Another common source of conflict is between head office and local offices. For example, in one wholesale distribution company, the Alpha Corporation, the central purchasing department had the responsibility of negotiating rock-bottom prices for the supply of goods. But it was the warehouses that bore the brunt of late deliveries, inefficient inventory levels and poor quality. The warehouses preferred to buy from local firms, even at slightly higher cost, if it meant they could reduce inventory levels without risking shortages. In this particular company a compromise was worked out, allowing the warehouses to blacklist suppliers that had failed to meet delivery standards. However, it was felt by all parties that this was not an ideal solution.

Another simple illustration of conflict between two departments – purchasing and production – was found in the Beta Corporation, a medium-sized manufacturing firm. Purchasing performance is measured by the purchase price of materials. Production performance is affected by the quality of materials; poor quality results in high wastage, reduces productivity, can damage equipment, and has other indirect consequences. In simple terms, purchasing wants to buy the cheapest materials; production wants to use the highest quality materials; they both have to compromise, to negotiate.

The best possible quality level for Beta Corporation as a whole depends on a perfect balance (or compromise) between the purchase costs of higher-quality materials and the production risks of lower-quality materials. However, neither department was in a position to judge this perfect balance, hence the conflict.

The bureaucratic way of dealing with such conflict is to develop a fixed standard or procedure. In a bureaucratic organization, the best available approach is to conduct an 'impartial' study to set the best possible quality level (according to some standard to be determined), and then instruct both departments to stick to this level. In other words, purchasing must achieve a fixed minimum quality standard, and production must plan to work with that level of quality. To reduce the manifestation of conflict, it will be made as difficult as possible to change the standard once it has been defined.

The trouble with a bureaucratic standard is that it is fixed. But the best possible quality level may change over time, thanks to new technology, improved techniques and equipment, substitute materials, changes in the capital/labour cost ratio, and many other factors. Purchasing has a trade-off between cost and quality, in which higher quality probably involves higher cost (Figure 1.1). Production has a trade-off in which higher quality probably involves lower cost (Figure 1.2). The combined cost curve is likely to be a complicated shape. Thus the graph in Figure 1.3 is the sum of the graphs in Figures 1.1 and 1.2.

The best possible quality level can be seen from the combined trade-off graph (Figure 1.3): it is the level corresponding to the lowest cost. But if either department can improve its trade-off curve, the combined curve will be altered, and therefore the best possible point will shift. In the example shown, the best possible quality level is A, but it would only take a very small shift in either the

Figure 1.1
Purchasing trade-off

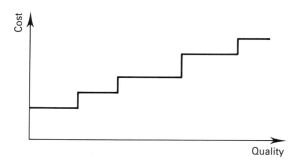

Figure 1.2
Production trade-off

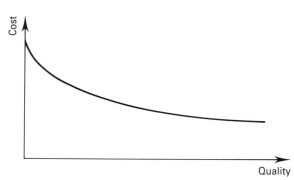

Figure 1.3
Combined trade-off

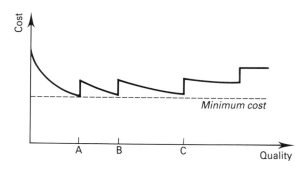

purchasing or the production curve for the best possible quality level to jump to B
or C.

Another complication is that quality is probably not a simple linear property of
the materials, but has several aspects or dimensions. So there may be some
aspects of quality that can be sacrificed more easily than others. For example, in
the Beta Corporation, the quality variables included width tolerances, stress
tolerances, and variations in surface texture. Instead of a two-dimensional trade-
off curve, it would be logically more correct, but far more complicated, to have an
n-dimensional 'curve'. In other words, a mathematical model showing how cost
depends on simultaneous calculation of several independent variables. Such
optimizations are practically impossible to calculate without a computer.

In negotiation jargon, a solution that is better for both parties than the current solution is known vulgarly as a 'win-win', or (more technically) non-zero-sum.[5] Bureaucratic procedures are not good at finding such win-win improvements.

The opposite of a bureaucracy is an 'adhocracy'.[6] In an adhocracy, the purchasing and production departments would engage in a dialogue to determine an appropriate quality level from one day to the next. The responsibility for different elements of the cost is likely to be much less rigidly divided between the two departments. Some joint accountability might be appropriate, to manage the total cost/quality trade-off for the best interests of the whole company.

More complex examples can be found, where more than two departments are involved, or where delay and uncertainty are introduced into the negotiations. Consider a large US consumer credit organization, the Gamma Corporation. One of the measures of performance is the level of bad debts, currently running at some $60M a year. Among the factors influencing the level of bad debts are the criteria used to determine the credit risk of a prospective debtor, the methods used to win new business, and the methods used for collecting delinquent repayments.

The best possible level of bad debt is not zero, because it is impossible to predict with certainty which customers might default. Therefore, if the Gamma Corporation had no bad debts at all, this would signify that it had acted with excessive caution, and turned away too much business. There is potential for conflict between the Marketing department, responsible for expanding the credit base, and the Financial Operations department, responsible for collecting the debts. However, what the Marketing department does this year will not affect the level of bad debts until next year at the earliest. This is because a debt is only defined as bad after the debtor has consistently failed to pay up, which for the Gamma Corporation must be at least several months after he has been allowed credit. The two departments must therefore negotiate without having all the facts. Which department is responsible for what proportion of the bad debts? What is the best possible point of credit risk, at which the increase in profit exactly balances the increase in bad debt? It is for negotiation between the two departments to determine where this point lies, and then to agree dynamic targets for each to achieve this.

1.2.3 Information systems

In the past, information systems techniques were geared to the computerization of bureaucracies rather than adhocracies. Many computer systems analysts will assume that every decision is the responsibility of a single department, with information being input from other departments where needed. The idea of corporate-shared data has become fashionable. Each department should have easy access to other departments' data, because information is a corporate resource, rather than belonging to a single department. Yet few organizations have made much progress in sharing the interpretation of data, and sharing the decisions made using the interpretations. One of the management techniques of successful adhocracies is known as MBWA ('management by walking around').[7] Where a company is too large or too geographically distributed for the managers to wander around physically, it will be necessary to supplement face-to-face communication with some form of Information Technology. Few companies have installed computerized information systems or office automation systems that come anywhere near the informality and serendipity of communication that can be achieved by wandering around.

An information system may be like an apartment, which we share reluctantly even with those we get along with.

But an information system is any set of procedures for the systematic processing of information, whether on a large corporate mainframe computer with shared databases and files, or on small personal computers (PCs) which may be stand-alone or networked. There are often complex negotiation and optimization problems involving several departments. Few companies are able to make full use of computerized information systems to address these issues. It is technically easier to build a simple interface between two departments, consisting of a single fixed standard quality, than to embark on a complex multi-user decision-support system. That does not mean that the technically simpler solution is the correct one. How can such systems be used to control tension between departments, in an intelligent and useful way, rather than requiring the conflict to be resolved and eliminated in the name of 'rationalization'?

In the Beta Corporation, a computer system was implemented as follows. The purchasing department was given a revised objective, not just to minimize the actual purchasing cost of the materials but to minimize the cost curve over a range of possible quality levels. In other words, they are rewarded for negotiating a low price for quality levels Q1, Q2, Q3 and Q4, even if the purchased materials are only at quality levels Q2 and Q3. Similarly, the production department was required to minimize wastage and other costs over the same range of quality levels. The managers' bonus depends on achieving a good average of hypothetical costs across the whole range of possible quality levels. The averages are weighted, so that more attention will be devoted to likely than to unlikely quality levels. The computer system is used in 'what-if' mode to estimate hypothetical· costs, calculate the averages, and recommend the best possible point at any given time.

Negotiation between purchasing and the alternative suppliers refers explicitly to these quality levels. This gives purchasing the flexibility to switch from one quality standard to another, either by changing the supplier or by exercising a quality/price trade-off option built into the supply contract. Meanwhile, production is motivated to seek ways of improving the manufacturing process, to allow them to accept cheaper materials without adding too much to wastage costs or compromising on the quality of the finished product.

In phase one of this project, the quality and selling price of the finished product were assumed to be fixed. It is envisaged, however, that the same opportunity for negotiated flexibility exists here as in the quality and buying price of the raw materials. Based on the success of phase one, the same concept may be extended to all interdepartmental relations within the Beta Corporation.

In the Gamma Corporation, the requirement was to work out a shared bad debt projection model, which would allow the relevant managers to determine the best possible level of credit risk, to maximize revenue and optimize bad debt levels. Note that the model would include factors outside the control of the Gamma Corporation, such as the prevailing level of unemployment. Already, some of the responsible managers had developed private computer models, using complex spreadsheets. But these models remained private, inaccessible except to their creators. Therefore nobody understood or trusted another manager's predictions or analysis. What was needed was an integration of these models into a shared model, which would be accessible (intellectually as well as operationally) to all the managers involved.

What about the Alpha Corporation? What they should have done is implemented a shared accounting system, so that the costs of poor delivery could be shared between the warehouse and the central purchasing department, and the benefits of reduced inventory levels too. The information system would have two business benefits. First, to allow the managers to control their work and their decisions against more complex, and thus more accurate, parameters than before. Second, to facilitate the communications between head office and the warehouses, so that decisions could be made on the fullest available information.

In this, as in the other examples, the computer serves as a kind of referee, helping to guarantee fair play between the rival departments. Clearly there are some important considerations for the people implementing such systems, to make sure the computer is perceived as a fair adjudicator. This is not always easy, sometimes not even possible, yet possible sometimes.

1.2.4 Reducing tension and complexity

One can easily have too much of a good thing. Although a certain amount of conflict and tension can be healthy, double that amount can cause personal stress and interpersonal strife. Just as IT can be used to preserve or increase healthy tension within an organization, it can also be used to decrease it where this is useful for the organization. Performance measures for given organization units can be defined so that they are unaffected by actions elsewhere, and so that managers can focus on what they can directly control.

For example, the accounting principle of **standard costing** is used to achieve this goal. The performance of a manager depends on the quantity of resources (including labour) used to provide some products or services. Since, in a large organization, the individual manager is not able to influence the price at which raw materials are purchased, or the salary rates of staff, it is common practice to cross-charge not at the actual cost to the enterprise, but at a notional standard cost. This means that fluctuations (known to accountants as **variances**), can be directly attributed to the manager responsible. If the cost of raw materials absorbed by production is higher than expected, this variance may be analysed into two parts: price variance (i.e. that resulting from a higher price paid per unit) and usage variance (i.e. that resulting from having used a greater number of units). Operational efficiency is based on usage variance; purchasing performance is measured on price variance. Meanwhile, customer profitability may be measured according to standard costs rather than actual costs. Standard costing is a mechanism for insulating the performance of one part of the organization from the influence of other parts of the organization.

However, the mechanism of standard costing has its drawbacks as well. In some organizations, standard costs may be difficult to set, and even more difficult to alter. Its handling of intangibles and hidden costs may be vulnerable to criticism. The point here is merely that this is a possible and practical mechanism, used within many companies, for decoupling the management of separate parts of the business.

1.2.5 Summary

The ambition of IT is to make organizations more effective and more creative.

Conflict in organizations does not always have to be eliminated, but can be managed by a judicious application of Information Technology (IT). IT is neutral: it can be used to increase, decrease or preserve the level of complexity and tension in an organization. If deployed unthinkingly, it may have an unpredicted and excessive effect on complexity and tension, either eliminating it altogether and causing inefficiency and stagnation, or increasing it wildly and causing too much complexity and hostility. If deployed wisely, in other words, deployed to serve the organization as a complex system of interacting people and activities, it may help direct the energies of the organization towards constructive and creative business ends.

1.3 Business process reengineering

1.3.1 Introduction

In the previous section, we looked at the possible benefits of maintaining some degree of tension within an enterprise. The goal of IT is not to eliminate tension, but to support what the organization requires. Our examples in that section were localized. Much interest is now focused on the needs of the organization as a whole, and of reengineering the enterprise and its processes. The concept of **Business Process Reengineering (BPR)** is usually credited to Michael Hammer.[8] (See Figure 1.4.)

BPR involves cross-functional modelling of business activities using diagrams and metrics to record what a business does, how processes are performed, including cost and value-added. Value chain analysis provides optimization of the business process model from which a change management plan may be constructed.

1.3.2 Role of IT

BPR provides a powerful incentive towards integrating computer systems, often because the benefits of BPR can only be achieved when the entire business process is automated.

IT therefore makes possible the reductions in business cycle-time and cost, and the improvements in quality, that BPR promises (see Box 1.1.). This is a key

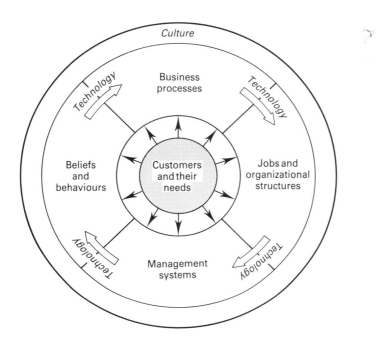

Figure 1.4
The cycle of business
process improvement
(*Adapted from
Michael Hammer's
reengineering
diamond*)

- Faster access to current information
- Improved correctness/consistency of information
- Broader access to information
- Elimination of physical information flows and transcriptions
- Elimination of unnecessary verification tasks
- Automation of manual tasks

Box 1.1
How Information
Technology supports
BPR
(*Thanks to Clive
Mabey*)

motivating reason for information coordination. However, there are two alternative technical solutions: the data-driven approach and the user-driven approach. We shall consider each of these in turn.

1.3.3 Data-driven integration

Let us start with a typical situation in a large company. A single business process is supported by a series of stand-alone computer systems, with limited or no interfacing between them. A complete view of the process is only possible by looking at all the separate systems, and putting information together manually (see Figure 1.5).

The traditional IT answer to this situation was to throw all the existing systems away, and replace them with a single homogeneous system, installed on a single corporate database. All information about the business process chain could then be obtained from this database (see Figure 1.6).

Figure 1.5
Process chain
supported by stand-
alone systems

Figure 1.6
Process chain
supported by central
(host) computing

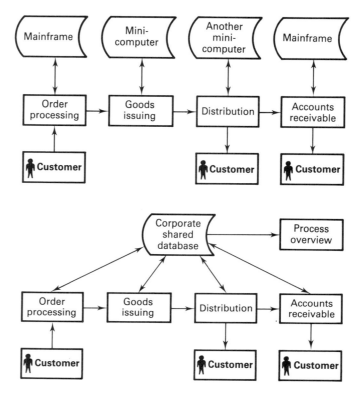

This traditional answer typically led to the kind of over-large project discussed earlier in the chapter. Transition from the existing systems to the new system would often be expensive and high risk.

1.3.4 User-driven integration

Client-server technology offers an alternative way of integrating the process chain. Instead of integrating on the database, it is possible to integrate on the desktop. The process owner, with an intelligent terminal (the 'client') can access information from a number of different sources (the 'servers'), which can be on a variety of technical platforms (see Figure 1.7).

1.3.5 Summary

One of the main forces for information coordination is the need to integrate business process chains. This potentially brings significant business benefits, such as increased quality and reduced cycle-time. However, there is more than one technical solution to this coordination. We shall return in later chapters to these technical opportunities.

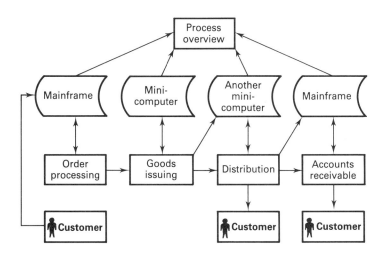

Figure 1.7
Process chain
supported by legacy
systems with desk-top
integration

1.4 Information model coordination

Information models are produced for several purposes within Information Engineering, and other systems and software methodologies. These purposes include the planning, development and clarification of information systems. The concepts and techniques for the production of an information model are described in the companion volume: *Information Modelling: Practical guidance*. This book is about the use of information throughout an organization.

Each information model has a particular scope, purpose and perspective. Since even the smallest enterprise has multiple purposes, with different areas of interest, it will potentially have many different information models. Some of these models will be explicitly documented; others will be implied by the data structure of given systems, or by the procedures and customs of the management team.

The differences between these models should reflect differences in scope, perspective and purpose. Moreover, these differences should reflect real differences between/within the organizations that manage and use the information systems. Or they should reflect real differences between/within the projects that design and develop these systems. This is because an information model expresses the structure and intentions of an organization, project or system. These differences demand coordination, which is the subject of this book.

Coordination of information models is really about coordination of the organizations, projects and systems. Coordination means identifying the differences, and determining which ones signify real contradictions, and which ones are trivial, illusory or temporary. It means eliminating certain types of contradiction, and tolerating others.

Some people argue against the multiplicity of information models. They do not deny that many different models exist in a typical information systems department (either explicit or implicit). But they argue that this is undesirable, and that information management should work towards a single global information model

Most organizations have legacy systems - old-fashioned computer applications they cannot easily discard.
Within these systems there may be much that is still of value.
Some organizations also have legacy management teams.

for the entire enterprise. In this book, we take a sceptical view of this goal. Some convergence is certainly worth striving for, but total convergence may not always be feasible.

However, even the proponents of total convergence and enterprise-wide information models can cite few, if any, organizations that have yet reached this goal. Therefore they need interim techniques to manage multiple models in the short term. This book describes techniques for the management of models, and of the differences and links between models. It also describes strategies for reducing the total number of models. These techniques and strategies will be of use to practitioners on both sides of this debate. The debate is not about how to climb the mountain, but where to pitch camp.

This chapter sets the scene for the book, by introducing some of the goals and difficulties of information coordination.

1.4.1 Goals of information coordination

Everyone preaches integration. It is a magic word. Computer manufacturers and software vendors boast how integrated, or how easy to integrate, their systems are. Writers bemoan the lack of integration; managers blame various things on the lack of integration. Like many magic words, 'integration' is a hopelessly ambiguous word. Sometimes integration appears as an end in itself, sometimes as a means to an end outside itself. Within information systems, there seem to be three main themes:

1. Building and implementing complex information systems (or suites of systems).
2. Integrating (i.e. consolidating) information and services from different sources.
3. Integrating business operations and support organizations with the aid of information and systems.

Some engineers may describe a system (consisting of several subsystems or modules) as integrated if it displays certain external behavioural properties (**blackbox integration**), while others may only describe a system as integrated if its internal construction satisfies certain properties (**whitebox integration**). What are these properties? Are there any reliable design guidelines for the designer who hopes to achieve blackbox integration with or without whitebox integration? We shall need to return to these questions later. Meanwhile, until we understand the concept of integration better, let us talk not about integration as such, but about the need to manage and use information systems in a coordinated way.

1.4.2 Difficulties of coordination

Everyone pays lip service to coordination. But if everybody really values coordination, then why is it not painless? There must be forces acting against it, which explain why people and projects 'do their own thing'. To coordinate projects

and systems usefully, we need to understand these forces. Put very simply, there
are three main forces: *working against coord*

1.	Technical complexity	Solutions to coordination problems are tricky, often inelegant, and require patience and cleverness. Systems developers and other engineers do not always have enough motivation and stamina to persist until a good solution is found.
2.	Management complexity	Awaiting solutions to coordination problems endangers the budgets and timescales of individual projects. Project managers therefore prefer to skimp on coordination in order to retain maximum control over the project. This increases the perceived probability that budgets and deadlines will be achieved.
3.	Conflict between users	The interests of different users often conflict. It is a political issue: to confront or not to confront. Some managers may want to avoid battles with rival departments, and therefore see the need to frustrate coordination efforts.

We have already seen examples of these forces in this chapter, and we shall
discuss techniques for dealing with them throughout the book.

Struggling against these forces will entail cost, which we may attempt to
measure in financial or other terms. To deal with these forces, therefore, we shall
need to acknowledge (and attempt to measure) the costs of coordination. We shall
then be in a better position to balance these costs against the (measurable) benefits
of coordination.

1.4.3 Information modelling – some definitions

This section provides a very brief summary of the concepts, principles and context
of information modelling. If you have read my previous book, you may regard this
as revision, or skip it altogether.

A model is a representation of the structure of information within an organization or part of an organization. It has a **scope**, whose exact boundaries are often
difficult to establish. It may represent either the present structure of business and
computer systems, or a desired future structure.

The modelling activity (usually called **analysis**) describes an area as a set of
constructs, which are named, defined and interrelated in a standard way. This activity is often seen as a process of **discovery** of pre-existing facts, but it is more useful
to see it as a process of **negotiation**: developing a consensus between different
stakeholders within the area. It is therefore important to be aware of the **perspective**
of a model: i.e. which stakeholders are included. (For example, the accountants'
view of an area is likely to be rather different from the engineers' view.)

The most common representation approach uses three main constructs to represent the area to be modelled: **entities**, **relationships** and **attributes**. This is the approach described in the previous book. Other possible approaches include **relational** models, and **object-oriented** models. Although the examples given in this book will mostly be entity-relationship-attribute models, the principles of coordination can be applied just as well to other models.

Having produced an information model, it can be used in many different ways. The intended **purpose** of a model influences its focus, and the appropriate style and detail. Some possible purposes include:

- To plan portfolios of computer-based information systems.
- To design, implement and maintain computer-based information systems.
- To evaluate existing systems (including commercial packages) for the degree of fit with the structure of the requirements.

Both the production and the use of an information model may be supported by a software tool. These tools are known as **Computer-Assisted Software Engineering** (**CASE**) tools. There are hundreds of CASE tools available, most of which only support specific portions of the software development lifecycle.

A handful of CASE tools support the whole life cycle, and support multi-project environments. These tools are usually centred around a database of models, known as an **encyclopedia** or **dictionary** or **repository**. (In this book, we shall use the term encyclopedia.) These are known as **Integrated CASE** (**I-CASE**) tools. These tools are of particular interest for readers of this book because they provide some intra-project and inter-project coordination facilities. Users of other CASE tools may need to carry out these coordination activities manually, or link several tools together to achieve the same level of automation.

Just as databases allow for data sharing between users, encyclopedias allow for metadata sharing between system developers and other information engineers. Many of the principles of database management also apply to encyclopedia management. In particular, the principle that each fact should be captured once, and any redundancy should be carefully controlled. Whereas the facts stored in the corporate database are facts about business objects and events, the facts stored in the encyclopedia are facts about business rules and systems. The encyclopedia is usually maintained on a host computer or server, using a relational database management system (DMBS); this itself may sometimes be one of the largest database applications in the company.

An information system may be like the Channel Tunnel, requiring some coordination between the two sides to be completed and successfully used, but which will itself greatly increase communications between the two sides.

To summarize, the three crucial properties of a model are its scope, perspective and purpose. We cannot coordinate models without knowing these properties: I shall try to demonstrate this claim through the book.

1.5 Complex systems development

1.5.1 Introduction

The first theme of coordination is building and implementing complex information systems (or suites of systems). An enterprise may commission or undertake system

	Large projects	Small projects
Characteristics	Integrated requirements based on large data model. (More than 200 entity types.)	Isolated requirements, based on small data model. (Fewer than 30 entity types.)
Potential Advantages	Financial benefit of scope Data sharing High reuse	Quick delivery Low risk
Potential Disadvantages	High risk Many failures 'Delusion of grandeur' False promises, System may be obsolete before delivery Monolithic block Moving target	Splintered, partial solutions Chaotic No data sharing Low consistency or coordination Poor data definitions Incomplete (or zero) business benefit

Box 1.2
Spectrum of large and small projects
(*Thanks to Michael Mills*)

development projects, and may also need to maintain and enhance existing systems. Implementation can be at least as difficult to coordinate as development and maintenance. This section carries out a preliminary exploration of these areas.

1.5.2 *Large development projects and programmes*

First let us put on one side the differences between large development projects and programmes. For the purposes of this chapter, we shall consider a development programme to be like a large project, only larger. A programme typically consists of several projects, with independent project managers and project schedules, but with some mechanism for coordinating between the projects. What is of more interest here are the differences between large development programmes or projects and small isolated projects (see Box 1.2).

The table should be regarded not as a strict alternative between small and large projects, but as defining the two ends of a spectrum. Obviously there are many intermediate possibilities. It would be good to establish a sensible pragmatic balance, which avoids the worst features of each extreme. However, there have been some projects that have managed to *combine* the worst features of each extreme, achieving incoherence and fragmentation even within a single model. (A **splintered monolith**!)

This concept may seem paradoxical, especially to those that have not experienced it directly. It happens because large models are typically produced by several analysts, who may not understand one another's work. (Imagine reading a novel in which each chapter was written by a different author.) Or because a large model is typically produced over a long period of time; if it is poorly documented, it may include inadvertent overlaps and gaps. Or because a large model is produced by forcibly merging two or more smaller models, without first reconciling differences in terminology or structure. These are all sadly familiar phenomena.

When models reach a certain size, even the most experienced analysts with the most sophisticated tools may experience insurmountable difficulties. One information model, for a very high-profile project in an organization brimming with expertise, grew to around 3,500 entity types. The project has not been a success.

The problems of large and small projects can be seen as problems of coordination. In large projects, the problems are mostly to do with **intra-project** coordination (i.e. internal coordination, within the project itself.) In small projects, the problems are mostly to do with **inter-project** coordination (i.e. external coordination, between the project and other projects and systems). However, even small projects may have serious internal coordination problems, and large projects will almost always have serious external coordination problems.

In a large multinational company, a major high-profile systems development project was divided, for political reasons, between Europe and America. This caused enormous coordination difficulties, not so much because of the geographical distance – team members and managers at various levels were constantly travelling from one project location to another – but the fact that the two halves of the project were in different time zones. Negotiation about data definitions (and everything else) took place over telephone conference calls. There was a 30-minute time window each day when the American team members had only just arrived in their office, and the European team members were impatient to go home for the evening.

Coordination over time is a key problem. Projects disband leaving a legacy of concepts to be coordinated with subsequent work. Flexible working and temporary teams exacerbate this problem.

The greatest risk to systems development projects occurs where the target organizations for the systems are themselves not adequately coordinated. Projects whose customers are consortia, or loose federations controlled democratically (or otherwise) by their members, have an appallingly high rate of failure.

Therefore, for projects of all sizes, we are going to need coordination techniques at three levels:

1. Techniques for intra-project and inter-project coordination, to reduce the costs, efforts and risks of given projects. (This may need to include coordination of the target organizations, and implementation of the systems into these target organizations.)
2. Techniques of planning (or replanning) projects, specifically to reduce the costs and risks of coordination that the projects will require.

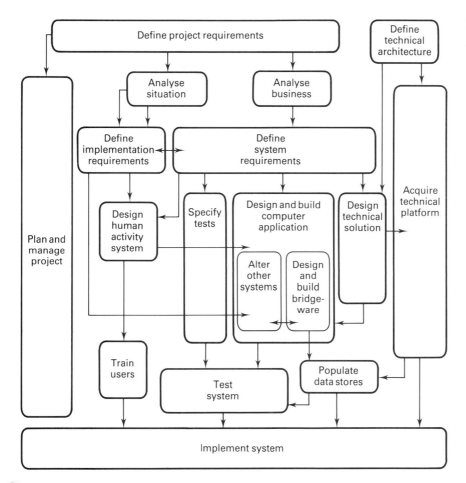

Figure 1.8
Some parallel
prerequisites of
implementation

3.   Techniques of planning the coordination activity itself, so that it can be systematically managed and balanced against the benefits gained from it. (These benefits may be intangible, hidden, or longer-term.)

We shall return to these topics in later chapters.

1.5.3 Implementing large systems

When a large information system has been developed, it has to be implemented. There are two main choices: 'big bang' implementation or 'phased' implementation. Each choice can be problematic.

   Big bang implementation is a high risk, simply because typically so many different activities must be synchronized (i.e. coordinated).

   If in Figure 1.8 we imagine large units of data or software being installed on large numbers of computers, with large numbers of users being trained in the use of large numbers of computerized procedures, and if we imagine that all of this activity needs to be synchronized, then the coordination difficulties will be clear.

Phased implementation is complex in different ways, and is often believed to be infeasible. For example, the financial accounts of a business are supposed to be complete and consistent. If the financial results are assembled in different and incompatible pieces, some from old systems and some from new, accountants and auditors will worry about their completeness and consistency. Examples abound, in which phased implementation apparently threatens the business by endangering the integrity of its information.

In other situations, the arguments against phased implementation are technical. Suppose the intention is to replace a large monolithic (or splintered monolithic) system. It will often be argued that the software quality of the old information system is poor, making it impossible to 'decommission' in stages. It must be run in its entirety, until it is ready to be switched off for ever.

Neither of these arguments are conclusive, but they often create a reluctance to undertake the complexities of phased implementation, and therefore a willingness to undergo the risks of big bang implementation.

Coordination techniques are required to defuse this dilemma.

1. Techniques to coordinate (i.e. consolidate or compare) information from multiple sources (including old and new systems), and to provide confidence in the quality of consolidated information.
2. Techniques to break an existing monolithic system into coordinated pieces that can be replaced at different times without endangering the integrity of the whole.
3. Techniques to design new large systems as a network or hierarchy of coordinated pieces, so that when their turn comes to be replaced, they can be easily decommissioned in stages.
4. Techniques to manage big bang implementations as large coordinated (i.e.. synchronized) projects, to reduce the risk to acceptable levels.

Implementation therefore raises four important coordination problems, and we shall return to these problems in later chapters.

1.5.4 *Implementing change into large systems*

It is astonishing that software developers so often complain that the systems of the past are monolithic, while at the same time designing new monolithic systems to replace them. It is as if they suffered from the fantasy that their designs would last for ever.

The more tightly integrated a large system is, the more difficult it becomes to make even small changes. When adding functionality, or changing the data structure, even an apparently trivial change can have a very wide impact. In the worst case, this can inhibit any enhancement to a system. When a system reaches this stage, it is considered ripe for replacement. However, it may still be necessary to maintain and upgrade such systems, and there are significant coordination issues here, similar to those discussed in the previous subsection with reference to the decommissioning of old systems.

1.5.5 Summary

In this section, we have stated some of the coordination needs of a typical systems development organization. Such an organization will typically be managed as a series of time-constrained projects, together with some on-going functions. Coordination itself is an important sub-function of Information Management (IM), often appearing in the formal IM organization under such headings as Data Administration or Development Coordination or Architecture Management or the like. Many of the coordination needs of both projects and ongoing functions can be satisfied using information model coordination as a vehicle.

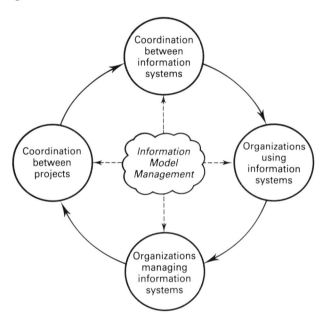

Figure 1.9
Coordination loop

1.6 Summary of chapter

In this introductory chapter, we have seen various areas where coordination and communication may be required:

- Between/within user organizations (via information systems);
- Between/within systems development and maintenance projects;
- Between/within information systems.

Information models are used by systems development (and maintenance) projects for establishing the requirements of user organizations, and for designing and implementing information systems. They are also used by information management organizations, for planning and managing systems and projects.

We can identify a cycle of coordination (see Figure 1.9): coordination within/between user organizations needs coordination between information systems, which needs coordination between development and maintenance projects, which in turn needs coordination within/between information systems management organizations. This book focuses on the management (i.e. coordination) of information models, to achieve these four connected coordination objectives. This gives one reason why an enterprise should have many information models. By having many different information models, it becomes possible to manage the many differences between/within organizations, projects and systems in terms of the differences between the information models that support them. If the enterprise were to have only one information model, the techniques of coordination to be described in this book would not be available to the enterprise.

Information modelling is a powerful technique of planning and designing information systems. Information coordination is a powerful technique of managing information systems, and of managing the enterprise itself as an information processing system, using the concepts and constructs of information modelling.

Notes

1. D. S. Pugh, 'Understanding and managing organizational change', *London Business School Journal*, vol. 3, no. 2., 1978, pp. 29–34.
2. M. Pedler, J. Burgoyne and T. Boydell, *The Learning Company*, London: McGraw-Hill, 1991.
3. An earlier version of some of the material in this section was published as R.Veryard, 'Tension and information systems', *Information and Software Technology*, vol. 29, no. 7, September 1987, pp. 358–61.
4. J. Dewey, *Human Nature and Conduct*, New York: Modern Library, 1930, p. 300.
5. H. Raiffa, *The Art and Science of Negotiation* Cambridge, MA: Harvard University Press, 1982.
6. H. Mintzberg, *The Structuring of Organizations*, Englewood Cliffs, NJ: Prentice Hall, 1979.
7. T.J. Peters and R.H. Waterman Jr, *In Search of Excellence*, New York: Harper & Row, 1982.
8. M. Hammer, 'Reengineering work: don't automate, obliterate', *Harvard Business Review*, July–August 1990, pp. 104–12.

2 Concepts

2.1 Introduction

This chapter introduces the general concept of coordination, and describes some of the views and models of coordination to be developed further in later chapters. After attempting to define what coordination is (and is not), we consider three main theories of how coordination works: hierarchies, markets and networks. Then we look specifically at the coordination of information systems and projects.

2.2 What is coordination?

Like many concepts (including peace and freedom) it is easier to define coordination negatively rather than positively.

2.2.1 Lack of coordination – the symptoms

Coordination is often invisible, and we can only recognize it in its absence. Thus in an orchestral concert, we may wonder what role the conductor plays, and we could only discover this by trying to do without a conductor. Lack of coordination forces itself on our attention – when you have to wait nearly an hour to change trains because the timetables are not synchronized – when there is no date within the next three months on which all six members of a committee are available for a meeting – when you have to stay in all day because you don't know exactly what time the gasman is coming – when you find that you and your partner have both sent Christmas cards (from both of you) to the same people – when someone makes an arrangement on your behalf, causing you to be double-booked – when an exciting new venture is cancelled in the belief that a key resource is lacking, just as the required resource becomes available elsewhere in the organization – when the repairman brings the wrong replacement – when tactical voting results in the wrong candidate being elected – (the list is endless . . .). Many people are capable of organizing their lives in a chaotic way – double-booking themselves and mislaying important documents – even without any help from anybody else.

One of the most poignant and elegant examples of lack of coordination is in a story by O. Henry. An impoverished couple, desperate to find Christmas presents for one another. He sells his father's watch to buy combs for her hair; she sells her hair to buy a chain for his watch.

The three most common symptoms of the lack of coordination are waiting, duplication (or waste) of effort or demand, and confusion/misunderstanding. Further consequences may be felt as inefficiency and lost opportunity. Where successful advancement or investment requires liaison, lack of liaison prevents real or lasting change. These symptoms are summarized in Box 2.1.

Although a good organization is robust enough to withstand imperfect coordination, there is a level of coordination below which the organization is no longer viable. This is particularly visible when a new organization is created

- Delay – waiting – work-in-progress
- Duplication – redundancy – overlap
- Confusion – cross purposes – incommensurate data – misunderstanding
- Lost data – gaps – poor utilization of resources – missed opportunities
- Inflexibility – prematurely frozen protocols – obsolete standards – stagnation

through merger. A merger has a cost, which is justified in terms of expected synergies, economies of scale, economies of scope, or whatever. Achieving these benefits requires coordination between the merged organizations. If the expected synergy is not realised, this is usually because of unanticipated difficulties in coordination. Incompatible cultures, incompatible systems, incompatible business operations. In the 1980s, a merger between two of the largest building societies in the United Kingdom (equivalent to savings and loan institutions in the United States) was called off, because the costs of aligning the computer information systems would have been prohibitive.

*A romantic liaison
between two people
can only tolerate
so much
misunderstanding.*

A lack of coordination is sometimes called a **contradiction**. This is not a logical contradiction, but an organizational or social or interpersonal contradiction. The process of coordination can then be thought of as the prevention or (more usually) the removal of contradictions.

2.2.2 Interaction between systems – a biological view

So what is coordination? Let us see if we can develop a positive definition of coordination, instead of a negative definition.

According to K.K. Smith,[1] the important issue in the vitality of living systems is not control, as earlier versions of systems thinking emphasized, but dynamic connectedness. It is not an issue of adaption or nonadaption. Rather it is the dynamic interplay between adaption and nonadaption. The future belongs to the symbiotic systems. Smith identifies five different levels of interaction as shown in Box 2.2.

	Communication	Two systems make some inner adjustments to each other, so there is a greater alignment between elements in one and elements in the other. However, these realignments are carried out in such a way that they in no way diminish the total autonomy of each entity.
Positive sum	Symbiosis	The exchange occurs in such a way that both systems sacrifice a part of their respective individual autonomies so that the superordinate system of which they are part may have greater autonomy in its relationship with other systems in its ecosystem.
	Fusion	The individual entities respond by treating their superordinate systems as all-important and surrender totally theirindividual autonomies so that thesuperordinate system will be maximallyautonomous in its relationship with otherentities of its kind in its larger ecosystem.By the entities giving up their autonomy in the interests of the super-ordinate system, they undermine their own capacity to continue as autonomous structures. Instead they become reduced to the status of elements in a larger autonomous system.
Zero sum	Parasitic	What one gains is another's loss.
Negative sum	Antibiosis	One, in its self-interest, actively harms the other.

Box 2.2
Biological coordination jargon: five levels of interaction between systems

We are only really interested in the first three levels, since we are after a positive coordination outcome. We shall see these three levels reappearing later in different guises: as blackbox, greybox and whitebox integration, or as market, network and hierarchical forms of organization; although these concepts are not exactly equivalent, there are useful parallels to be drawn.

The alliances between separate organizations can often be seen in biological terms. Some slime mould cells act independently when it is easy to get food. But when food is scarce, they attract each other and, in the process, develop a way of moving along the ground in search of more favourable feeding places. After arriving at new pastures, they unhook from each other and act individually again, until the next period of scarcity.[2] This is a form of temporary symbiosis. We might see certain strategic alliances between large computer manufacturers in this light.

With his usual whimsical abuse of Greek myth, Freud described these biological forces as a conflict between Eros (Love) and Thanatos (Death). 'The goal of the first is to establish at any time larger unities and preserve them. The goal of the second is, on the contrary, to break connexions and destroy things. . . . In biological functions both basic instincts combine mutually or they act the one against the other.'[3]

Kenwyn Smith sees symbiosis in two kinds of human organizations:

> One may be characterized by the existence of a central planning center where overall policy for the collectivity is formulated and then passed down to the parts in terms of specific actions for them to take in the service of both themselves and the collectivity. The alternative is a pooling process where the ideas of component groups are raised and then debated as mutual adjustments are made. The U.S. Congress is illustrative of the former while the SALT or START talks between the Soviet Union and the United States are like the latter.[4]

From the point of view of general systems theory, both of these examples involve a two-level abstract hierarchy, involving the collectivity and the individual. However, we shall find it more useful to refer only to the former example as a proper hierarchy, since it involves control from above, and the latter as a network or confederation.

2.2.3 *Coordination between activities*

Malone and Crowston define coordination as 'the act of working together harmoniously'.[5] They offer a conceptual framework for coordination as requiring four basic components: **actors** performing **activities** directed towards **goals**, with goal-relevant **interdependencies** between the activities.

> For example, an automobile manufacturing company might be thought of as having a set of goals (e.g. producing several different lines of automobiles) and a set of actors (e.g. people) who perform activities that achieve these goals. These activities may have various kinds of interdependencies such as using the same resources (e.g. an assembly line) or needing to be done in a certain order (e.g. a car must usually be designed before it is built).[6]

They argue that interdependences can be analysed in terms of **common objects** that are involved in some way in both activities. Thus a resource may be a common object; a design blueprint that is communicated from a designing activity to a production activity may also be a common object.

We shall see the crucial importance of common objects in later chapters.

2.2.4 *Scope of coordination*

All organizations need both internal and external coordination. Internal coordination is between the parts of the organization itself, and the systems directly supporting the organization. External coordination is with other organizations. For large organizations, the main problems of coordination are internal. As an organization gets larger, the need for internal coordination grows exponentially. For smaller organizations, the main problems of coordination are external.

A merger between two or more organizations is not instantaneous. Although the legal formalities may be completed at a particular instant, it takes time to become one organization in a practical sense. There is a transition period, which may even start before the legal formalities are completed, and may continue for a long time after. For months, if not years, the old organizations are still visible.

By organization, we should not think only of traditional enterprises. A joint venture, or participation in a common business, itself creates an implied organization. A franchise operation may include one franchiser and many franchisees: this can be regarded as an organization whose marketing must be coordinated. Many industries have dealer networks, which can likewise be regarded as organizations. Various names have been used to denote different kinds of stable long-term relationships between independent exchange partners, including: cooperative arrangements, relational contracting, joint ventures, quasifirms, global coalitions, and dynamic networks.[7]

Thus the distinction between internal and external coordination can be blurred, since the boundaries of the organization itself are blurred. What is important is the need for coordination.

2.3 Three theories of coordination: hierarchies, markets and networks

There are three main theories of coordination. These are used by different writers both as descriptive and as prescriptive theories: they may explain how coordination actually happens, or they may recommend how it ought to happen.

In this section, we shall describe the theories in their most general form, without specific reference to information systems. In the following chapter, we shall see how the three theories lead to different approaches to information systems planning. The hierarchical theory leads to top-down planning; the market theory leads to protocol planning; the network theory leads to organic planning.

2.3.1 Hierarchical theory of coordination

A hierarchy is held together by administration, command and control. Each part is precisely defined to perform a specific function. Efficiency in a hierarchy is thought of in terms of the division of labour. Ideally, each function is carried out by a single part, with no overlaps. Control functions are carried out by additional parts.

If a hierarchy is required to be fault-tolerant, or to allow for maintenance without halting operations, then some redundancy will be required, comprising back-up parts. This (known as **redundancy of parts**) is allowable although it compromises efficiency.

British Airways was created in 1974 by a merger of British European Airways (BEA) and British Overseas Airways Corporation (BOAC). Two separate cultures are still visible, two decades later.

When Texas Instruments took ownership of JMA Information Engineering in 1991, the two companies had long since aligned their structures and working methods. Coordination had been prompted by the companies participating jointly in the same business, not by common ownership.

Hierarchies incur what economists refer to as **agency costs**, which has to do with the imperfections of delegation, and the fact that different levels and locations within a hierarchy have divergent goals. Although in theory each manager, at each level of the hierarchy, acts as a conscientious and disinterested agent for the manager at the level above, and the top manager acts as an agent for the shareholder, in practice each manager adds (or subtracts) something of her own objectives and values to the task, working partly for the organization and partly for herself. Even close supervision (which imposes a burden both on the person being supervised and on the person supervising) cannot entirely eliminate self-interest or occasional laziness.

There are therefore three kinds of agency costs: **monitoring costs**, incurred by each manager who does not entirely trust her hierarchical subordinates, **bonding costs**, incurred by each manager who is not entirely trusted by her hierarchical superiors, and **residual loss**, incurred by the organization from not getting full value from the manager, despite monitoring and bonding.

(Obviously there is a trade-off between these three: the more you spend on monitoring and bonding, the less the probable residual loss.)

In addition to agency costs, a hierarchy is subject to **decision costs**. These are the costs of making, communicating and documenting decisions, and the opportunity costs of making poor decisions. (In large organizations, it may take years before these costs come to light.) These costs are summarized in Box 2.3.

Box 2.3
A hierarchy incurs internal coordination costs

Agency costs:
- monitoring costs (incurred by supervisor)
- bonding costs (incurred by supervised)
- residual loss (incurred by organization)

Decision costs:
- information processing costs (communication, documentation)
- opportunity costs (due to poor decisions)

In a hierarchical organization, decision-making authority can be centralized or decentralized. As authority is pushed down the organization, upward communication costs are reduced, but there may be an increase in agency costs resulting from the divergence of goals. For each organization, there is an optimal degree of decentralization, being the point at which the total internal coordination costs are minimized.

It is worth noting that effective use of IT can reduce both monitoring/bonding costs and decision processing costs.[8] Sometimes IT enables greater centralization, sometimes greater decentralization, depending on the balance of these costs. In organizations whose middle management has been entirely devoted to internal coordination, IT can significantly reduce the number of middle managers needed. (However, politically adept middle management can usually prevent IT being excessively effective.)

2.3.2 Market theory of coordination

A market is a system of agents, providing products and services to one another. A market is held together by exchange, based on formal contracts.

In economics, a market is defined as **efficient** if no agent has the power to distort the market. Various forms of monopoly are regarded as inefficient, since the monopolist may exact higher prices or degrade the quality of service without redress.

For an engineer, a system of automated agents providing products and services to one another is **robust** if no agent has the power to interrupt or destroy the functioning of the system, and is **efficient** if no agent has the power to distort the system. If an agent has a monopoly on providing a particular essential service, then its failure causes the system to fail, and its inefficiency causes bottle-necks in the system as a whole. Fault-tolerant systems are designed to ensure that no agent has such a monopoly. (This also makes maintenance much easier, because each part is able to be disconnected and replaced, without halting the operating of the system as a whole.)

Markets incur what economists refer to as **transaction costs**, as shown in Box 2.4. These apply to the operational and contractual costs of supplying and purchasing products and services between independent organizations. (The terms 'transportation' and 'inventory' need to be understood metaphorically with respect to services.)

Operational costs:
- search
- transportation
- inventory holding
- communication

Contractual costs:
- writing contracts
- enforcing contracts

Box 2.4
A market incurs external coordination costs

2.3.3 Network theory of coordination

In the broadest sense, a network can be regarded as any system of interconnected parts. In this sense, hierarchies and markets can be regarded as forms of network. However, there is a third form, which is how we intend to use the term 'network' in this book (see Box 2.5).

Sociologists use the term 'network' to denote a system held together by informal communication, based on trust. It is a 'flat' organizational form, in contrast to the 'vertical' organizational form of the hierarchical form. Fashion in management theory favours network over hierarchical forms, at least for human organizations.

You might think that machines cannot communicate informally. Computerized information systems are formal by definition, and so the idea of informal links between systems would be nonsense. How can a machine trust another machine?

But if a machine leans on another machine, relies on its robustness and integrity, depends on the internal structure of another machine, this could be regarded (metaphorically) as a form of trust. When we say that machine A 'trusts' machine B, this is perhaps just a shorthand way of saying that the designers of machine A trusted machine B (or its designers). Trust is 'inherited' by the machine from the designers.

Box 2.5
A network incurs both internal and external coordination costs

Membership costs:
- establishing trust
- breaches of trust (failure)

Exclusion costs:
- lost opportunities

So for the purposes of this book, we shall use the term 'network' to refer to a tightly linked flat structure, in contrast to a 'market', which is an open structure.

Nearly coordinated networks

In parts of the City of London, as in many other cities, there are overhead walkways that cross over roads, pass through buildings, and enable pedestrians to get quickly and safely from A to B. These walkways have been extended over the years; starting from the Barbican development, each new adjacent building has added to the walkway network.

If all the walkways in a network had to be at exactly the same level, this would place extreme restrictions on the architects, and make it impossible to link two networks together. To overcome this, the network includes some gentle slopes, and the occasional stair. But if the network is riddled with stairs, so that a person walking from A to B is constantly having to ascend and descend, this will greatly reduce the advantage of the walkways over walking at street level. And of course, people in wheelchairs need at least one route, not necessarily the shortest, that does not include stairs at all.

To achieve this, it is necessary to ensure that each walkway, if not at exactly the same level as the walkways on all other buildings, is at least at a similar level to its neighbours. This allows for gradual gradients, which may be necessary if the ground itself slopes. This is **near coordination**, as opposed to total coordination. It is clearly a network solution, since it is not centrally planned, and extends itself through piecemeal activity in a complex and unpredictable manner.

2.3.4 *Comparison of the three theories of coordination*

As we have seen, hierarchies and markets incur different kinds of costs: agency costs and transaction costs. IT can be used to reduce both.[9] Sometimes a hierarchy will be the more cost-effective form of coordination; sometimes a market will be more cost-effective; sometimes IT will tilt the balance one way, sometimes the other. Networks can be highly efficient, but because they are not open, they can be vulnerable to corruption.

The transaction costs associated with markets are those of writing, executing and enforcing contracts. Williamson[10] identified three factors that influence these costs: (1) uncertainty, (2) asset specificity, and (3) frequency. These factors translate into 'make-or-buy' decisions: whether it is better to provide a service from within the organization, with hierarchical coordination, or from outside the organization, with market coordination.

In computer systems the same principles apply: is it easier to perform a function internally, or to call an external (reusable) module?

In practice, most organizations combine all three modes of coordination in complex ways. Thus for example, a regulated market consists of a basic market with an administrative (i.e. hierarchical) superstructure to impose controls. Most commercial organizations are divided into cost centres or profit centres, allowing certain limited market transactions between them. Complex market transactions may need to be based on trust as well as formal contracts, since the cost of agreeing a complete and legally watertight specification of a complex product or service can often be prohibitive.

Quality management systems (including those following the international standard ISO 9000) recognize that the quality of software products and services delivered by a systems development project cannot always be determined by inspection or functional check alone; verification may be required throughout the development process. This means that the relationship between the purchaser and supplier of software needs to involve some level of trust and mutual collaboration, and cannot be simply a market-driven commodity transaction.

2.4 Limits to coordination

This book adopts the pragmatic view that total coordination is neither possible nor desirable. This view is not universally accepted. Ultra-liberals such as von Hayek believe that a perfect market is possible. Stalinists used to believe that a perfect hierarchy was possible, allowing total coordination by central planning; Hitler tried to implement the teutonic concept of Gleichschaltung, which implied total synchronization of German society through technology, metaphorically linking all society to the same grid, the same source of electricity. The idea that techno-logy will enable or impose coordination that had not been possible by political action alone is a surprisingly popular one.

That Hitler and Stalin were in favour of total coordination is not itself an argument against it. After all, Hitler was a vegetarian, but that is not a good reason to eat meat.

Many proponents of total coordination fall into the category of **hedgehog**, derived by Isaiah Berlin from a fragment of ancient poetry (a hedgehog is a person who knows one big thing, contrasted with a fox who knows many small things). Hedgehogs 'relate everything to a single central vision, one system less or more coherent or articulate, in terms of which they understand, think and feel – a single, universal, organizing principle in terms of which alone all that they are and say has significance.'[11] For the hedgehog, everything can and should be managed and

The fox knows many things, but the hedgehog knows one big thing.

coordinated by this principle, which is elevated to religious or ideological status.

The hedgehog also believes that we all have the same basic goals. All people and organizations want to survive, although they may adopt different strategies. We all need the same things, and we all have the same underlying values, although there may be superficial differences in how these manifest themselves in behaviour.

However, the pragmatic view, that total coordination is neither possible nor desirable, seems to be gaining ground, as evidenced by the collapse of central planning in the communist bloc, and by the move away from 'ivory-tower' strategic planning in large capitalist enterprises. The Catholic doctrine of 'subsidiarity' has been extended to fix the principle of decentralized planning and decision-making into international agreements.

There are five main reasons why total coordination is not practically possible:

1. An organization is made up of parts with different (although overlapping) purposes and objectives.
2. Parts of an organization may deploy different, and perhaps even competing, methods and conceptual apparatuses to calculate, rank and measure their objectives, and to undertake their activities. Indeed, some parts of the same organization may be locally structured as hierarchies, others as networks.
3. Coordination mechanisms incur some cost; there is a level of coordination at which the additional cost of further coordination outweighs the additional benefits.
4. Stable evolution of a system or organization often requires the possibility of one part to change in advance of other parts. Even if it were possible, total coordination may degrade and fragment over time, thanks to external forces.
5. Although coordination is supposed to be an antidote to chaos, there are circumstances where excessive coordination itself actually causes turbulence and chaos.

We shall explore each of these reasons in turn.

2.4.1 *Different objectives*

In a market, each of the actors is presumed to be acting out of self-interest. Their goals therefore conflict. Even in a hierarchy, there will often be different opinions and interpretations about the corporate goals. Two designers on a project may have strongly opposed opinions about the design priorities.

We referred above to the concept of a **fox** as a person who knows many little things. Foxes are

> those who pursue many ends, often unrelated and even contradictory, connected, if at all, only in some *de facto* way, for some psychological or physiological cause, related by no moral or æsthetic principle. (They) lead lives, perform acts, and entertain ideas that are centrifugal rather than centripetal, their thought is scattered or diffused, moving on many levels, seizing upon the essence of a vast variety of experiences and objects for what they are in themselves, without, consciously or unconsciously, seeking to fit them into, or exclude them from, any

one unchanging, all-embracing, sometimes self-contradictory and incomplete, at times fanatical, unitary inner vision.[12]

The fox believes that we all have different motives and goals. Some organizations may want to increase profit, to replace human workers with machines; other organizations may want to grow, to create employment for human workers; other organizations may want to survive, or contribute to broader social goals. Indeed, many organizations set conflicting objectives at the highest level: e.g. growth and profit, in situations where long-term growth can only be achieved by sacrificing short-term profit.

In a large public utility company, for example, operating in different regions, each region had differing requirements from the customer accounting system. One region had a rapidly shifting population and needed facilities within the system to track customers and support debt control. This was of no benefit to other regions, who wanted to minimize workload of customer record maintenance.

2.4.2 Different concepts and methods

Within an organization, there will necessarily be some division of intellectual labour. Not everyone needs to be familiar with the details of accounting practice, or with employment legislation; not everyone needs to know the detailed engineering design of a product, or the exact readership profiles of the magazines in which the company advertises. Each of these domains will typically 'belong' to a different department.

Different specializations

Different specializations usually deploy different jargons, and different measurement principles. For communication across specializations, one of the following is required:

1. Overlap between jargons.
2. Specialists in more than one area, who speak two or more jargons and can translate between them.
3. Ability of specialists to communicate in plain language when talking outside their specialist domain.

However, it would be a serious constraint on specialists if the occasional need to communicate outside their specialist domain prevented them from using jargon at all. Specialist jargon is developed not just for elitist secrecy and ego, but also for accuracy and reliability. Would you want to fly in an aeroplane that had been designed in language so simple that even the non-executive directors of the aerospace company could understand the blueprints?

Two descriptions are better than one.

Two loudspeakers are needed to hear stereo.

Therefore, there will sometimes be a need to communicate between members of the same specialization, or for specialists to store and retrieve information in a form that is perhaps incomprehensible or uninteresting to members of other specializations.

Two eyes are needed to see in three dimensions.

Integration and consistency mean you only have a single unified view of the world. This is of course dangerous when this view is wrong. But even when it is

Mystics claim to see with the 'third eye', hear with the 'third ear'.

correct, it may be limiting. Multiple descriptions aid calibration, allow cross-checking and learning, bring new patterns to the fore.

Example: the Zeta Corporation used three or four different distribution channels. Given identical data, each division calculated which channel was the cheapest, and all came to the same conclusion. The other channels were therefore closed down. This may have been the most efficient solution for the Zeta Corporation in the short term, but led to inflexibility and vulnerability in the longer term. When the chosen channel became more expensive, it proved hard to re-establish the others.

2.4.3 *Cost of coordination*

We have already seen that the different forms of organization, the different coordination mechanisms, all incur costs and risks of one kind or another. It follows that, at some point, the benefits of coordination are outweighed by the costs and risks.

One of the paradoxes of bureaucracy is that, although each separate attempt at coordination may appear to be rationally justified, the benefits are not additive. If this is ignored, an organization can easily extend its attempts at coordination beyond what can be rationally justified. For each person doing real work, there are several others trying to coordinate her. It would be unfair to name any of the many organizations, in both the public and private sector, which commit this collective error.

Of course, the costs and benefits of coordination change over time. Consider the different patterns of television viewing in affluent families during the past few decades. In the 1960s, a lucky family might have one television set, and was therefore required to coordinate its viewing. Everybody had to watch the same programme at the same time; if two viewing requirements conflicted, a choice had to be made.

By 1990, it has become common in the OECD countries for a middle-class household to possess several television sets, and one or two video recorders. Advances in technology have made it unnecessary for these affluent households to make difficult choices. This is not an unusual pattern: although technology can sometimes make coordination easier, at other times it can make coordination irrelevant or unnecessary.

Note that this change also required a change in social attitudes. In the 1960s, although some families could easily have afforded another television set, it was thought that viewing ought to be a shared experience, and that even when clashes of programme caused arguments, this was an essential and healthy part of the family bonding process. By 1990, this thought had been abandoned, and the family had transformed into the household: an uncoordinated set of consumers occupying the same house. Some people might moralize and generalize from this example, to argue that the process of coordination itself has human value, in addition to the direct benefits from coordination. However, the same argument can be applied in reverse, since the process of liberation from coordination is also thought to be valuable in its own right. Within industry, the dilemma of liberation or coordination (alias solidarity) generates bitter arguments for and against syndicalism and trades unions: since many old-fashioned syndicalists believe that worker solidarity is a good thing in itself. Collective wage bargaining is a form of coordination (either hierarchical or networked) that has attracted orchestrated political criticism from those who believe it conflicts with the requirements of market coordination.

2.4.4 Stability and progress

Robust systems survive by absorbing fluctuations. The tighter the structure, the less permissible are fluctuations within the systems, therefore the greater the probability that fluctuation will provide a threat to that structure. Furthermore, productive change is inhibited. If hundreds of small pieces have to be altered simultaneously, in order to make progress, such progress may never happen, or may be postponed until it is too late.

Organizational change and renewal therefore thrive on a tension between order and disorder. In a classic paper, Hedberg, Nystrom and Starbuck propose several aphorisms for the Learning Company, of which two are particularly relevant here:[13]

- Cooperation requires minimum consensus.
- Improvement depends upon minimum consistency.

2.4.5 Turbulence

Turbulence is a phenomenon that has been studied since Leonardo da Vinci, and it is only now starting to be understood. Turbulence means unpredictable fluctuations in the behaviour of a system. We see the chaos in fast-flowing streams, and we feel the bumps when we fly through storms. A storm is a piece of turbulence in the global weather system. Turbulence can also be found in commodity or stock market prices, or in complex ecological systems.

Large highly interconnected networks of systems are found to be vulnerable to intermittent and unpredictable bursts of chaos. This effect has been found by both TRW and Xerox in different computer configurations. The effect has also been produced by Japanese scientists within superconducting switches. There appears to be nothing wrong with the design of these systems; the problem appears to be something inherent in the complexity of networks when they contain feedback loops of a certain kind; mathematicians refer to this property as **non-linearity**.[14]

Although this effect is not fully understood, it seems that this turbulence can only be avoided by isolating subsystems from one another, rather than linking them all together. This therefore provides another argument against total coordination; the analysis of non-linearity giving us a mathematical explanation of the ancient Greek concept of **hubris** and the more recent concept of Murphy's Law.

Computer models for economic predictions are vulnerable to this turbulence. The more complex the models become, the more parameters and factors are added to increase accuracy, paradoxically the less reliable they seem to become.

2.4.6 Conclusions

This section has argued that total coordination is not feasible or desirable. The remainder of the book will assume that coordination is sometimes a good thing, but should not be elevated above all other goals, nor taken to inappropriate extremes. One of the most difficult aspects of managing coordination is knowing where to stop coordinating.

(Technocrats may think this is not a problem; you just do as much as you are allowed to, since that will never be enough. But this is not a book solely for technocrats. It is a book for responsible managers as well.)

2.5 Purposes of information coordination

The first half of this chapter has been discussing coordination in general. We can now apply this to information coordination in particular.

The potential benefits include: Information Sharing, Reuse and Comparability. These benefits may be required to make the business more efficient (by making the information systems more efficient or effective). This should make the benefits quantifiable, and directly comparable with the costs of achieving them. Sometimes the business can benefit from the economies of scale available from Information Processing, or economies of scope.

Alternatively, they may be required to fulfil some aspect of the business strategy directly. Measures to achieve strategic benefits tend to be more difficult to cost-justify than measures to increase operational efficiency, and should be planned as part of an Information Systems Strategy Planning exercise.

2.5.1 Levels of coordination

Coordination between information systems is sought for two reasons. We shall refer to it as **enterprise coordination** if the lack of coordination would affect the business directly, and **technical coordination** if the lack of coordination would merely increase the costs/risks or reduce the quality/productivity of computer systems development and/or operation.

Strategic business benefit comes from enterprise coordination. For example, lack of enterprise coordination may increase costs of specific business processes. Some business opportunities may be not worth doing at all in the absence of adequate coordination, because costs are too high.

Technical coordination may deliver either enterprise coordination, or system lifecycle cost savings. Enterprise coordination will often (but not always) require technical coordination.

Thus it is important to understand the difference between enterprise coordination and technical coordination. Since this difference is often ignored by technically minded information engineers, I shall devote one section to examples of enterprise coordination, and the following section to examples of technical coordination, before going on to discuss how both may be achieved.

2.5.2 Enterprise coordination

There are several types of enterprise coordination required by a typical business enterprise, affecting key business performance measures such as market share and profit. Often, it is part of the business strategy to establish and maintain such coordination. This provides a powerful argument to information systems planners, to ensure that the computer systems support the required enterprise coordination.

1. Single point of management

Objects of interest to the business are managed in a consistent way, by concentrating all decisions about the object in one place. For example:

1. Customers have a single contact point, allowing all business conducted with that customer to be coordinated and optimized.
2. Products have a single management point, allowing all development, manufacturing and marketing of a single product to be carried out in a coordinated way.
3. Functions are coordinated, e.g. marketing campaigns for different products may be coordinated, or funds management may be coordinated, to minimize the firm's exposure to currency fluctuations.
4. Processes are coordinated, thus ensuring that business processes are carried out effectively and efficiently, e.g. shipments are combined to reduce total delivery mileage, or inspection is carried out before assembly, to reduce wastage.

Some of these decisions may be centralized at head office; others may be allocated to branch offices, but in a clearly defined way.

2. Force business to coordinate

If two system development projects need to talk to each other, it is because the business areas themselves need to talk to each other. Sometimes there is a lack of communication within the organization, and the information systems are being developed to alleviate this. We saw some examples of this in Chapter 1.

In many organizations, there is a push towards devolution and the empowerment of staff. Getting decisions made at the point of action involves coordination of various concepts to support the decision. These concepts were perhaps previously understood by different people in different departments. Business Process Reengineering may involve breaking down these private domains.

The production of this book, for example, demanded coordination between three teams: one producing the inside pages, another separate team producing the cover, and a third team preparing the entry into the publisher's catalogue.

3. *Consistency of behaviour*

If a company is selling the same product in several different countries, it may attempt to set different prices in each country. In other words, the pricing is a local decision. However, if there are significant variations in price from one country to another, multinational customers will purchase wherever the product is cheapest, and then reship. Traders may even buy in the cheapest country, and sell in the more expensive countries, thus undercutting the company itself. Some computer manufacturers attempt to control these 'grey imports' by retaining a monopoly on repairs; they refuse to provide spare parts for computers except in the original country of sale. Other manufacturers merely ignore the problem. For some companies, however, it can be a serious drain on profits.

Wider examples can be found involving interorganizational coordination (e.g. price-fixing cartels), or even intergovernmental coordination (e.g. harmonization of taxes and duties).

4. *Consistency of data*

For an organization to communicate effectively, it is necessary for them to speak a common language. When data are summarized and compared, it is useful for them to have been calculated in a consistent manner.

A long time ago, a computer manufacturer designed a new range of tape drives. These were to be linked in a chain, with a vacuum pump at the end of the chain. The tape drive had a part number (say 4711), and the vacuum pump had a different part number (say 5822).

When sales and marketing started to sell these tape drives, however, it was decided that the vacuum pump could not be separately priced. The price list included a tape drive without vacuum pump (part number 4711) and a tape drive with vacuum pump (part number 5822). Salesmen were instructed that each order should include at least one tape drive with vacuum pump. Orders were taken and passed, in the usual way, to the production section for manufacture and shipment.

Customers who had ordered two off part number 4711 and one off part number 5822 expected to receive three tape drives and a pump. However, the production and shipment systems expected the customers to be satisfied with two tape drives and a pump. When the first customer complained, this was attributed to clerical error. By the time the real cause of the problem had been identified, it was already causing serious embarrassment to the company.

5. *Comparability of business*

Consistent measurement and presentation of business performance mean that the performance measures from different parts of the business can be fairly combined, compared and contrasted. This benefit relates to management's ability to exercise strategic and tactical control over the business.

2.5.3 Technical coordination

The Roman architect Vitruvius, a contemporary of Jesus Christ, identified three elements of quality: **firmness**, **commodity** and **delight**. I was surprised (and delighted) to find this definition of quality being repeated by Bill Gates, founder of Microsoft.[15] For software, Gates glosses the three components as shown in Box 2.6:

Firmness	Consistency
Commodity	Be worthy of the user's time and effort in understanding it
Delight	Engagement, fun

Box 2.6
From Vitruvius to
Gates – definitions of
quality

We can see enterprise coordination as connected with the benefits to the enterprise, the fit-for-purposeness of an application system, which Vitruvius calls its commodity. Firmness/consistency includes a number of technical quality characteristics, including reliability and maintainability. This is closely connected with what we are here calling technical coordination. The following benefits are related to the operational efficiency and effectiveness of the information systems themselves.

1. Data quality and integrity

Consistency of data can be important, even in situations where it does not bring any direct business benefit. A standard data format may simplify data processing, may simplify aggregation and comparison and analysis. And it allows data and system components to be reused.

2. Reuse of data

Information sharing means that the same information becomes available to different parts of the business. Since the acquisition and maintenance of information are themselves an expense, it benefits the organization if the same information can be exploited many times. Once data have been entered into a computer system, it is a waste of time and effort to enter it into another computer system. Furthermore, when several different parts of the business are using the same information, errors and inaccuracies will be more quickly noticed and eliminated.

In some situations, lack of integration between systems results not merely in inefficiency but in irreversible loss of data (see Box 2.7).

3. Reusability of system components

Reusability means that once built, Information System components can be used many times. This includes technical components (such as programs and algorithms, data definitions and routines) and also human components (such as user skills). As with information sharing, reuse enhances quality (but only if the reused components are appropriate and properly used).

Box 2.7
Examples of lost data

System	Data lost	Reason	Consequence
Credit card system	Date of purchase	A customer buys some goods from a merchant, using a credit card. The customer's credit card slip is transmitted electronically from the merchant to the bank. There is a minimal interface between the merchant and the bank, designed many years ago, which only includes the amount and omits the purchase date.	The customer bill doesn't show the date of purchase, but the computer entry date. This causes the customer some confusion, and forcing the customer to record or reconstruct the actual date.
Job costing system	Product data	Job costs are calculated on the basis of timesheets completed by engineers. These engineers are reluctant to spend extra time completing timesheets, and there is no interface between the scheduling system (which does maintain the relationship between jobs and products) and the costing system.	This means the job costs have to be apportioned between products on a semi-arbitrary basis.

Development costs can be saved by having standard components. It reduces the number of design decisions, and reduces the amount of testing (since the test effort can be reused).

Conservative fashion (also known as tradition) uses standard solutions rather than solve every problem from scratch. An often arbitrary decision may be made, which everyone then adheres to. Standards often have great value – they offer stability, but at the risk of inertia.

Some systems are built with high levels of reuse, which implies low levels of redundant functionality. This is thought to make the systems cheaper to maintain and enhance, since changes will only have to be made in one place, rather than in several places. However, if we see systems (of human-computer activity) as being parts of learning organizations, and if we take the ideas of General Systems Theory seriously, we should consider the potential advantages of redundancy of function and requisite variety.[16] 'Redundancy (variety) should always be built into a system where it is directly needed, rather than at a distance.'[17]

4. Economies of scale in resource usage

One of the reasons for sharing resources across several systems (or several organization units) is to gain economies of scale. For example, since the organization incurs a cost for each DBMS used (both software licences and internal support costs), there may well be a cost advantage if all organization units use the same DBMS.

However, if the different organization units have different requirements, it will sometimes be the case that the cost of compromise (i.e. using a DBMS that is inefficient for the given purpose) is greater than the cost savings from the economies of scale. These are often extremely difficult calculations to balance.

5. Economies of scale in decision-making

If you are going to buy a machine, and the choice is between spending $1000 on a cheaper model or $1500 on a more expensive model, then you would want to consider whether the additional power and functionality of the more expensive model was worth the extra money. Suppose that the only way you would know for certain is by carrying out a benchmark study. If the study itself will cost more than $500, then it would be more sensible to do without the study and simply buy the more expensive model. (Many companies are prevented from doing the sensible thing, because capital expenditure comes from a different budget than evaluation studies, but that is a different problem.)

However, if you want to buy a thousand machines, it could be worth spending $10,000 or more comparing the options, gathering the information to support a better decision. Thus we can get economies of scale in decision-making, by sharing the information costs between a thousand separate purchasing decisions. This will only work, however, if all the thousand purchasing decisions take proper heed of the supporting information. Thus, to get these economies of scale, we seem to need standardization.

6. Uniformity of control

Uniformity of functionality and controls make for greater user-friendliness. Let us consider some analogies. When you drive a strange car, there is uncertainty about the various levers on the steering column; sometimes you want to signal a left turn, and operate the windscreen wipers instead. Or in a strange hotel room, you cannot find the light switch in the middle of the night. Faced with such inconveniences, many people would prefer that all cars had the same controls in the same places, or that all hotel rooms were laid out in the same way.

Or consider differences in the highway code for car drivers. In some countries (including the United Kingdom), when joining a roundabout, you give way to people already on. In other countries (including France), the people on the roundabout give way to those wishing to join (priorité à droite). Some countries do not have roundabouts at all. Some countries do not even have a highway code.

An organization may desire uniformity for its internal operations. This enables staff to be interchanged ad lib between different functions, and simplifies the development and maintenance of computer software. But this argument may not apply to the external information systems, the so-called strategic ones. Standardization may make it easier to poach market share from your competitors, but also makes it easier for your competitors to poach from you. So standards are two-edged.

2.6 Methods of information coordination

2.6.1 *Achieving enterprise coordination in an organization*

Enterprise coordination requires clear and appropriate coordination policies, determined (usually) as part of the strategic planning process, and implemented (often) through layers of management. We shall return to planning issues in Chapter 4, and to the political issues in Chapter 8.

2.6.2 *Should technical coordination match enterprise coordination?*

We have said that the purpose of technical coordination is often to achieve some specific enterprise coordination. We have also seen that there are three main coordination mechanisms: hierarchical, market and network.

This prompts the question whether technical coordination should take the same form as enterprise coordination. Does it make sense, for example, to implement a network of information systems to serve a strict hierarchy, or a hierarchy of information systems to serve a market?

Sometimes not only enterprise requirements but also technological factors may influence the architecture of the information systems. A technical architecture that matches the enterprise architecture may simply not be available or feasible.

However, experience suggests that although implementation of mismatching technical architectures is possible, it will be much more difficult to manage. The reasons for such a technological mismatch need to be well understood, and carefully explained to the stakeholders, since they will be required to alter the way they plan and control the information system support. Hierarchical systems, for example, have to be planned and designed hierarchically, and if no hierarchical decision-making and issue-resolution mechanism exists, it may have to be created specially for the purpose. We will return to this question in the final chapter.

2.6.3 Data ownership

In a hierarchy, the data are owned at the top. Agents are merely the custodians of data.

In a market, the data are owned privately by the agents, who may make formal contracts to provide them to other agents.

In a network, the data are owned privately by the agents, or collectively by the local network. Communication within a local network may be informal; communication outside the local network may be based on wider network transactions or market transactions.

Most organizations combine the hierarchical principle with the market principle. The concept of internal cross-charging is common to most commercial organizations, which implies market transactions between parts of the same organization.

This tells against the oft-cited principle of treating data as a corporate resource. If a cost centre or profit centre has expended effort in collecting and processing some information, why should it provide this free to other cost centres? Since other services are subject to cross-charge, why should information services be exempt?

2.6.4 Coordination within / between systems

Sometimes, coordination can be achieved by integration and homogeneity. Sometimes it is more appropriate to tackle the symptoms of contradiction, rather than to eliminate them by full integration. There are several ways of doing this, including insulation, redundancy, and standard interface protocols – 'open systems'.

1. Homogeneity

Until recently, the majority of large application systems were designed and implemented as centralized host systems. Such systems can generally be assumed to be **homogeneous**. The characteristics of homogeneity can be seen in Box 2.8. Many distributed systems still retain these characteristics.

2. Insulation

Insulation means that parts are shielded from other parts, keeping their interactions to the minimum necessary. In the design of houses and offices, we can see several examples of this:

- Sound insulation enables people in adjacent rooms to sleep at different times, or to listen to different music. (People in open-plan houses have to coordinate their lives much more.)
- Firewalls or firedoors to contain and compartmentalize the risk of failure.

Analogous insulation possibilities exist in information systems. For example, databases are often designed to contain 'firewalls'. This is an important technique, and we shall return in later chapters to the techniques for placing these firewalls, and for providing the necessary links across them.

This brings us back to the difference between a market and a network, namely the degree of formality in the interface. In a network, there is 'trust' across the interface. For example, the data quality within one application system may depend on the data quality in another application. Problems of data integrity can easily ripple across the network. If there is a serious software crash, it may be difficult to trace the source of the fault.

A market interface, on the other hand, is much less permeable to data quality problems. As in a real market, applications must apply the principle of 'buyer beware', revalidating data integrity rather than relying on the quality of the data received. Software faults can be much more easily located. A market interface may also be less permeable to other problems, such as software virus infection. However, such insulation has its own costs, since much of the validation will arguably be redundant. The interface can be regarded as a formal contract or agreement, and the double-checking of data quality can be regarded as the cost of enforcing the agreement.

Box 2.8
Assumptions of
homogeneous systems

- Single global name space
- Global shared memory
- Global consistency
- Sequential execution
- Failure is total
- Synchronous interaction
- Locality of interaction
- Fixed location of components
- Direct binding
- Homogeneous environment

3. Redundancy of function

In some circumstances, change is impossible without redundancy. Many real-time computer systems are designed for constant operation: you just cannot switch off the system that controls a nuclear power station, even for a few seconds; such systems always incorporate the principle of redundancy, usually by duplicating parts.

Furthermore, self-organizing or even self-improving systems must include some redundancy. Whereas redundancy of parts is a feature of mechanistic hierarchical control systems in which spare parts are added to a system, **redundancy of function** is a feature of intelligent networks in which extra functions are added to each of the operating parts, so that each part is able to engage in a range of functions. Requisite variety is built into the system where it is needed, rather than at a distance.[18]

4. Standard interfaces

The concept of **open systems** has attracted much interest from purchasers of computer hardware and software, and considerable hype from suppliers. The vision is that if there is a standard interface to which all suppliers conform, it will be possible to plug anything to anything else. All hardware and software become interchangeable commodities.

The IT industry has discovered that defining and agreeing such a standard interface is easier said than done. It is possible (but unnecessary) to be extremely pessimistic or even cynical about the open systems movement. Suppliers have an uneasy dilemma: they can conform exactly to standard, provide no non-standard features (even if they are better than standard), and compete solely on cost, performance and delivery. Or they can try to provide something extra, and be accused of rebelling against the open systems community.

Analogies abound. There is no worldwide standard voltage for electrical appliances, and there are several different standards for sockets (see Figure 2.1). It would of course be dangerous to standardize the sockets without first standardizing the voltages. But we probably have to accept the fact that the different local standards are now too entrenched, for a worldwide standard ever to be implemented. Standards may be restrictive. Designers have been attempting for 50 years to replace the QWERTY keyboard without success.

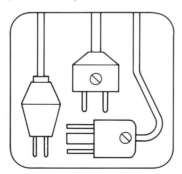

Figure 2.1
No world-wide standard for electric plugs

The railways provide another interesting example. By a feat of network coordination, most of Europe operates on the same railway gauge. However, nineteenth-century Russia decided to adopt a different gauge, for fear of invasion from the West. Standardization enables the strong to attack the weak, but it also allows the small to infiltrate the large. It is therefore a highly political issue, although technocrats refuse to recognize this.

In IT, standards have been developed for Electronic Data Interchange (EDI), which provides a fairly limited language for communicating data between organizations. This is a useful basis for inter-company coordination, but does not provide the coordination itself.

For example, a small software company Alpha may subcontract the duplication of floppy disks to company Beta, the printing of manuals to Gamma, and the warehousing and shipment to Delta. There must be communication between the companies, which could be paper or electronic. It would be fairly straightforward to design a logistics system for Alpha, which sent orders to Beta, Gamma and Delta, and received status reports back (see Figure 2.2). The logistics system would then be linked to a payments system, that would receive invoices from Beta, Gamma and Delta, and initiate cash transfers back. The idea of EDI is to make such interfaces easier to build, because there are common protocols for such business entities as orders and invoices.

Figure 2.2
Single company Alpha being serviced by Beta, Gamma and Delta. (Fat lines show material, thin lines show information)

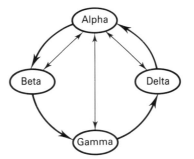

But suppose there are several software companies, Alpha-1, Alpha-2, etc, using the same trio of Beta, Gamma and Delta (see Figure 2.3). If Beta, Gamma and Delta liaise directly, they may be able to achieve significant economies of scale. For example, duplicated disks and printed manuals could be delivered to the warehouse in larger batches. An Alpha-controlled logistics system would not support this; a network of symbiotic logistics systems would be needed. This would be much more difficult to design and implement, and goes way beyond simple EDI.

5. Near coordination

Earlier in the chapter, we discussed the concept of near coordination, using the example of the overhead walkways in the City of London.

How is near coordination possible with information systems? Interfaces can be imperfect or incomplete, requiring manual intervention. Interfaces may involve a delay or cost, instead of allowing cost-free real-time update. With such interfaces,

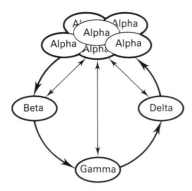

Figure 2.3
Many companies being
serviced by Beta,
Gamma and Delta.
(Fat lines show
material, thin lines
show information)

there is near coordination, reducing but not entirely eliminating the symptoms of contradiction.

6. *Open Distributed Processing*

Probably the most influential work in the area of open distributed processing has been done under the umbrella of the Advanced Network Systems Architecture (ANSA). The ANSA model adopts several principles for market-linked systems,[19] based on the client-server model of computing. These principles characterize the interfaces themselves, as well as the mechanisms for implementing and controlling them (see Box 2.9).

The ANSA model has also been influential in introducing the concepts of trading and federation.[20] In **federation**, separate systems can interoperate but still maintain control of their own domains. **Trading** refers to the process by which clients can use the attributes of a service as well as its name to find the appropriate servers and services on a network. A **trader** (or **broker**) acts as an intermediary between client and server. These concepts belong without doubt to the market mode of coordination.

These principles were behind the NASA Astrophysics Data System (ADS), which is already claimed to be the largest distributed system in the world, and is expected to incorporate over 100,000 users within 2 years. It uses a wide variety of hardware and software, to allow scientists all over the world to share text, numerical data and images from outer space.

The problem faced by scientists before ADS was the fragmentation of data and processing, residing in different formats on a wide variety of machines. It was difficult to discover what data there were, or what applications had already been written by other scientists at other institutions.

For the end-user, ADS provides 'one-stop-shopping' – the ability to retrieve and process data regardless of its location or technical format. For the computer industry, ADS demonstrates the feasibility of such networks with heterogeneous hardware and operating systems, and the feasibility of evolving such networks without disrupting existing operations using existing standards and protocols.

Box 2.9
ANSA principles of
distributed systems

Separation

- Assume every module is on a separate physical platform (the most complex case for the designer). Optimize by sharing platforms (co-location), but without changing the internal design of any module.
- Each system is responsible for processing its encapsulated data
- All interactions with services are through defined interfaces
- All detected interaction faults and failures are named and reported

Heterogeneity

- Assume heterogeneity
- Abstract away from unnecessary diversity, while still retaining the benefit of specialization

Federation

- Each system controls its own policies and services locally
- Cooperating systems negotiate the sharing of services
- Cooperating systems identify the available services via a context-relative naming scheme
- A trading facility is provided through which federated cooperating systems can organize and control the sharing of services

2.6.5 *Coordination within/between projects*

If two or more parallel projects are building or maintaining systems that will need to coordinate, it is almost certain that some coordination will be needed between the projects. Since projects are human organizations, they may also be coordinated as hierarchies, markets or networks. We might expect that hierarchically coordinated projects are best able to build hierarchically coordinated systems, and so on. Of course, it is not quite as simple as that. We shall return to this issue in Chapter 5.

2.7 Summary of chapter

Now we know what coordination is, why (and how much) we want it, and (broadly) how it can be achieved. Now we are ready to look at the concepts and techniques of information coordination, creating and managing the underlying information models for:

- scoping and coordination of projects,
- scoping and coordination of systems.

The next two chapters will look at planning and scoping of projects and systems, and therefore at the scoping of information models.

Notes

1. K. K. Smith, 'Rabbits, lynxes, and organizational transitions', in J. R. Kimberly and R. E. Quinn, *New Futures: The challenge of managing corporate transitions,* Homewood, IL: Dow-Jones Irwin, 1984, pp. 269–94.
2. E. Jantsch, 'Evolving images of man: Dynamic guidance for the mankind process', in E. Jantsch and C.H. Waddington (eds.), *Evolution and Consciousness: Human systems in transition,* Reading, MA: Addison-Wesley, 1976, pp. 230–42.
3. S. Freud, *Outline of Psychoanalysis,* 1938.
4. K. K. Smith, *op. cit.*
5. T. W. Malone and K. Crowston, 'What is Coordination Theory and how can it help design cooperative work systems?', *CSCW 90 Proceedings,* October 1990, pp. 357–66.
6. *Ibid.*
7. J. L. Bradach and R. G. Eccles, 'Price, authority and trust: From ideal types to plural forms,' *Annual Review of Sociology,* 1989, pp. 97–118.
8. V. Gurbaxani and S. Whang, 'The impact of information systems on organizations and markets', *Communications of the ACM,* January 1991, pp. 59–73.
9. *Ibid.*
10. O. E. Williamson, *Markets and Hierarchies: Analysis and anti-trust implications,* New York: Free Press, 1975.
11. I. Berlin, *The Hedgehog and the Fox,* London: Weidenfeld & Nicolson, 1953. His list of hedgehogs includes: Dante, Plato, Lucretius, Pascal, Hegel, Dostoevsky, Nietzsche, Ibsen and Proust.
12. I. Berlin, *op. cit.* His list of foxes includes: Shakespeare, Herodotus, Aristotle, Montaigne, Erasmus, Molière, Goethe, Pushkin, Balzac and Joyce.
13. B. Hedberg, P. Nystrom and W. Starbuck, 'Camping on seesaws: Prescriptions for a self-designing organization', *Administrative Science Quarterly,* vol. 21, no. 1, 1976, pp. 41–65.
14. J. Briggs and F. D. Peat, *Turbulent Mirror: An illustrated guide to chaos theory and the science of wholeness,* New York: Harper & Row, 1989, p. 62.
15. T. Peters, *Liberation Management: Necessary disorganization for the nanosecond nineties,* New York: Alfred Knopf, 1992, p. 688.
16. G. Morgan, *Images of Organization,* London: Sage, 1986, pp. 98 ff.
17. *Ibid.,* p. 100.
18. *Ibid.,* pp. 98 ff, citing Fred Emery and W. Ross Ashby.
19. *ANSA Reference Manual,* Cambridge, UK: Architecture Projects Management Ltd, 1989. See also D. S. Marshak, 'ANSA: A model for distributed computing', *Network Monitor,* vol. 6, no. 11, November 1991.
20. *ANSA Reference Manual, op. cit.*

3 Planning

3.1 Introduction

A large British insurance company produced an information systems strategy some years ago. This was supposed to provide a stable framework for information systems development over an extended time period. This long-term IS strategy relied on a fixed view of the business, and a fixed view of the organization to support the business. But the insurance business is now moving very rapidly, mergers have taken place, and the organization has been restructured radically to keep up with the business. System development budgets have been cut, and IT spending is under increasing pressure. Corporate data models, on which the plans were based, are out of date and discredited. As a result of these pressures, the long-term plans have been all but abandoned. The systems development department now concentrates on solving short-term problems.

Many companies are in a similar situation. The grand visions of the past are put aside, and the focus is on short-term measures to support an increasingly dynamic business. Under these circumstances, is any planning possible at all? And what happens if we don't plan – do we merely drift into a yet worse mess, with integration further off than ever?

To try and answer these questions, in this chapter and the next, we shall discuss the theory and practice of **information systems planning**. This is an activity that is sometimes carried out as a single exercise before any systems development projects are allowed to start. Alternatively, it may be carried out cyclically, with periodic replanning exercises, or even (in very large organizations) continual adjustment to cater for changing requirements and opportunities.

The result of a planning exercise is, of course, a plan. This plan is sometimes expressed as a schedule of projects, sometimes as a blueprint of systems, sometimes as a set of policies and/or standards. It may include a high-level business case cost-justification for all systems development, together with any technical infrastructure or organizational change that may be required.

In the previous chapter, we saw that there were three basic approaches to coordination: hierarchical, network and market. We can find the same three basic approaches to information systems planning. These three approaches result in different types of plan. All attempt, in one way or another, to create a framework for system development, enhancement and repair projects. All, therefore, provide a starting point for coordination between projects and between systems.

Within information systems development, there are three main tasks of coordination: beginning, middle and ending.

- **Scoping**   Dividing a problem area into (semi-)independent sub-areas, whose solutions can be developed (in parallel or sequence) with minimum interaction effort, and minimum integration risk.

- **Interaction**   Liaison and reconciliation between the separate developments, to minimize integration risk.
- **Integration**   Putting the separately developed pieces together to achieve a coherent solution to the original problem.

Planning includes some scoping, usually based on an outline information model of the whole enterprise, or some reasonably large part of it, known as an **information architecture**. The three planning approaches all involve the production of an information architecture, which is used for scoping. Most scoping techniques involve some form of clustering.

The structure of the chapter is as follows. After describing the three main approaches to information systems planning, we consider how the three approaches affect the cost-justification of a technical infrastructure. In the following chapter we look in detail at the scope, purpose and perspective of an information architecture, and at the techniques of scoping.

3.2 Why plan?

This book is not about the design of individual information systems, satisfying a set of requirements, built by individual projects. It is about programmes of designing many coordinated systems, satisfying the complete requirements of a large organization, forming a 'whole'.

What do we mean by the word 'whole'? It denotes coherence, lack of fragmentation. If a structure is whole, its parts are also in a sense whole, not fragmented but coherent. This may be because all parts are guided by the one single process, by a development programme which follows the same principles at all levels, from the preliminary sketch to the tiniest detail. Such a development programme will of course contain many projects, in series or in parallel, each developing one part. Any two parts are related, in sometimes very complex and indirect ways, but remain compatible, consistent. And yet the boundaries between parts can be clearly perceived, each part is visible and makes sense on its own, as well as within a wider context.

In most development programmes today, this vision of coherence is at best only partly achieved. We can analyse what goes wrong; more importantly, we can identify what improvements can be made in planning and executing these programmes, subject to the culture and environment of the organization.

Common sense and experience show that such wholes cannot be implemented in a single step. Such projects are too large to be successful, producing a system too monolithic to be meaningful. The best we can achieve allows the whole to grow in many steps, over many years. Its final form cannot be predicted, except perhaps in ambiguous generalities, partly because the form is sensitive to details that cannot (and should not) be worked out in advance, but partly (and more importantly) because the organization itself learns during the development: the systems do not merely support the organization but transform it, or rather allow it to transform itself.

There are two common approaches to such multi-system design, with multi-project development. One is called piecemeal, and the other is called preconfiguration.

Piecemeal means that each system is built according to its own needs alone. Its features are determined by its direct costs and benefits. Each project is started and steered in isolation of other projects; communication between projects only takes place if of immediate benefit to the projects themselves. Piecemeal growth, by itself, will not create coherent wholes. This is exactly why people produce plans.

Preconfiguration means that each system is built to fit a prearranged position, within a planned framework or blueprint. The aim of such planning is to create coherent wholes in advance, and thereby provide order and organization in the large. The trouble with this form of planning is that it often fails to achieve the sought order. In the worst case, such a plan can be a mixture of meaningless generalities and ill-considered rigidities.

It is worth noting here that there is an important ambiguity in the word 'plan'. This word may be used to refer to a preconfiguration or blueprint, as in a building plan or an urban development plan. It may also refer to a scheme or schedule of activity, as in a military plan of action, or development programme. It may even refer to a combination of both.

3.3 Development versus maintenance

Within some project planning methods, there is a vision (explicit or implicit) of eliminating maintenance. This vision is misplaced. Indeed, in this section we shall question the very distinction that is drawn between development and maintenance. We shall argue that the distinction is not useful, as a systems plan should include both development and maintenance projects, and that it will become increasingly meaningless, as the future brings not an elimination of maintenance, but a transformation of both development and maintenance. The success of a project should not be measured in the amount of activity of information technologists, nor by whether they are following this or that way of satisfying the business requirements, but by the satisfaction of the business requirements themselves.

Development of new systems often creates a starting point for further maintenance. When first implemented, a system may represent a strategic or operational opportunity; such opportunities may only be fully converted into competitive advantage through the fine-tuning of intelligent and planned maintenance.

3.3.1 What is wrong with maintenance?

One of the problems with maintenance is that hardly anyone wants to do it. New development not only carries more status, but it is thought to add more weight of experience to a CV. So although maintenance is usually more difficult than developing new systems, it is avoided by many of the people who would be able to do it well, and may be left to those who are unable to demand more glamorous work. Alternatively, it is handed over to outside contractors, not all of whom are conscientious and loyal.

This can apply not only to the work itself, but also to the management of the work. Maintenance activity can sometimes be reactive, rushed, forced to deliver incompletely tested work, unable to tidy up the loose ends or bring the documentation up to date.

As a consequence of these pressures, it is difficult to carry out maintenance efficiently, or even competently. Each act of maintenance makes the system more tangled, and the documentation more incomprehensible or inaccurate. Instead of being an intellectual challenge, maintenance becomes an alienating frustration. It is remarkable that despite these pressures, many maintenance departments are better organized than the corresponding development departments.

But the real problem with maintenance is not the status and job satisfaction of the maintenance workers and their managers, but the inability (even of the best run maintenance departments) to fully satisfy the demands of the end-users.

It does not seem unreasonable for the end-users to want a system to be permanently available during business hours, with any operational or design faults being rectified as soon as they are discovered. Furthermore, in every organization, there is constant pressure on the end-users to innovate and improve their operations, and to respond promptly to changes in the environment. Many of the things the end-users want or need to do, in order to remain competitive, require changes or small additions to existing information systems.

These are reasonable things to want, but it would be a naive manager indeed who would expect to get this level of service. In many companies, the IT department cannot even cope with correcting the known faults in the system, and has practically given up hope of delivering any meaningful enhancements. Faced with this situation, end-users sometimes invent ways of by-passing the controls built into the computer system, giving them what they want in the short term, but possibly making things worse in the future.

3.3.2 *What prevents maintenance being presented in a better light?*

It is commonly assumed that there is a clear difference between development and maintenance, that they are different activities requiring different skills, tools and attitudes, as in Box 3.1.

However, in many organizations, the effective boundary between development and maintenance is based not on the type of activity, but on the size alone. Thus conversion of a large existing application system from one operating system to another is regarded as 'development', simply because it requires several man-years effort, whereas the creation of a new management reporting facility is regarded as maintenance, simply because it can be completed in a few man-weeks. This means that the maintenance manager is at a disadvantage, since s/he

Box 3.1
Perceived differences
between development
and maintenance
(*Thanks to Mel
Southerden*)

Beliefs about Development	Beliefs about Maintenance
Creating a system where none existed before	Altering the quality, functionality, user interface and/or technical platform of an existing system
CASE tools (analysis workbenches, code generation)	Reengineering tools, testing tools (debugging, dump and trace)
Project-based	Support-based
Large (coherent) chunks of work	Small fragments of work
Straightforward, capable of being done right first time	Complicated work done under extreme pressure, therefore error-prone
Budget under IT management control	Budget uncontrollable by IT management
User involvement in project	No user involvement required
Documentation correct	Documentation out of date

is typically responsible for spending a great proportion of the IT budget, without anything major to show for it (since, by definition, anything major is not counted as maintenance).

End-users often exploit the artificial distinction between development and maintenance, sometimes deliberately fragmenting a major enhancement into several minor enhancements, in order to keep the decision from being escalated to higher management.

3.3.3 *Eliminate maintenance by preventing it*

If you cannot increase the supply, why not reduce the demand? What happens in many organizations is that maintenance requests are discouraged, or prevented from reaching the maintenance team. Bureaucratic procedures and other communication barriers may be erected, or maintenance may become so expensive, long-winded, unreliable and unproductive that the business simply cannot afford it.

Even during development, altering the specification is discouraged or banned (by change control techniques) for fear that the system will otherwise never be completed. This postpones the maintenance until after implementation, when it becomes someone else's problem.

It might seem that the sensible way of solving the maintenance problem would be to make maintenance more effective. But the tactics that are adopted often seem to be focused more on eliminating maintenance, in the same way that one might talk about eliminating smallpox, or the traffic in hard drugs.

3.3.4 Attack maintenance via new development

The best way to reduce maintenance in the longer term is to replace the existing systems with more flexible, modular, high-quality systems. It is not necessary that these new systems support all future requirements from the start, provided that future requirements can be added in with the minimum of cost and disruption.

Architects have already discovered the benefits of flexible and modular design. In 1990, for example, the London-based TV news company ITN moved from a building where it would take months to rig up a new studio, to a building where it only takes hours. Architects are also becoming increasingly aware of the possibility, indeed in some complex situations the necessity, of postponing some design decisions until after construction. The Rare Books Library at Newnham College, Cambridge, for example, was built without air-conditioning, its humidity was monitored for 14 months, and then a de-humidifier was added. The important point here is that this addition did not represent an oversight by the architects; the option to add an appropriate air-conditioning unit, after monitoring the behaviour of the building across all four seasons, had been written into the original contract and allowed for in the original design.[2] Within IT, an approximate equivalent can be found in the object-oriented concept of **deferred methods**.

3.3.5 Attack maintenance by proactive management

Maintenance often comes as a surprise to the manager. Better planning can take the surprise out, and lead to more efficient maintenance. This can be done at two levels.

At a micro level, expressing the structure of the existing system in the form of a requirements model (through reverse engineering techniques) allows the assumptions and inflexibilities of the existing system to be analysed. Sometimes, a precisely targeted piece of maintenance, removing a specific inflexibility, is a good investment, saving several future maintenance tasks. This could for example involve creating data tables in order to remove data from program code, or replacing data access code with standard subroutines. Although these opportunities are not new, they tended in the past to be identified and planned rather unsystematically. With a good information model, it becomes possible to identify these opportunities more easily, and to plan them more systematically.

At a macro level, there are several engineering models that predict the amount of maintenance a system is likely to need, depending on age and other factors[3] (see Figure 3.1). This allows the maintenance activity to be budgeted and

Figure 3.1
Predicted cost of
maintaining 3GL
application system

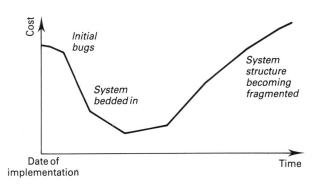

scheduled in advance. It also allows the optimum time for system replacement to be calculated, so that systems are replaced before they become too difficult to maintain.

3.3.6 Attack maintenance via re(verse) engineering

Many companies adopt the same accounting conventions for software as for physical assets, including depreciation. Thus after several years, a system may have a book value of zero, enabling it to be discarded and replaced without upsetting the shareholders.

However, such a system represents a great deal of past effort. Some of this effort, of course, represents solutions to problems that no longer exist. Some technical problems may disappear with advances in technology. But much of the intellectual effort that went into the old system may still be valid; it would be of value if it could only be extracted and recycled.

CASE technology has become very useful in engineering forwards, from a model that represents the complete requirements through to a generated system. Reverse engineering takes all or some of an existing system, and works backwards to a model, which can then be cleaned up, integrated with new requirements, and engineered forwards again to a new system.

The long-term research objective of reverse engineering is to be able to produce a perfect and complete model of any existing system. At present, the available tools and techniques are some way short of this. But if we accept that any recycling is better than none at all, then we have to admit that reverse engineering has an enormous value already, if we can only avoid placing unreasonable demands on the technology. One of the most important areas of reverse engineering is to support the transition from existing systems to new systems, analysing the data structure of the existing system in order to design efficient bridges and interfaces.

In the past, the main alternative to custom-made application software was to purchase application packages. Although the good packages are often highly parametrized, to allow minor differences in requirements to be handled without modifying the software, major changes can be extremely hard to handle. Furthermore, packages are very difficult to integrate, unless you buy all your packages from the same vendor, and sometimes not even then.

As CASE technology becomes more widespread, an intermediate alternative is emerging: application templates. An application template is a complete solution, including specification models and all generated code. As with application packages, a template usually does not fit the business requirements perfectly; however, unlike application packages, a template can be easily altered and extended. Since the underlying data model can be made consistent with home-grown data models, the generated systems can be easily interfaced or integrated. Furthermore, with Integrated CASE tools (I-CASE), several templates from different sources can be fitted together, to build complex application portfolios.

3.3.7 *Conclusions*

It should be clear from this discussion that IS planning should cover development and maintenance together.

1. Produce a single plan for all development and maintenance. The same criteria should be used for evaluating and ranking development and maintenance requests, to remove any incentive to disguise development as maintenance, or vice versa.
2. Understand the factors that positively or negatively affect the maintainability of systems. Not only development but also maintenance itself may affect subsequent maintenance. Raise the priority ranking of these factors when making design trade-off decisions.
3. Integrate the tools and techniques used by development and maintenance. Ensure that the development skills (e.g. analysis) are available to mainten-ance teams, and the maintenance skills (e.g. sensitivity to actual system usage) are available to development teams.
4. Ensure every new development project devotes an appropriate proportion of its budget (e.g. 25 per cent) to post-implementation enhancements.
5. Make sure that development contracts are consistent with service level agreements for maintenance, in costing assumptions and design criteria.
6. Having done steps 1–5, organize the department to remove the separation of development and maintenance resources, and establish positive serviceability targets through the entire software life cycle.

We shall explore the combined planning of development and maintenance activity in this chapter. Other topics of maintenance and maintainability will be discussed in a later chapter.

3.4 Top-down planning (hierarchical approach)

Let us start by considering a methodology that produces preconfigurations as part of the planning process. **Information Engineering** (IE), based on the writings of James Martin[4] and Clive Finkelstein,[5] probably contains the most successful top-down planning approach of any methodology (see Figure 3.2). In the IE approach, an Information Strategy Plan is developed by deriving a **Business Systems Architecture** (BSA) from the Information Architecture. The BSA is a precon-figured portfolio of Information Systems. A long-term development schedule is then prepared, to build the systems one by one over a period of several years, until the BSA is completely implemented.

Figure 3.2
Top-down
development based on
information
architecture

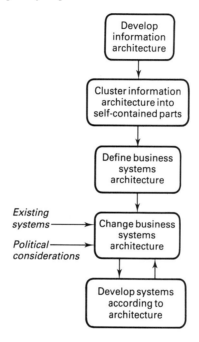

3.4.1 Coherent structures

A business systems architecture needs to be not an inflexible monolithic structure but a **coherent structure**.

This concept is defined in Box 3.2 and illustrated in Figure 3.3.

The level of coherence that has to be achieved within **Financial Accounting** is greater than the level of coherence that has to be achieved between Financial Accounting and **Management Accounting**.

To illustrate this, consider a change to financial accounting policies. This would have to be implemented consistently across the enterprise, probably at the end of the financial year, in order to maintain the consistency of the published accounts. However, changes to management accounting policies can be implemented mid-year. Management accounting policies may be out of step with financial

- Flexible, stable, not rigid
- Quasi-hierarchy of areas

  need not be strictly hierarchical, can have overlaps

  also allows for matrix management (joint ownership / sponsorship of applications)

- For each area, there are some things shared and controlled within the area, that are not shared and controlled outside
- An area may be the scope of a development or repair project or subproject

Box 3.2
Features of a coherent structure

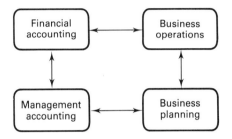

Figure 3.3
Example of business systems architecture (extract)

accounting policies: for example, there was a time when many firms used historical costs for the published financial accounts, but used inflation accounting policies for internal management accounting purposes. In other words, there may need to be changes in one area that do not immediately affect other areas. Without this condition, it may be impossible to implement any changes at all.

3.4.2 *Advantages of top-down planning*

- Enables corporate information systems to be composed of discrete modules which fit together
- Achieves appropriate consistency of information
- Permits separate design projects to proceed by themselves
- Control instead of chaos
- Senior management involvement
- Sharing costs of database infrastructure

Box 3.3
Advantages of top-down planning

The advantages of top-down planning are shown in Box 3.3. James Martin uses the fable of the Tower of Babel to demonstrate the need for centralized coordination. 'With cheap computers and user-friendly languages, if everyone designs his own data, it will be like the Tower of Babel. A high price will be paid in lack of management information, inability to improve procedures, and future management costs.'[6]

3.4.3 Limits to top-down planning

However, experience shows several potential problems with this approach.

1. The derivation of the Business Systems Architecture (BSA) from the information architecture can be very difficult. The aim of the derivation is to define systems with the fewest interfaces. However, because the information architecture is merely a high-level sketch, the derivation is an optimization based on incomplete knowledge. The systems architect has to make educated guesses as to the scale of interfaces between systems.
2. In practice, the BSA is usually compromised, by political and pragmatic considerations, before any development starts. There is no formal technique for modifying the BSA to cater for these considerations, and some methodologists appear to regard any such compromise with silent disapproval.
3. Since the BSA is designed to fit together, some of the components can only be cost-justified in terms of supporting the others. These components are known as 'infrastructure'. Indeed, some Information Engineers believe that the main purpose of the BSA (perhaps even the main purpose of Information Strategy Planning) is to persuade companies to invest in 'infrastructure'. But there is no agreed method for analysing the detailed requirements for such 'infrastructure'.
4. Although the BSA defines broad scopes of projects and systems, it provides no guidance for resolving more detailed scoping issues or inter-project differences.
5. The BSA ignores the existing systems. Since many of these systems will continue to be operated for many years, this is unrealistic.
6. There is no method for changing the BSA once the development has started, to cater for new insights and changed circumstances. There are three non-methods:

    (a) Change the projects and systems as required, but do not make changes to the BSA, which therefore becomes obsolete.
    (b) Change the BSA in an ad hoc piecemeal manner, to follow and reflect the changes to the actual projects and systems.
    (c) Create a new BSA from scratch. If this is done thoroughly, using the official IE techniques, and ignoring the original version of the BSA, there will usually be major differences between the two versions. It will then be politically necessary to adjust the second version (in an ad hoc piecemeal manner) so that it more or less resembles the first version.

7. Even if the information architecture is reasonably stable (in the sense that small changes can be absorbed without requiring radical structural change),

this stability is not necessarily inherited by the BSA. Some Information Engineers believe dogmatically in the stability of the BSA, which actually inhibits them from making necessary changes. Alternatively, the changes are 'damped', to prevent wild fluctuations.

8. The BSA assumes that the boundaries between the enterprise and its environment are fixed. There are no longer many organizations that dare make this assumption.

For these reasons, Information Engineering is widely (but wrongly) perceived as a methodology aimed at greenfield situations. There can be an uncomfortable mismatch between what the methodology prescribes and what actually occurs.

The proponents of the top-down planning approach use the story of the Tower of Babel to argue for central coordination and common terminology. However, the story can equally be interpreted to draw the opposite conclusion. The people of Babylon set themselves an over-ambitious task, their tower threatened to reach the heavens. Providence intervened, interfered with their ability to coordinate their activities, interfered with their ability to understand one another, at which they gave up the attempt to build a single coordinated centrally planned structure, and dispersed. The Tower of Babel can be seen as a metaphor for a collectively shared lofty vision, and the hubris (i.e. non-feasibility) of attempting to achieve total coordination.

3.5 Organic planning (network approach)

The approach outlined in this section differs from the piecemeal and the preconfiguration approach – it attempts to generate coherent wholes without a preordained framework. The plan that is produced must be understood strictly as a scheme of activity, without a preconfigured structure. To avoid confusion, we shall call this a **strategy**, composed of a series of policies and principles, and a schedule of projects. Here is how we arrive at this strategy. (Note that the starting point, and the first two steps are much the same as in the top-down planning approach; subsequent steps diverge.)

1. By discussion with senior management, discover the business objectives and goals. By observation of the organization and its environment, discover its business strengths, weaknesses, opportunities and threats.

2. Build a high-level conceptual model of the functions and entities of the organization. We call this an information architecture. It may include new concepts (generalizations, consolidations, opportunities for cross-fertilization between different areas of activity) as well as familiar concepts. Making the conceptual structure explicit in this way allows the development of such new concepts to be rationally managed. In some cases, it may be appropriate to consider changing the boundary between the organization and its environment.

3. Survey the existing and planned systems, together with the interfaces between them. By comparison with the information architecture, assess the

quality and adequacy of the systems and their interfaces. By discussion with senior management, discover the major system problems and opportunities.

4. Establish a set of system development principles, and establish the procedures and support groups and technical infrastructure to carry them out. These principles will be based on the standard set adumbrated below, but will need to be tailored and interpreted for the particular organization, depending upon its present situation (e.g. current skills portfolio), its priorities (e.g. long-term versus short-term, speed versus cost versus caution) and its culture and style (e.g. are decisions usually quick or drawn-out, democratic or handed-down, obeyed or challenged, closed or reopened?).

5. Identify some important projects that will need to be carried out in the next three to five years. Rank them in importance and urgency, consider the logical sequence of development and any political factors, and produce an outline schedule. *The effort devoted to these major projects should be less than half the total available resources.* (The remainder will be allocated to tactical projects and infrastructure.)

6. Finally, some tactical planning: identify some small and medium projects to be carried out in parallel with the major projects during the first year.

For steps 1 and 2, techniques of Business Process Reengineering may be used. This provides a radical critique of the business activities, and often results in identification and elimination of redundant activity, or opportunities to alter the boundaries of the organization.

3.5.1 Projects

Following the arguments of a previous subsection, projects include enhancement and repair projects as well as new development. Routine maintenance (e.g. bug-fixing, or amending data hard-coded into programs) need not be included, unless the need for a fix prompts a redesign effort. (Note: the definition of 'routine' is a management question, not a merely technical one. For example, instead of repeatedly amending hard-coded data, it may be sensible to remove the data from the program into a separate set of tables. Or instead of coding a new algorithm every time a new discount formula is negotiated, it may be possible to parametrize the formula. This may require more time and effort than a single amendment, but less than a series of such amendments.)

The architect Christopher Alexander, who developed this approach originally for the purposes of town planning (as an alternative to the top-down approach adopted by both Ebenezer Howard and Le Corbusier), uses a metaphorical language to describe this: *whole, repair, fabric, centre, healing.* We shall adopt his metaphors, and then try to define what they mean for information systems.

The overriding principle is that every project must 'make whole'. It should repair and maintain existing wholes (this implies respect for the coherence of existing structure, although a project may abandon any particular mechanisms); it should create new wholes; it should establish a continuous fabric of wholes around itself. Thus a good project is not merely fabricating new fabric, but repairing and patching torn/worn places in the existing fabric. (Christopher Alexander calls this 'healing'.)

Each project has a 'centre'. This may be either an entity type or a process. Around this centre is arrayed several other entity types or processes. The rule is that, as one such centre is produced, it must contribute to larger structures, and also bring together smaller structures – it must be both unifying and unified.

For example, consider a project that is centred around the EMPLOYEE entity type. It will bring together, perhaps, aspects of personnel, payroll, work allocation, and other related applications. It therefore unifies many views of EMPLOYEE into a single structure. And at the same time, EMPLOYEE may be recognized as a special case of PAYEE, so that payments to employees may be unified into the larger structure of all outward payments.

For another example, consider a project centred around the ISSUE PURCHASE ORDER process. It will bring together aspects of supplies, contracts, subcontracts, service contracts and perhaps even insurance policies. It therefore unifies several views of the same process. And at the same time, it contributes to a larger structure, containing deliveries and invoices and payments to suppliers.

In general, an entity type contributes to a larger structure by being a subtype of a more general entity type, or by playing a role shared with other entity types. And a process contributes to a larger structure by taking part either in the life cycle of a given entity type, or in a control loop. Or both.

Peripheral entity types will contribute by being part of the horizon of a central entity type, or by providing a supplementary information structure (e.g. an historical or geographical breakdown). Peripheral processes will contribute by establishing the preconditions for a central process. But these peripheral entity types and processes become in turn the centres of their own, smaller areas.

Thus we can restate our goal as follows: to weave a fabric of centres, such that each centre supports one or more larger centre, and is supported by smaller centres. Furthermore, the fabric should be complete: there should be no 'negative space'.

In traditional design of computerized information systems, the spaces between systems are often merely the areas that nobody has bothered about. This is **negative space**. But the redress for this ill is not total automation, which leaves no space at all, but deliberately created space. Space in which the system users can be imaginative and innovative, freed of the burdens of repetitive and inflexible administration. This is **positive space**. (Although these concepts of positive and negative space are metaphorical, they can be linked to concepts about human-centred systems design, being developed in Scandinavia and elsewhere.[7] The relevance of these concepts increases as Information Engineering moves from its traditional base of 1970s-style automation of clerical transaction processing, and towards cooperative decision-support systems. Many people now believe that user-friendliness is profoundly affected by system scope and structure, and is not simply a matter of having the right front-end.)

3.5.2 *Measurement*

As seen above, one of the difficulties of the preconfiguration approach is to quantify the benefits from interfacing and integration. With the approach proposed here, each project identifies (is forced to identify) its own integration requirements, which must be expressed in terms of business/user benefit. Ideally, this approach should be linked with full Business Process Reengineering, so that the business benefits and organizational risks of integrating a particular chain of processes will be properly understood and managed.

3.5.3 *Systems development principles*

In this approach, projects are selected, planned and managed according to a set of principles. Each organization may define its own principles, but here is a reasonable set to start from:

1. There is a maximum project size. This may be defined in various ways, and will vary from one organization to another. The Information Strategy should provide firm guidelines ruling out excessively large projects, and restricting projects to what is feasible with existing project management skills and procedures. (It may be intended to enhance these skills and to redesign these procedures, but until the project management infrastructure is in place, large projects should not be contemplated.)

2. There is an ideal mixture of project sizes in progress at a given time. Within the maximum size already defined, there will be large, medium and small projects. A rough guideline should be established for the relative numbers of such projects, or for the proportion of resources devoted to projects of different sizes. (This will enable, among other things, a skills development path for project managers.) There should also be a mixture of high-risk and low-risk projects, and a mixture of urgent and non-urgent projects. Time-critical projects should be mixed with innovation-critical projects, and projects requiring much attention from senior management should be mixed with projects requiring relatively little attention.

3. The projects in progress at the same time should not all be concentrated on the same small corner of the overall fabric, but should be distributed between different functions, different groups of users. This allows not merely political balance but also systems balance and resource balance.

4. Each project must have an identifiable centre, and contribute to an identifiable larger whole, more significant than itself. Those managing the project must be able to show how their project will contribute to the overall fabric. The growing *awareness* of such larger wholes is an essential success factor towards our goal. Some of these wholes may be predicted, but some may emerge as you go along, and must be allowed to develop without preconceptions or forcing.

5. A larger whole has a discernible life cycle. First, one project hints at a more general structure, which it is outside its own scope and terms of reference to

explore. Then other projects help to indicate the outlines of the larger whole, which gradually takes shape as each project enhances our understanding of it. A series of further projects then completes the whole.

6. A project will usually play simultaneous but different roles with respect to different larger wholes. Each project should therefore aim to do three things. First, it should help to complete at least one major whole that is already clearly defined. Second, it should help to pin down some other, less clearly defined whole(s), previously only hinted at. Third, it should hint at some entirely new whole(s), which will only clearly emerge with later projects. A project may use both 'development' and 'maintenance' tools and techniques.

7. Each project should be expressed clearly in advance. A communicable vision of the project can be provided through a well-defined portion of the information architecture, which the project is to analyse, or for which the project is to design a system.

8. Each project must create, and each system must have, coherent and well-shaped decision space next to it.

9. Each system must either be a simple and compact unity, or it must be made up of several simple and compact parts, one of these being major and the others minor, hanging onto it.

10. Interface bridges with other systems are built afterwards, incrementally. The bridges should serve the systems, and the systems serve the users. You do not design the systems to serve the bridges.

11. Because the information architecture represents the conceptual framework, this will evolve as the organization develops new concepts. Each project may feed new insights back to the Information Architecture, making it richer and more powerful.

A summary of these concepts is shown in Box 3.4.

- No preconceived system architecture necessary
- Each project builds a coherent/whole system
- Each project contributes to larger wholes, increases overall coherence
- Large projects consist of coherent subprojects
- Coherence is defined through
  - Clustering of information architecture
  - Entity-specific business objectives
    (e.g. CUSTOMER or PRODUCT)
  - Business Process Reengineering

Box 3.4
Features of organic growth

3.5.4 *Conclusions*

We can agree with Le Corbusier that the plan is a generator, generating both activity and structure. The question is how the plan is to be formulated: does it specify the structure itself, or does it merely specify a method by which the

Le plan est le générateur.
Sans plan, il y a désordre, arbitraire.
Le plan porte en lui l'essence de la sensation.
(*Le Corbusier* Vers une Architecture)

structure will evolve? This section has suggested the latter approach.

A similar evolutionary approach has been tried by Christopher Alexander and colleagues in California. They developed a set of principles for urban development, and then conducted a large-scale simulation to test the principles. A group of architecture students surveyed a real area of the city, discovered what kinds of buildings would be required in a redevelopment of the area, and used the principles to grow a series of coordinated designs, without any zoning or grand design. Although such an artificial experiment cannot be regarded as a definitive proof of the approach, the obvious merit of the models and drawings gives some plausibility to its claims, at least as an alternative to traditional town planning.[8]

Empirical experience with the approach recommended here is admittedly limited. The plausibility of the approach rests on the known difficulties with the other approaches, and on the analogy with architecture and urban development. But the arguments for the preconfiguration approach are usually based merely on the comparison with the piecemeal approach. This statement of a third option should at least serve as a challenge for the proponents of preconfiguration to develop a new and stronger justification.

3.6 Exchange planning (market approach)

Having considered planning approaches that correspond to hierarchies and networks, let us now look at the market approach to planning. We start with an analogy, taken from a market-based approach to planning and controlling local transport services, and then apply this to planning and controlling information systems.

3.6.1 Local transport interfaces

A complex journey by public transport may involve many changes. To get from Ashford to Dallas, I may have to get a mainline train to Waterloo station, a bus to Victoria, then another train to Gatwick airport, followed by a direct plane (if I'm lucky) to Dallas Fort Worth airport. At each interchange I may have to walk several hundred yards, and wait upwards of an hour. Each leg of the journey involves a different transportation company.

Some people have no choice but to use public transport. Others will use public transport in preference to their own cars only if it is safe and convenient. If the walking distances are short, and if the interchanges are pleasant places to wait, this not only benefits the passengers, but by increasing passenger revenue also benefits the transport companies themselves. Therefore there is some incentive for these companies to coordinate.

Some cities have a central transport planning department, with total control over all public transport services. Timetables are synchronized, so that the bus arrives at the station at least two minutes before the train leaves. Private transport companies (if they exist at all) are given licenses to operate exactly specified services.

In other cities, there is a free-for-all between rival companies. Timetables and routes are arranged for the convenience and competitive advantage of each transport company. Profitable routes are packed with rival vehicles. Powerful companies try to establish hubs, at which most or all of the services are operated by the same company. A passenger conveyed to such a hub then becomes a temporary captive of the company, and is forced to change onto another vehicle from the same company. Since passengers spend money while waiting at hubs, there may even be little incentive for the company to reduce the waiting times between its own services.

There is however a third option, which we can characterize as the market option.[9] In this, instead of hubs being controlled by individual transport companies, each aiming at its own competitive advantage, the hubs are controlled by the local community. Transport operators are invited to provide services into the hub, on specified conditions. Competition between transport operators is encouraged.

3.6.2 Interface engineering

In the organic approach, as we saw above, interface bridges with other systems are built afterwards, incrementally. The bridges are to serve the systems, and the systems serve the users. You do not design the systems to serve the bridges.

Here, the opposite seems to hold. We are designing the bridges or interfaces first. But this difference is not as strong as it appears. The bridges are designed first, true, but according to an understanding of what the systems themselves and their users are likely to need. A bridge (or interchange) between two or more information systems is itself an information system.

To plan such interchanges or bridges, some protocols or interfaces need to be defined. These will be based on the types of communication anticipated between the systems. The ANSA principles of Open Distributed Processing, mentioned in Chapter 2, can be expected to provide a strong basis for planning detailed protocols for specific applications.

The detailed input for this planning will probably be some analysis of the **speech acts** between systems, together with the **public objects** to which these speech acts refer. This approach is used by such methodologies as SAMPO (Speech-act based office modelling approach),[10] which emphasize the cooperative or collective features of work and the role of communications in coordination of the collective efforts. SAMPO provides methods for analysing and describing office communications. This is an area that awaits future exploration, and is linked to ongoing research in **electronic promising**[11] and **electronic contracting**.[12]

When the interfaces have been clearly defined, this makes the use of commercial application packages easier. The development of industry standard protocols and interfaces will almost certainly prompt the development of commercial packages as interchangeable commodities. Therefore market-based planning will want to make maximum use of packages, both those available presently and those that may become available in the future.

3.7 Infrastructure and its cost-justification

3.7.1 Introduction

One of the main reasons why top-down planning is thought necessary is that it includes or enables the planning and funding of infrastructure. This section discusses the alternatives to top-down or central planning.

3.7.2 What is infrastructure?

There are several levels or types of infrastructure in IT:

- Production infrastructure – the hardware, software, procedures, skills, and other facilities required to run information systems.
- Development infrastructure – the hardware, software, procedures, skills, and other facilities required to build and maintain information systems.
- Information infrastructure – the central core databases, on which all information systems are dependent, such as Customer database or Product database.
- Decision-support superstructure – general-purpose query and data manipulation facilities that sit on top of the information systems, including report writers, data extracting, spreadsheet and graphics facilities.
- Management overhead – including all required administration and coordination.

Note that it depends on your perspective whether you regard something as infra- (below) or super- (above). Whether something counts as infra- or super-, it is a technological investment that transcends the requirements of a single information system (see Figure 3.4).

Figure 3.4
What is infra? What is super?

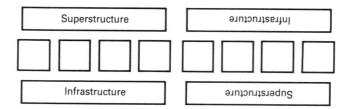

3.7.3 Planning and accounting

Although planning and accounting are closely linked within most organizations, it is not necessary that they follow the same structure. Planning says: this is a good idea, it will generate more benefit (over time) than it costs. This infrastructure is worth having, because it **can** be paid for. It does not necessarily specify how it **will** be paid for, in terms of how the costs will be allocated between different organization units over time. This is a matter for accounting.

Obviously, nothing should be planned unless there is a cost distribution algorithm that will leave everyone no worse off (and at least some better off). How can we prove (or at least produce a plausible and reasoned argument) that something can be paid for?

The investment decision may be made by a single manager or board (single funding), or may be shared between several different managers (joint funding). In the case of joint funding, there will be some agreement in advance how the costs and risks are to be shared, although this agreement may sometimes be vague or implicit, with the details to be negotiated later, perhaps after the actual costs and benefits can be measured.

In a hierarchical organization, the infrastructure is usually owned centrally, with some hierarchical charging mechanism to allocate actual costs to the relevant organization units. In a market-oriented organization, infrastructure is owned by the unit or units that have funded its development, who can charge horizontally for its use.

Among market-oriented organizations we include highly decentralized holding companies, where the subsidiaries may trade voluntarily with one other, or not, without interference from the parent company. We also include confederations and associations of companies, with separate ownership, but with some shared operations or interests. For example, many Stock Exchanges and Commodity Exchanges can be seen as nothing more than an organization owned jointly by member companies (i.e. brokers and dealers) for the purposes of infrastructure; these members may elect a council for central planning of investment in infrastructure, or they may adopt the market approach, with the larger members selling operational services (i.e. infrastructure) to the smaller members.

There are four combinations of these factors, with one or two approaches per combination, making five alternative approaches altogether (see Box 3.5).

Box 3.5
Coordinated funding –
alternative approaches

	Single funding	Joint funding
Hierarchical transactions	1 Centralized	2 Decentralized 3 Coalition
Market transactions	4 Entrepreneurial	5 Joint enterprise

1. Centralized

Top management estimates the total benefits, which are compared with the estimated total costs and the project risks. Although the organization units may be consulted before the investment decision is made, and may participate in the detailed specification of requirements, they are usually given no choice whether they use the infrastructure or not. Top management has the power to allocate charges between organization units as it sees fit.

2. Decentralized   A provisional allocation of the costs between organizational units is produced. If the manager of each organizational unit is prepared to bear his/her share of the costs (based on a calculation that his/her estimated benefits exceed his/her estimated costs), then the investment goes ahead.

3. Coalition   The organization units funding the investment need not include all of the organization units expected to benefit from the investment, as long as they can estimate enough benefit between them to justify the project. The use of the infrastructure can be extended later, which will bring further reduction in costs to the original participants, but this is an added bonus.

4. Entrepreneurial   One organization unit invests in infrastructure, on the assumption that this infrastructure will be of use to other organization units. Depending on the nature of the organization, the use of the infrastructure can then be traded horizontally, either on the basis of a negotiated financial cross-charge, or in return for some other benefits.

5. Joint enterprise   A group of organization units agrees to fund infrastructure costing more than they together can justify internally, on the assumption that this can be traded with other organization units later.

From a rationalist point of view, the central planning approach is clearly best. It is the only one that completely balances the total costs with the total benefits, and ensures everything is included, nothing is counted twice, and all risks are properly considered. So why do we not do all our planning this way?

The rationalist point of view ignores two things. First, that the amount of information available at the centre is limited. Its knowledge is necessarily less (in quantity, accuracy and timeliness) than the sum of the knowledge of the parts, since there will always be some selection, distortion and delay in reporting information from the periphery to the centre. This selection, distortion and delay are repeated at every level of the hierarchy, even with the most up-to-date computerized communication systems. And second, that the ability of the centre to handle complexity is also limited. In a totally centralized system, it is only in the centre that decision-making skills can be developed, and these skills will always be overstretched.

Therefore, based on inadequate information, and limited capacity for coping with complexity, the centre may not be able to make any better decisions than the periphery, and its mistakes will be bigger and more disastrous. After all, if central planning worked perfectly, the Soviet Union would not have collapsed.

To say this is not to dismiss the idea of central planning altogether. Many centralized organizations do survive and thrive. Central planning is common in Japan and Western Europe, and is not unknown in the United States of America.

All successful organizations have a moderate amount of central planning, balanced against some local autonomy. The right balance varies from one organization to another, and from one culture to another. Some organizations, seeking the ideal balance, swing violently from one extreme to the other: total decentralization one year, followed by central power the following year. Pragmatists (and Taoists) stick to the middle way.

One of the problems with the coalition solution is the fear of the free rider. Managers of organizational units often find it difficult to forget that they are competing with one another. Thus if one manager doubles revenue at reduced cost, only to find that another manager has trebled revenue and halved cost, the first will be made to feel a failure. Even if the costs are shared equitably between organizational units after the project has been completed, the manager(s) who took the original risk may feel inadequately compensated for having taken the risk in the first place. (We shall return to some of the issues surrounding coalitions in Chapter 8.)

3.7.4 Who pays for infrastructure?

With any resource that is to be shared between several users, there is always a problem allocating costs. Whatever algorithm you come up with, someone is bound to object. Indeed, it is perfectly possible to come up with an algorithm under which everybody believes themselves disadvantaged. (Technocrats take this outcome, perhaps rather optimistically, as a sign that justice has been done after all.) Note: the planned distribution algorithm may include contingent elements, as long as the risks are properly balanced. In other words, there may be different algorithms for different scenarios.

Since the actual benefits from the use of the resource are likely to differ from the expected benefits, there will inevitably be some users who would do better sharing costs according to the expected benefits, while others would do better sharing costs according to the actual benefits. Even when algorithms are agreed in advance, based on the expected benefits, it is common for user departments who have done comparatively less well to argue for a 'fairer' redistribution of costs.

However, there is an important difference between social distributive justice and distribution within an enterprise. Whereas a human society usually contains people who do not contribute economically to the society, and have no prospect of doing so in the future (perhaps the old, the severely handicapped, etc.), an enterprise should not include any parts that do not and never will make a net contribution to the objectives of the enterprise. This applies both to profit-making organizations and NFPs (Not-For-Profit organizations), although in the case of NFPs, the contribution may be difficult to express in economic terms.

However, this may not be reflected in the internal accounting systems. Some organizations have so-called cost centres, to which costs are allocated, but whose benefits are not directly accounted for. This does not prevent planning, as long as the benefits from the investment can be estimated.

3.7.5 Town planning analogy

If a builder puts an office block in the middle of nowhere, who pays for the transport links and utilities? There are several possible approaches:

- The builder pays, and this cost is absorbed by the tenants of the office block, in return for the privilege of seclusion. However, this makes the area very attractive to other builders, who can then take advantage of an existing low-cost infrastructure. This may then erode the benefits to the first tenants.
- One builder (or a consortium of builders) must plan to build enough office space to cost-justify the required infrastructure.
- The local authority and utility companies pay, and this cost is spread across the area/region/country.
- The local authority and utility companies pay, and this cost will be spread across future users of the infrastructure.
- The first office block makes do with inadequate infrastructure, until more office blocks are built nearby. When sufficient 'critical mass' is attained, a proper infrastructure can be cost-justified and built by central planners or entrepreneurs.

Note: there are important planning questions as to whether we want a cluster of office developments in this particular area. What we cannot afford is to have infrastructure that brings less benefit than it costs.

The differences between London Docklands and Paris La Defense are instructive here. In London, although the funding of public transport links became something of a political question, the Conservative government was able to demonstrate the success (in their own terms) of its hands-off approach to planning, since large amounts of cheap office space was made available to civil service departments and private sector companies, mainly at the expense of Canadian and Scandinavian property companies, without public funding. However, critics of the Docklands project would adopt different evaluation criteria.

3.7.6 IT example

One large organization had the following planning dilemma. Several large application systems were being developed. Each would require substantial investment in telecommunications. Furthermore, the telecommunications links had a significant installation lead time. The group responsible for installing these telecommunications links therefore put pressure on the systems development projects to specify the number of users that would be connected to each system and from which locations. The systems development projects, however, were not able to determine this, because the user organizations were undergoing a fundamental rethink of their locations.

One solution might have been for the telecommunications group to provide telecommunications links to all major office buildings, on the assumption that these could be allocated to the different application systems at a later date. There would, of course, be a risk that the capacity thus installed might not be best distributed, but this would be offset by the advantages of being able to plan well in advance.

However, because the telecommunications group had no budget for such anticipatory planning, and could only install telecommunications links based on the business case for a specific application system, the organization was unable to exploit this planning flexibility. The telecommunications infrastructure had to be tightly coordinated with the development projects, as a matter of policy.

This kind of coordination may appear to be necessary to ensure money does not get wasted on unnecessary infrastructure. However, it often prevents planning decisions being taken at the best time. Either the development projects must seek premature closure on questions of user distribution, or the telecommunications group must risk delay or excessive expense in trying to provide links at short notice.

3.7.7 Reduce extent of infrastructure

The problem can be eased, if not solved, by applying the principle of **subsidiarity** (introduced in Chapter 2). This principle states that central planning only applies to those things that require central planning.

Some IT planners seem to think that because **some** IT investment has to be centrally planned, it is therefore a good idea to apply central planning to **all** IT investment. Log-rolling tactics are used, in which large investment packages are put together, from which every decision-maker will gain something. This approach is ultimately unmanageable, since nobody can realistically assess the total costs and benefits of such a large package. Investment decisions are taken for the wrong reasons, development and implementation projects are inflated in size and risk, and there are too many failures for comfort. A better approach is to prune down all global infrastructure proposals, to exclude any facilities that could be provided locally, and concentrate on small manageable elements of centrally planned infrastructure.

3.7.8 Conclusions

There are several alternative approaches to the planning and design of infra-structure. The choice of approach will depend on the enterprise circumstances and culture. If central IT planning is merely a devious way of burying investment in infrastructure that could not otherwise be justified, then it should be exposed and abandoned. This section argues for focused planning, to enable each component to be judged on its merits. Although investments sometimes cannot be judged in isolation from one another, that is no reason to go to the other extreme. If central planning is required for elements of infrastructure, then focused techniques should be developed for planning and accounting for these specific elements.

3.8 Summary of chapter

In the past, an organization could expect to keep its form more or less unaltered for decades. Nowadays, there is no organization safe from either take-over or sell-off, or that can afford to turn its back on opportunities of merger, joint venture or partnership. The boundaries of the organization become more fluid. This means that the 'modernist' information systems planning methodologies of the 1970s must be replaced by 'post-modernist' planning, to cope with the competitive environments of the 1990s.

> In the world of management and organizational change and development, the modernist tradition can be easily seen. It is the organization development scenario of demolish and/or rebuild around a central purpose, represented in town planning and architecture as demolish, clear, rebuild, start again on a green field site or new town development tradition.
>
> Post-modern organizational change might involve the quest to adapt existing organizations, recognize and build on existing features and strengths – restore rather than re-develop. It may recognize, too, that purposes are unclear, multiple, conflicting. It also brings into focus, but does not resolve, the relationship between a Learning Company that survives and prospers (against some criteria) and a company which is 'good' in some moral, ethical, social responsibility sense, in a world where 'good' is difficult or impossible to define.[13]

In this chapter, we have seen three contrasting approaches to information systems planning. Clearly, each approach provides a somewhat different starting point for systems development projects, and for coordination during development. The choice of planning approach will depend on the culture and circumstances of the enterprise. However, for coordination to be successful, there are some common requirements, regardless of the chosen planning approach.

1. Systems must be defined as coherent modules, with well-defined interfaces between them. Either these modules and interfaces must be defined by the information systems plan itself, or a task must be scheduled fairly early within the systems development process to define them (perhaps based on preliminary ideas sketched during the planning exercise).
2. Projects must be defined as coherent quantities of activity. Again, either the project scopes and inter-project interfaces must be exactly defined by the information systems plan, or they may be roughly defined, with a clear procedure for promptly resolving any issues of scope or interface.
3. There must be a clear statement of which information objects and other resources are to be shared between several/all systems, or between several/all projects, together with the policies and mechanisms for such sharing.

To the extent that a high-level Systems Development Plan does not address these requirements, a separate Development Coordination Plan will be required, to formulate and agree the necessary policies and other structures, to enable successful coordination.

Notes

1. Le Corbusier, 'If I had to teach you architecture', *Focus*, no 1, Summer 1938, p. 12. Reprinted in Dennis Sharp, (ed.), *The Rationalists*, London: Architectural Press, 1978.

2. R. Banham, 'A drip in Sidgwick Avenue', *New Society*, 9 August, 1985.

3. M.M. Lehman, 'Programs, life cycles and laws of software evolution', *Proceedings of I.E.E.E.*, vol. 68, No. 9, 1980, pp. 1060–76.

4. J. Martin, *Strategic Data-Planning Methodologies*, Englewood Cliffs, NJ: Prentice Hall, 1982.

5. C. Finkelstein, *An Introduction to Information Engineering*, Sydney: Addison-Wesley, 1989.

6. J . Martin, *op. cit.*, p. 4. Prentice Hall even reproduces a picture of the Tower of Babel by Breughel the Elder, portraying it as having been rather a successful construction project, as far as it went.

7. For an excellent overview, see M. Nurminen, *People or Computers: Three ways of looking at computer systems*, (English translation), Lund Sweden: Studentlitteratur, 1988.

8. C. Alexander, H. Neis, A. Anninou and I. King, *A New Theory of Urban Design*, New York: Oxford University Press, 1987.

9. C. Alexander, S. Ishikawa, M. Silverstein with M. Jacobson, I. Fiksdahl-King and S. Angel, *A Pattern Language: Towns, buildings, construction*, New York: Oxford University Press, 1977, pp. 92–5.

10. E. Auramäki and K. Lyytinen, 'SAMPO as an Information Systems Design methodology – A comparison with some data-modelling methodologies', in P. Van den Besselaar, A. Clement and P. Järvinen, (eds.), *Information System, Work and Organization Design*, North-Holland: Elsevier, 1991, pp. 271-81.

11. S. Kimbrough, 'On representation schemes for electronic promising', *21st Hawaii International Conference on Systems Sciences*, January 1988.

12. R. Lee, 'A logic model for electronic contracting', *Decision Support Systems*, vol 4, no. 1, March 1988.

13. M. Pedler, J. Burgoyne and T. Boydell, *The Learning Company*, London: McGraw-Hill, 1991.

4 Planning techniques

4.1 Introduction

In the previous chapter, we discussed different approaches to the planning of information systems. Long-term plans for information systems development are increasingly based on some kind of high-level model of the business entities and functions (often referred to as a **strategic model** or **information architecture**). In this chapter, we shall discuss techniques that can be used in this planning. The techniques broadly apply to all three planning approaches, but with some differences in flavour.

The first step is to create a broad understanding of the business (or business area) for which information systems are required. This is achieved by a modelling exercise, producing a strategic information model known as an information architecture. The second step is to input the information architecture to a scoping process, which uses clustering techniques to define the contents and boundaries of projects and systems.

This chapter will address each step in turn. First we shall look at a messy example where poor system scoping, in the absence of a proper architecture, is causing considerable problems.

4.2 What goes wrong without plans – an example

Some readers may find the following example implausible. Let me assure you that although some of the details have been altered to avoid identifying the company, the essential facts of the case are true.

4.2.1 Situation

The company, a multinational, pays commission to its agents on a monthly basis, based on documented commission claims submitted by the agents. Some agents are paid by cheque, others receive payment directly into their bank accounts. In some countries, each agent also receives a monthly statement, showing how the commission payment has been calculated.

4.2.2 Projects

The company is migrating from an old payments system to a new payments system. During the transition period, some of the agents will be paid by the new system, the remainder by the old system.

The new payments system is being developed as part of a large redevelopment programme of accounting systems. When this programme was planned, the generation of agents' commission statements was not regarded as a high priority, and this was therefore excluded from scope. However, another part of the organization has decided to sponsor a project to develop an information system for generating the commission statements. These statements will itemize the transactions that have taken place during the month, and notify the agent that the payment has been forwarded to his bank. The commission statement system requires more detailed transaction data than the payment system, since the payments are based on accumulated figures.

The new commission payment system is being developed by a different team, in a different location, from the team developing the commission statement system. Meanwhile, a third team is modifying various other accounting programs, and making the split between the old and new payment systems.

4.2.3 Problem

In the old system, there was a single identifier for the commission claim submitted by the agent. There were some problems with this identifier, but at least there was only one. There are now three different identifiers.

- The team developing the new payment system has designed a new identifier.
- The team developing the commission statement system has designed a new identifier.
- The old payment system operates with the existing identifier.

Furthermore, the identifier from the commission statement system is not passed through to either of the payment systems. This means that some matching has to be carried out to update the commission statement database, and there is a possibility of duplicate matches. Thus the correctness of the data cannot be guaranteed.

4.2.4 Why did it happen?

Despairing experts inside the organization attributed this misunderstanding to two main reasons:

1. The new payment system was scoped too narrowly. As far as the analysts on the project were concerned, commission claims came into existence when they were passed on to the payment system from other systems. This was therefore the point when the identifier needed to be created. In reality, of course, the claims exist much earlier in the business process.
2. None of the three projects was fully aware of what the other two projects were doing. There was no reference to a common data model to guide each development.

4.2.5 *Conclusions*

There are three conclusions we might draw from this example:

1. The necessity of an architecture. Had the projects all been operating against an agreed information architecture, the need for a common identifier ought to have been recognized at an early stage, and the necessary coordination activity triggered.
2. The necessity of adequate scoping. Had the payment system been more cleanly scoped, the problem might have been avoided.
3. The desirability of a single development planning organization, so that all projects are at least initiated from the same place in the organization.

The third conclusion might sound good, but we have already seen that central planning can be extremely problematic, especially in decentralized organizations. In the company from which the example is taken, the required degree of central planning is not compatible with the structure and culture of the business.

The second conclusion is certainly an important factor. This is why we shall consider scoping techniques in some depth later in this chapter. But however well scoping is done, there will be always be the need for some communication between what is inside the scope and what is outside.

This brings us back to the need for an architecture. We shall discuss this in the next section.

Coordination without an architecture is like doing a jigsaw on your lap.

4.3 Architectures

All information models have scope, perspective and purpose. If the purpose of a model is planning and scoping, we call the model an **information architecture**. In this section, we discuss the main differences between an information architecture and other types of information model.

4.3.1 *Purpose*

First let us expand on the purpose of an information architecture.

One of the possible purposes of building an information model is to develop a strategy for the business. The information architecture may represent the principal activities or functions of the enterprise (structured hierarchically, or as a value chain) as well as its important entity types. A model of the whole enterprise can be clustered into sub-models or business areas, each of which is then the subject of detailed analysis and IS development projects (see Figure 4.1).

But the purpose of such strategic models need not be restricted to IS development plans. Strategic models can express the changing intentions and conceptual structures of the business, which may need to be reflected by new Information Systems, but which also may be communicated via Information Systems.

Thus an information architecture may have several related purposes:

1. To provide a framework for formulating opportunities to obtain direct

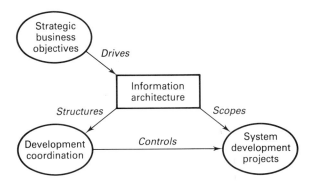

Figure 4.1
Purpose of information
architecture

competitive advantage from information and information systems.
2. To establish and maintain the link between the strategic business objectives and the systems development projects.
3. To define the scope of business areas and of data analysis projects.
4. To provide a framework for coordinating analysis and design projects.
5. To provide a framework for planning and implementing the necessary technical and organizational infrastructures.

4.3.2 Perspective

The perspective of the information architecture is usually said to be 'strategic'. This is a somewhat abused word, and we shall need to clarify what it means in our context.

Computerized information systems have the power to change the way the members of the organization think about their work. The more the organization relies on computers, the more power the systems have. This is one of the reasons why the conceptual structure of the systems deserves serious attention from the management of the organization.

At the most general level, the kinds of questions raised by an information modelling exercise are of relevance to top management, in their formulation of the business strategy. Defining such entity types as customer, employee, competitor, market, product and organization, and determining their identity rules, can lead to significant strategic insights. For example, high street banks have traditionally equated customer with account holder. This means they have been unable to recognize when a person holds more than one account; each communication with a customer (including financial transactions and marketing promotions) relates to a single account; this is not only operationally inefficient, but may also reduce the quality of service perceived by the customer. Furthermore, customers without accounts (e.g. a person who buys travellers cheques for cash) are not recognized at all. Likewise, insurance companies have equated customer with policy holder.

To cite a personal example: when I was working in Chicago, I opened a card account with a well-known charge card organization, billed in dollars. When I returned to the United Kingdom, I asked that my billing be switched to sterling. This turned out to be impossible, because the billing currency was implied by my card number. Eventually I had to cancel my dollar card and get a new card with a different number. Various complicated transactions were required to transfer the balance (including the annual fee) from one to the other. Meanwhile I have one card for business expenses and a separate card for personal expenses; the company appears to be unaware that I am the same person.

For this organization, integration between North American and European customer operations may not be significant, because there are perhaps not very many customers that move backwards and forwards. But there are a great number of customers that hold two cards; this is therefore likely to be more significant.

To cite another personal example, last time I parked my car at Heathrow airport, the parking company used my car registration number as a search key to retrieve my credit card number from their database, where it had been stored the previous time I had used their services. Unfortunately, I did not want to use the same credit card as before, because I was travelling on business instead of privately, so on this particular occasion their attempt to save time misfired.

These examples of customer-oriented integration, or lack of integration, are strategically important for many, if not all, service companies. Financial service companies in particular are now trying to change their perception of customer, to one that encompasses a whole spectrum of dealings with an individual. This requires a realignment of information systems, but goes further than this: it requires a realignment of the business itself.

Thus the questions addressed by an information modelling exercise, i.e. *who are our customers, what are our markets, who are our competitors, what are our products*, these are important strategic questions for an enterprise. The most important question of all, especially for publicly owned or Not-For-Profit (NFP) organizations, may be: *how many organizations are we?* Thus in the 1960s and 1970s, many national PTTs (Post, Telephone and Telegraph companies) divided themselves into a separate telecommunications organization and mail organization. In the 1990s, the UK Central Electricity Generating Board divided into a power generation company and a power distribution network. A theatre may split into a company to run the building, and a separate company to produce plays. A charity may consist of a fund-raising organization and a fund-spending organization.

NFP organizations ought also to think strategically about the social need they are addressing, in the same way as a commercial enterprise thinks about its products. A social need will often have a life cycle similar to a product. (Consider, for example, the changing needs associated with polio or AIDS.)

Meanwhile, the question *how many organizations are we?* applies also to commercial enterprises. An oil company or chemical giant may divide itself into separate pieces; a tobacco giant may be forcibly attacked and dismembered; a computer manufacturer may fragment itself between numerous joint ventures.

These questions can be seen as questions about an intended future, rather than merely describing the present situation. The techniques and concepts of information modelling can be used to address these questions systematically, and to ensure correspondence between the business strategy (which may be fixed or dynamic, planned or emerging) and the information systems.

Another strategic question concerns the scope of the organization itself. One of the strategies for gaining competitive advantage is to change the information processing interface between the organization and the outside world. To analyse such opportunities, we need to define the information model independently of whether the underlying activities are done within the organization or outside.

For example, airlines may scope their models to include travel agents, regarding them not as external customers but as autonomous and unreliable departments. Wise manufacturing companies recognize that loyal customers make an excellent unpaid sales force, as do independent service engineers, whose continued employment depends on the continued purchase and use of the equipment they have been trained to maintain. As a more general rule, the strategic thinker always thinks twice where the boundaries of the organization lie. They may stretch outside the company's own offices, or outside the company's own employees, or into areas where the company has at best partial control. Thus the perspective of an information architecture is the management of the unity, purpose and scope of the business.

4.3.3 Scope

The purpose of the information architecture includes the management of the scopes of projects and systems. The strategic perspective of the information architecture addresses such issues as the scope of the organization, particularly as this affects the organization's relationships with the outside world. But the information architecture itself has a scope, which is not quite the same thing.

The scope of the information architecture can be the entire enterprise or organization, together with its immediate environment (including customers, suppliers and other business partners). This enables a systems development plan for the entire enterprise to be drawn up, including opportunities to automate links with the computer systems of business partners.

In very large organizations, it may not be possible to create meaningful models for the entire enterprise. Instead, the scope for the information architecture may be a single operating division or business unit. If the enterprise has hierarchical management, and hierarchical business strategies, it may be thought appropriate to create a hierarchy of increasingly abstract information architectures, but this is seldom a realistic prospect.

In some situations, an architecture is created for a portion of the organization only. This allows the scope of a single project or system to be defined, by a consideration of its immediate neighbourhood, which may include objects inside the organization or outside (see Figure 4.2).

This is frowned upon by top-down planners, but is considered useful by pragmatists.

Figure 4.2
Information
architecture limited to
neighbourhood

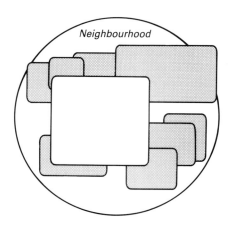

4.3.4 *Public and pivotal objects*

Any object which is explicitly addressed by a major business strategy is likely to be needed within the information architecture. These may be referred to as **strategic** objects. Strategic objects may be either public (participating in all or many business areas) or pivotal (providing the strategic linkages between business areas). The strategy tells us which objects have to be shared or common.

1. *Public objects*

Public objects are those elevated for strategic purposes above the interests of a single project or system. This implies a distinction between **public objects** and **local** or **private objects**. Whereas private objects have an owner (the project or system or user), public objects have a **custodian**. The owner of a private object has unlimited rights over the object (and what it represents in terms of information), including the ability to change the structure of the object without notifying anybody else. The custodian of a public object has certain responsibilities towards other users of the object, which we shall return to in Chapter 5.

The following example is taken from a seminal paper by H-J Pels.[1]

Box 4.1
Entity types belonging
to two systems

System	Own	Foreign
Purchasing	ARTICLE, BACKORDER	ORDERLINE
Sales	CLIENT, ORDER, ORDERLINE	ARTICLE

In Box 4.1, the entity type ARTICLE is public, under the custodianship of the Purchasing system/project. The entity type BACKORDER, on the other hand, is private to the Purchasing system/project, and is invisible to the Sales system/project (see Figure 4.3).

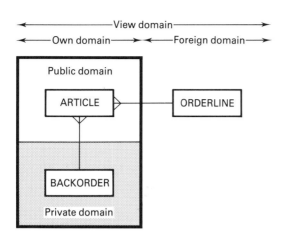

Figure 4.3
Separation of model
into public and private

The distinction between public and private/local only works, of course, if there are some of each. Some intrepid data administrators attempt to make all objects public. This usually leads to excessive coordination overhead, with little genuine business benefit. It is usually better that only a minority of objects are public, unless you want to spend all your time managing public objects.

2. Pivotal objects

A project should have a centre or focus; so should a plan or architecture. For example, if a business strategy revolves around the customer, then we should expect to find the entity type CUSTOMER at the centre of the information architecture. But consider which entity types you would expect to find in the centre of the information architecture, based on the following CEO statements quoted in Box 4.2.

Box 4.2
Focus of business
strategy – How does
this influence
information
architecture?

- 'We are a market-led company.'
- 'We need to become a market-led company.'
- 'We are a quality-oriented company.'

If a company believes itself to be (or becoming) market-led, we should surely expect the entity type MARKET to have a prominent position within the information architecture. If a company takes quality seriously, we should expect to see quality measurement and quality improvement processes, supported by strategic information.

Sometimes the information architecture will reveal a contradiction between the stated mission of the enterprise and the actual management practice. For example, in many companies, despite paying lip service to marketing or quality, the actual centre turns out to be accounting entity types: COST CENTRE or ACCOUNT. Sometimes the entity type MARKET does not appear at all, nor anything equivalent. This would suggest that the concept of market does not actually pervade their thinking.

The fact that the information architecture reveals the actual strategic thinking of management entails the need for it to be produced directly from the strategic information needs of top managers, or with their active participation. If it is produced indirectly by technicians or middle managers, the likelihood of error is increased. Even if technicians or middle managers have better or longer-term strategic vision than their bosses (as most technicians and middle managers believe), there is no point in working to an information architecture that does not fit the strategic vision of the company as a whole.

4.3.5 Modelling contents and constructs

An information architecture typically includes both the data objects (entities, relationships, attributes) and also the business activities (processes, inter-process dependencies).

Figure 4.4 shows what must be in the information architecture.

Figure 4.4
Essential contents of information architecture

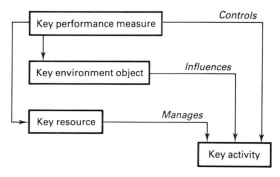

- Key resources – physical and non-physical assets of the organization which may be used or reused, people inside and outside the organization who support the organization.
- Key environment objects – things, people and bodies whose actions may affect the organization (including competitors).
- Key performance measures (KPM) – these will be attributes of key entity types – possibly one of the key resources or environment objects – they will almost certainly turn out to be derived from something else when we come to the detailed analysis. (A possible exception is when the KPM is measured for you by an outside agency, such as your market share.)
- Key activities – a function usually manages a key resource and/or influences/ monitors the environment and/or controls the business against a key measure.

4.3.6 Building the information architecture

What is the difference between building a strategic information architecture and a detailed analysis data model? Should the same techniques and standards apply? Some might argue that the attitudes required for detailed analysis and development are too pedantic for strategic planning. It all depends on what you think the information architecture is for. And what are the consequences of getting it wrong.

My argument here is that the techniques and attitudes are much the same. However, since the purpose and scope are different, the perspective should also be different. It is indeed necessary to be pedantic, but only about the strategic things. Part of the question is to identify what these strategic things are. This section provides some clues.

The information architecture should mostly eschew detail. We certainly do not want a model with more than 400 entity types. However, this is not an excuse for superficiality. There may be a few pivotal entity types and processes that deserve careful analysis, because they contain the germs of enormous strategic opportunities.

One form of abstraction found in detailed data models is classification. The information architecture does not normally include classification objects – it may therefore be less abstract than the information and activity models produced in detailed requirements analysis, in the sense that its entity types are more direct, albeit perhaps more generalized. For example, such classification as the demographic category of a customer would probably be left as an attribute in the information architecture, but could well become separate entity types in more detailed development models.

However, a strategic information architecture should at least identify opportunities for generalization and abstraction, so that projects can be given clear and minimally overlapping scope. This means that the definitions of the major entity types should be thought out fairly thoroughly. Even if the entity type has no formal identifier, it should at least have an identifying strategy. (In other words, some thought needs to have been given to the kind of identifier that would be appropriate.) However, the relationships and attributes need not be defined in detail.

Although the information architecture may be called a strategic model, it does not necessarily include all the information required by top management to make strategic decisions. Long-term market planning, capital planning and acquisition, and cultural change are all strategic issues – they could be suitable for business area analysis, perhaps resulting in the development of Executive Information Systems. So we may identify some broad Subject Areas, but the details of these areas will not be excluded from the information architecture, because they are not relevant to its purpose.

Thus the information architecture is not simply a top management model. It is focused specifically on information systems strategies, and not on general business management.

There are several crucial things that must be addressed by the information architecture:

- **Unity**   How does the public object bring together different aspects of the business?
- **Leverage**   How pivotal is this object? Can small changes here have a large impact (positive or negative)?
- **Intention**   What are the strategic intentions relating to this object? In

other words, what changes are foreseen for this object? What should it become?

- **Meaning**   What is the object all about? What is its significance to the business? In other words, what is it?
- **Source**   Where does the object originate?
- **Destination**   Does the object get exported?
- **Structure**   What are the components and structure of the object?

Let us look at each of these in turn.

1. Unity

The information architecture expresses the unity of public objects. For example, a financial services company might want to issue a single telephone number to its customers, which can be used for any possible service the customer might require. (Instead of having to dial one number for account enquiries, a different number for reporting a stolen credit card, a different number for making an appointment to see the manager, and so on. Or imagine if the customer has to notify the same bank twice when s/he changes address, because the different departments do not talk to each other.) This is known as 'one-stop service' or 'one-call service'. It cannot be implemented without the information systems that support these services being somewhat integrated.

The first example can be satisfied by unity of the servicing process; the second example can be satisfied by unity of the customer address data. In both cases, we can fulfil the business strategy by elevating the process or data object to public status, which gives it global validity across the business.

A third example shows how the information architecture expresses changes in business thinking. A small financial company thought of itself as being in the loan business. It lent money to private individuals, which it raised through issuing bonds on the international markets. The people who received loans had always been regarded within the company as the customers, but the bond-holders had not been. It was realised by top management that there would be a strategic benefit to the company if the bond-holders were regarded as customers too. This would encourage the members of the organization to deal with the bond-holders in a more positive way, and encourage the development of profitable services aimed at the bond-holders. By building 'brand loyalty' among bond-holders, it would also protect the company from attack by large international predators.

This vision was reflected in the strategic information model by including both loan-holders and bond-holders in the entity type CUSTOMER, and including both loan-related services and bond-related services in the entity type PRODUCT. Some of the members of the organization could relate easily to these generalizations, but others found it difficult at first to see the implications of such abstract statements. But when these extended conceptions of CUSTOMER and PRODUCT were implemented in new computer systems and databases, this served to propagate and reinforce the new thinking throughout the organization.

2. Leverage

When formulating a strategy, the idea is to identify pivotal objects that will have maximum impact on the health of the information systems, and on the business.

A business strategy based on organizational learning, or total quality management, will be usefully supported by information systems that cross through many areas of the business. These information systems will be based on pivotal entity types and processes.

Pareto analysis is a useful technique which finds where the majority of the costs or risks or customer problems are being incurred, or where the opportunities are concentrated. For example, if we have received 500 occurrences of CUSTOMER COMPLAINT during a given period, and over 400 of them refer to late deliveries, while only two customers have complained that the documentation is only available in English, we might reasonably conclude that DELIVERY was strategically important, while DOCUMENTATION LANGUAGE was not. The information architecture should support and be supported by this kind of business analysis.

3. Intention

Sometimes an enterprise will have two or more business concepts, with some similarities and some differences. A strategy may be declared, to bring these concepts closer together (or further apart). This strategy can be expressed and supported by modelling the two or more concepts within the information architecture, which is then used to plan information systems which will facilitate the intended changes.

Here is another example: suppose the present computer systems only support a single trading currency, but the business strategy is to allow each customer to be billed in more than one currency. This strategy can be expressed as an intention to move from Figure 4.5 to Figure 4.6. Such a change may have several direct and indirect effects on the business.

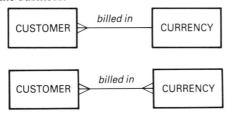

Figure 4.5
A single billing currency will be defined for each customer

Figure 4.6
Each customer may be billed in more than one currency

The information model shows clearly whether the customer may have only one billing currency, or may have many. If the customer may have many, then the data model contains a many-to-many relationship. Such a relationship automatically raises some data and process issues. The data and process models will be complete and consistent only when these issues have been settled.

1. If the customer may be billed in more than one currency, then we need to know precisely which currency is to be (or was) used for which bill.

2. There may also be business rules demanding that certain transactions be in the same currency (e.g. bill and payment, or bill and chargeback).

3. A decision process is implied, to choose which currency is to be used for a given bill. Is this decided by a predefined algorithm, or by the customer, and how or when is this decision communicated to the company? How much flexibility can be allowed for? What controls are required? Until what point in the process cycle can currency be changed?

4. What are the consequences of making the system more flexible? What proportion of customers is likely to benefit, and is there any negative impact on the remainder? (For example, is extra information demanded from them?) What is the likely overall impact on profitability?

By exploring the data issues, the business issues can be addressed more systematically.

The same kind of situation can arise in a manufacturing environment.

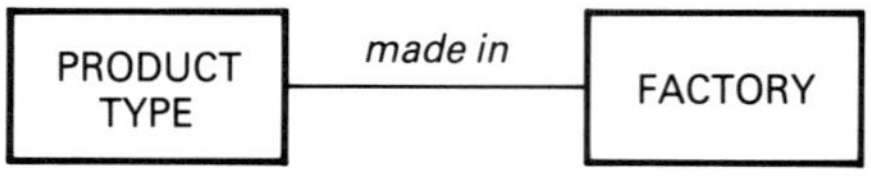

Figure 4.7
Each factory makes a single type of product. Each type of product is made in only one factory.

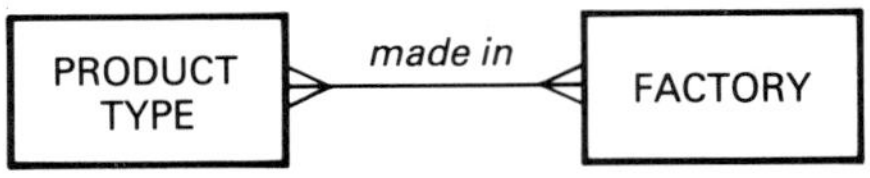

Figure 4.8
Factories will be equipped to make a variety of product types.

Suppose the present factories only produce a single type of product, but the business strategy is to move to a more flexible manufacturing arrangement. This strategy can be expressed as an intention to move from Figure 4.7 to Figure 4.8. Such a change may have several direct and indirect effects on the business.

• Manufacturing scheduling – may become more complex because there is now a choice of production location.

• Delivery of products to customers – may become simpler, because a single sales order may be supplied from a single factory.

• Engineering and production design – may be able to share components, skills, facilities and equipment between production of different types of product, wherever possible.

• If each type of product uses different raw materials, and if each factory must maintain separate stocks, inventory holdings may increase.

4. Meaning

We could give many examples of inadequate thought about the meaning of strategic objects during the planning stage, causing project problems and/or coordination problems later. Here is one. In the oil business, petrol is sold, not directly to motorists but to petrol stations. Some departments refer to the petrol station as the customer, while others refer to the motorist as the customer. In one oil company's

Information Plan, however, there was a major entity type CUSTOMER, completely overlooking this ambiguity. This caused problems for several projects, and for Development Coordination. Such homonymy was too broad to be sorted out within a single development project, and needed to have been addressed at a strategic level.

The same confusion might arise in a manufacturing company, which might have conflicting understanding about who the customer is. Some managers may think of the distributor or retailer (who directly purchases the product) as the customer, while other managers may focus their attention on the end-consumer. Again, if this confusion is unresolved, and information data architecture includes a single entity type called CUSTOMER, the architecture may not provide an adequate framework for subsequent projects.

5. Source

Where does the object come from? If, for example, we have decided that the entity type MARKET is the strategic centre of everything, who defines what the markets are? Does the organization create them itself, or does it wait until other (larger) organizations have created markets, and then seek to exploit them? This makes a difference as to how we see the stability of the markets. Information systems will be required to collect and analyse business feedback by market, so this may be a crucial factor running through all areas of the business.

Where do new products and services come from? Are they copies of competitors' products and services, or do they spring fully-formed from the heads of the 'boys in the back room'? This makes a difference to what counts as a product at all, and to how products are identified. Different information systems may be required, to refer to products at various stages of product development.

If quality is to be the strategic focus of the company, where does our conception of quality come from?

6. Destination

If information is provided as a commercial service to external customers, or bundled into other commercial products or services, then it has a strategic significance for the enterprise, which can be recognized and analysed within the information architecture. Taking account of the external destinations (usages) of such information objects can result in IS development plans that include 'strategic' systems to provide competitive advantage to the enterprise.

7. Structure

The identification and content of major entity types can be important for an Information Systems Strategy Plan. The information architecture should reflect the structure of the 'real' world. Thus the structure of markets, the relationship between markets, products and customers, the internal organization structure of commercial or industrial customers, these are factors that should be considered.

4.3.7 Maintaining the information architecture

If the architecture is to be a living object, it must change. Stability does not mean inability to change, it means that small changes are possible without destroying the whole.

There are several ways that the feedback from development projects to the architectures could be managed.

1. One option is not to allow any changes to the architecture to be carried out during on-going development projects, but to schedule a periodic replanning exercise, in which the architectures are entirely reformed to incorporate any new insights.
2. Architecture contains aggregates of business objects – all changes are fed back. The components of the architectures are initially defined in vague and generic terms. As the detailed analysis is carried out, these definitions can be replaced by one that specifies the objects encompassed. Once a component of the architecture is so defined, any change to an object included in its definition automatically affects it.
3. 'Panning for Gold' – the architecture coordinator dips a sieve into the torrent of detailed changes to the models, the trivial stuff passes through, and the large stuff remains. (Does he keep everything that remains in the sieve, or only if it glisters ?)

There are of course costs associated with changes to the information architecture. These must be balanced against the benefits of having an accurate and up-to-date architecture (see Box 4.3).

Box 4.3
Costs of changes to
Information
Architecture

Need to analyse impact on current projects/systems
Communication of new architecture to interested parties
Risk of delay and changes in scope to current projects
Risk of maintenance to current systems

What we need is a measure of the scale of change, so that we can monitor and control the amount of change undergone by the architectures.

We have said that the information architecture documents the **meaning, source, destination, structure, unity, intention** and **leverage** of **public** and **pivotal** objects. Therefore, any insights affecting these points need to be fed back to the information architecture from the individual project models (requirements or design models).

In the organic planning approach, described in the previous chapter, each project is required to contribute to the architecture. Each project should therefore aim to do three things. First, it should help to complete at least one strategic object that is already clearly defined. Second, it should help to pin down some other strategic object, less clearly defined and previously only hinted at. (This may involve promoting an object from local to public status.) Third, it may hint at some entirely new object, of potential strategic/public interest, which will only clearly emerge with later projects. This itself implies feedback to the information architecture itself, which may grow organically as projects build upon one another.

4.3.8 Summary

> * Avoid detail – but analyse the strategic 'pivots'
> * Model should be generalized – but not too abstract
> * To plan strategic systems, you do not need to specify strategic information requirements
> * Document the meaning, source and structure of public and pivotal objects

Box 4.4
Summary of information architecture guidelines

4.4 Scoping and clustering

4.4.1 Introduction

Clustering addresses the task of dividing a problem area into (semi-)independent sub-areas, whose solutions can be developed (in parallel or sequence) with minimum interaction effort, and minimum integration risk. Depending on your perspective and specific purpose, it can be either a method of putting small sets of objects together, or a method of dividing a large set of objects into subsets. These small sets or subsets are known as **clusters**. The word **clustering** itself can refer either to the process of defining a series of related clusters, or to the result of this process, i.e. the series of clusters itself. Each cluster can then be used to define the **scope** of something, which may be a design project, a departmental responsibility, or something else, by enumerating what it is to contain.

For information systems planning purposes, the problem area is described by an information architecture. However, we shall start by discussing some general concepts of clustering, before looking specifically at carving up an information architecture.

Some useful work on clustering in a problem-solving context was done in the early 1960s by Christopher Alexander, then at MIT. This work was taken up by Tom DeMarco, and applied to the structuring of information systems. As we have seen in the previous chapter, Alexander has largely moved away from the top-down approach to problem-solving implied by his first book, but it is a useful source for the concepts of clustering, which can be applied by top-down planners and others.

4.4.2 Project funding

In some organizations, users try to get every system requirement satisfied in the first project, because they do not know if there will be a second. This increases the size, timescale, cost and risk of projects. Scoping is fraught with difficulty, since leaving things out tends to have political implications. Indeed, scoping often becomes more a political activity than a technical one.

To get around this problem, some user trust has to be established. It is easier to tolerate a queue if the queue moves quickly, and if there is no danger that the queue will be aborted before one reaches the head of the queue.

To depoliticize scoping, the mechanisms for project funding may have to be addressed. In particular, the following steps should be considered.

1. Guarantee continuity of funding, with fixed criteria.
2. Shift from cost-based budgeting to investment-based planning. There is no limit to projects with demonstrable benefit payback, provided that the risk-reward ratio is better than the market cost of capital.

4.4.3 *Concepts of clustering*

1. *Purposes of clustering*

Scoping is usually achieved by dividing the entire problem area into small objects, and then clustering the objects together to form coherent subproblems. The purpose of clustering is to group objects together that can be worked on together. For example, to divide a large complex problem, consisting of a large number of small interconnected problems, into several groups of related problems.

Following from such a clustering, we usually construct organization structures (such as projects, departments and teams), and match the responsibilities to the clustering. We hope that at least some planning and design decisions can be taken for an individual cluster, without considering other clusters.

Another somewhat different use of clustering is to group things together for presentation purposes. For example, when displaying a large entity-relationship diagram (ERD), it is useful to establish neighbourhoods which correspond to some underlying structure or clustering. This makes user communication and documentation more effective. Thus clustering enables us to define the scope of a system, project, task, organizational responsibility or deliverable.

Clustering can also be used to bundle a series of information services into a commercial offering, or a series of product enhancements into a new version or release.

2. *Criteria for good clustering*

A good clustering minimizes interaction effort (during development and maintenance) and integration risk (i.e. failure to meet enterprise or technical coordination requirements).

In a good clustering, each cluster is highly coherent (i.e. it coheres, or sticks together), and there is little overlap or coupling between clusters. There is more similarity or affinity within one cluster than between two clusters.

Sometimes consistency of size is adduced as an additional criterion. In other words, each cluster should be more or less the same size. This does not affect interaction effort or integration risk. It may sometimes be convenient for the clusters to be similar in size, but it may sometimes be inconvenient. Thus if you have several project managers of equal ability, experience and aspirations, you may prefer to define several projects of the same size, based on equal-sized clusters. But if you have several project managers of different ability, experience or aspirations, you would not want to give them equal-sized projects. In any case, size should never be used as an excuse for incoherent or fragmented clusters.

3. Stability

Since the problem will undoubtedly change its shape while we are working on it, there is also an implied criterion of stability. Does the clustering remain valid, although the details change? Perhaps the clustering becomes less than ideal, in the sense that if we were starting from scratch we should prefer something else, but it may be inappropriate to change it. There should be some 'stickiness', to prevent the clustering from changing all the time. However, we do need a mechanism for abandoning a clustering if and when it is totally wrong.

Even if we do not set out to do this explicitly, the clustering will also be used to control change. Some changes (such as additional requirements) may be formulated in a way that is convenient to the current clustering. The clustering itself provides a language for identifying and formulating change. This is healthy up to a point. However, in some cases, good opportunities may be ignored or rejected (or worse, distorted so that they lose their original value), because they cannot be fitted into the framework provided by the clustering.

Extreme radicals rather welcome a periodic reclustering, turning everything over to uncover new opportunities. They will redraw diagrams, in the hope that by changing the neighbours of an object, new insights will appear. Thus they enjoy (and are likely to promote) instability. This can often be an extremely refreshing attitude, and in some organizations it is necessary. However, non-radicals hate this, and prefer things to remain in the same place wherever possible.

Thus the 'stickiness' of the clustering (how far things should change before a reclustering is appropriate) needs to provide a proper balance between the radicals and the conservatives.

4. Naming of clusters

Do not expect the clusters to correspond to existing concepts. It is precisely because we do not trust existing concepts that we have gone to all the trouble to perform clustering according to an algorithm, instead of guesswork.

. . . Today we have naming of parts . . .

Alexander even advises caution if the parts appear post hoc to resemble existing concepts. This is because people can easily be misled by the apparent continuity of the name, and ignore the formal definition of a cluster in terms of its actual contents.

> The designer must resist the temptation to summarize the contents of the tree in terms of well-known concepts. . . . If he tries to do this, he denies the whole purpose of the analysis, by allowing verbal preconceptions to interfere with the pattern which the program shows him.[2]

However, sometimes a clustering will appear to group unrelated things together, and to make no sense whatsoever. Naming of clusters is always going to be difficult in such cases, if the clusters themselves do not mean anything. There are two possible explanations for such a nonsense clustering. The first explanation is that it does make sense, but not in an immediately obvious way. The true sense of each cluster may only emerge after some difficult thought, and only after this true sense has emerged can the clusters be meaningfully named. The second explanation is that the clustering really is nonsense. Errors and anomalies can sometimes result in unemployable clusters, on the 'garbage-in-garbage-out' principle. Do not be too quick to reject the clustering as nonsense, but it is always worth checking that the information used as input to the clustering is correct.

5. Hierarchy

In some cases, we can form clusters of clusters of clusters, thus forming a hierarchy. This clustering in stages can sometimes significantly affect the result. The lowest level clusters will be different, according to the number of stages.

Top-down or bottom-up? Do we construct the lowest-level clustering first, and then put them together to form clusters of clusters, or do we construct a broad clustering, and then divide each broad cluster into smaller subclusters? If the latter, what is the scope of the clustering? Can the clustering within broad cluster A be influenced by the contents of other broad clusters, or must it restrict itself to the contents of A?

The answer to these questions depends on the chosen coordination style. The analyst carrying out the clustering should include everything that she has the capability of changing, depending on the results of the clustering. In a decentralized organization, there may perhaps be little point in broadening the scope of the clustering.

Note: although Alexander originally proposed a top-down clustering approach, he assumed that all the requirements have been identified, with the smallest possible decomposition. 'The more specific and detailed we make the variables, the less constrained [the structure] will be by previous conceptions, and the more open to detailed and unbiased examination of its causal structure.'[3] You cannot do this prior to analysis. Perhaps this means we should recluster everything between analysis and design. And I think this is correct: if you have two or three related analysis projects reaching the end of phase at the same time, the design area scoping should be carried out across all analysis areas, and not isolated for each analysis area.

It is usually assumed that the broad clustering is good enough to allow further subdivisions to ignore the contents of other broad clusters. But consider this: if there is a small inaccuracy introduced at each level, and if there are several levels, the accumulated inaccuracy at the lowest level might well be significant. It is better to have a self-correcting method.

Because the higher-level clustering necessarily ignores the lower-level of detail, we will almost certainly get different results if we redo the clustering after the detail has been determined.

This is related to the political problem of constituencies: a majority of a majority of a majority does not necessarily form a majority.

6. Heuristics and algorithms

There are several different heuristics for clustering data and activity. For each heuristic, there are different algorithms, which calculate the affinities and interactions between objects in different ways, or which may classify and weight the factors differently. Certain CASE tools include specific algorithms. (Usually each CASE tool only contains one chosen algorithm.) At present, however, we are not interested in the specific algorithms (how), but in the thinking behind the algorithm (what), which we call its heuristic.

A **heuristic** defines what types of connexion shall be deemed to possess clustering force. An **algorithm** defines how to measure the clustering force of each connexion, and how specifically to combine forces. (The techniques of specific algorithms are beyond the scope of this book.)

Everyone uses the word 'heuristic' to mean something different. So this is how I am going to use the word.

We can distinguish between two forms of clustering: **affinity clustering**, which produces homogeneous clusters of objects of the same type, and **interaction clustering**, which produces heterogeneous clusters of objects of more than one type. For example, a heuristic to produce clusters of entity types would be an affinity clustering, whereas a heuristic to produce clusters of entity types and processes, based on the interactions between them, would be an interaction clustering.

7. Clustering decision

Often there are certain objects that obviously go together into clusters, and then some other objects where it is not clear whether they should belong in this or that cluster. To resolve this kind of problem, we need a 'gravitation' rule (see Figure 4.9). This will often need to be provisional: we assign the object to one or other cluster, based on available information, supplemented by intuition or instinct, with the option to move the object later if it proves uncomfortably placed.

Figure 4.9
Gravitation rule

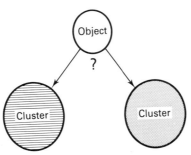

A heuristic is **complete** or **conclusive** if it can always resolve all clustering issues without reference to any other heuristic. In other words, every object always has one cluster that it is more strongly drawn to than any other cluster. (This is not necessarily a good thing.) Without a single complete heuristic, we shall need several incomplete heuristics, with a **precedence rule** telling us which to apply first.

4.4.4 Types of cluster

1. Business areas and design areas

Much of what we have said so far can be applied at several different levels or stages. In Information Engineering, there may be a clustering at the end of Information Strategy Planning (ISP), to divide an enterprise into business areas, and a further clustering at the end of Business Area Analysis (BAA) to divide a single business area into design areas. Each design area becomes the scope of a business system.

(In some versions of the IE methodology, the information engineer is instructed to produce design areas (or business systems) first, and then cluster these together to produce business areas. However, although we are given criteria for this definition of business systems, we are not always given explicit criteria for the second step of defining business areas.)

2. Data stores

A **data store** is a cluster of data objects that are to be implemented on the same hardware using the same software, and presented to the user as an integrated system. From a housekeeping point of view, for such physical processes as backup and recovery, it is usually managed as a single item. However, it may sometimes be appropriate to adopt a different heuristic for scoping the logical data stores and the physical data stores. Thus the physical data stores may be physically distributed across a network, or across client/server technology, but this may be invisible to the user.

3. Application modules (or systems)

An application module is a cluster of activity objects that are to be run on the same hardware, with the same underlying software, and presented to the user as a single system. As with data stores, there may be differences between the logical scoping and the physical scoping, to enable the designer to exploit client/server technology.

4. Business benefit packages

A benefit package is a coherent set of advantageous changes to the business operations and/or management.

A project is usually cost-justified by the expectation that it will achieve some direct or indirect business benefits. The planning and management of a project will be easier if the changes enabled by the project are a coherent set, and more difficult if the benefits are spread across a number of projects.

Information Engineering plans projects on the assumption that the business benefits (based on business objectives or CSFs) fall into the same natural clusters as the business functions in the information architecture. This is a useful simplification, but is not the whole truth.

4.4.5 Geo-political use of clustering

Clustering is crucial as a technique for handling complexity. Before we consider the detail of clustering techniques for information systems, let us consider another distant example of clustering.

People seem to prefer to be grouped into political units together with similar people. This is what leads to nationalism, since people apparently want to belong to a political cluster whose affinity rule is based on nationality. This is a non-trivial problem, as demonstrated by the existence throughout history of independence movements whose fervour leads to terrorism on one side, and anti-terrorist oppression on the other side.

One of the problems of drawing political boundaries is that there will almost inevitably be minority communities left 'on the wrong side'. (Although genocide and forced migration are often practised, under a variety of morally repulsive euphemisms, they rarely (thank God!) achieve total elimination of the undesired groups.) An interesting question, that has not been properly addressed by political scientists, is whether it is better (in terms of social harmony and justice) to have small minorities (less than 10 per cent, say), or larger minorities (more than 25 per cent, say). It may be that a mathematical study of clustering techniques and their consequences would provide some clues.

However, since the membership of national groups is often subjective, any geo-political clustering based on nationality is likely to be unstable. Consider Yugoslavia, whose previously friendly citizens almost overnight divided themselves into hostile nation states. Religious affinities may suddenly become more relevant, as they did in Spain in 1492, and in Germany in the 1930s.

Some forms of representative democracy require a country to be divided into constituencies, each of which can elect a representative to a parliament. A constituency is a cluster. Governor Elbridge Gerry of Massachusetts invented a technique of biased clustering (known in his honour as **gerrymandering**) to ensure that the favoured party, in his case the Republicans, attained an advantage.

Note: in the first-past-the-post system, if all the constituencies were demographically identical, we should expect all the seats in a general election to be won by the same party. A random division of the country into equal-sized constituencies might well come close to this result. On the other hand, if a constituency consists only of like-minded people, it will become a 'safe seat', in which it is hardly worth voting. Demographic changes do necessitate changes in the constituency boundaries from time to time, although there is little public clarity about the method used to redraw these boundaries (in the United Kingdom, by the Boundary Commission).

4.4.6 *Alternative clustering heuristics*

Now let us concentrate on information clustering. In this section, we shall look at the clustering of data and/or activity objects.

1. *Clustering by organization/management requirements*

In this heuristic, data and activities are clustered according to their usage by parts of the organization, or their contribution to the management objectives of parts of the organization. This results in systems that should match organization structure. But what does this mean? The systems should provide communication within organization units, but probably not between organization units.

2. *Clustering by geographical requirements*

This is similar to #1, in that data and activities are clustered according to their usage by different locations of the organization. This results in systems that should match geographical structure. But what does this mean? The systems should provide communication within locations, but probably not between locations.

3. *Use of existing clusters*

Existing clusters (i.e. existing systems or organizations) can be used in two ways to define new clusters: positively and negatively.

Positive use of existing clusters defines new clusters to (more or less) replicate existing clusters. For example, activity clusters are based on existing systems; data clusters are based on existing data stores. This will make implementation (and bridging old-new) much easier. It may be the best heuristic for short-term benefits, but is unlikely to provide a good basis for long-term improvement.

If the project boundaries more or less correspond to organizational boundaries (as with a functional organization), this probably makes intra-project coordination easier. But it could make inter-project coordination harder.

Negative use of existing clusters defines new clusters to deliberately cut across existing systems and data stores. This is not a complete heuristic, and should be used in conjunction with another business-oriented heuristic. In this context, however, it may be useful to specify that, other things being equal, it may be better to break rather than respect existing boundaries.

The advantage of defining new systems and data stores that cut across existing system and data store boundaries is that it may create an opportunity to increase integration, and enhance data integrity. If the existing systems are bad enough, doing something completely different *must* be an improvement. However, it requires much planning, much work, and much coordination and control. In this sense, it is a poor clustering heuristic for the short term, but may be an excellent heuristic for the long term.

4. Hub clustering

In this approach, a single object is chosen in advance as the central or **hub** object, and the area is defined as anything connected (in a predefined way) to the hub object. For example, the concepts of **horizon** and **inverse horizon** can be used to define clusters around an entity type. If a chain of one-to-many relationships can be constructed, all in the same direction, then a derived one-to-many relationship can be defined as their sum. The **horizon** of an entity type A is the set of entity types B_i with a one-to-many real or derived relationship to A. In other words, for each occurrence of A there is at most one occurrence of B_i. The **inverse horizon** of A is the set of entity types B_i with a many-to-one real or derived relationship to A. In other words, for each occurrence of B_i there is at most one occurrence of A.

A cluster can also be defined with an activity as the hub. The cluster around a business process may include prerequisite and controlling processes. Thus for example, authorization and error-correction processes may be implicitly included in the scope of a project, although they may use different data to the hub process, and may not have been explicitly identified when the project scope was defined.

5. Bundle clustering

In this approach, a generic type of communication is chosen as the focus of the cluster, and the area is defined as anything communicated. This may then be an information flow or **bundle.** For example, if we analyse the communication from warehouse to factory, we may define a cluster including product data and expediting processes.

Whereas systems scoped according to clustering heuristics #1 and #2 provide for communication *within* an organization unit or location, bundle-clustered systems are consciously scoped to provide for communications *between* organization units or locations.

6. Non-binary clustering

Many clustering heuristics, such as those outlined above, assume that affinity is a binary relationship between objects. P is similar to Q, Q is very similar to R, R is slightly similar to P. (In mathematical terms, we should want to define this as a function from pairs of objects to a quantity: $F:<p,q> \rightarrow a.$).

There are some more complicated concepts of affinity, that cannot be broken down to such a binary form. These are much more difficult to work with. Such non-binary affinities may be relevant for clustering based on data integrity, but are usually not necessary.

7. Negative clustering

Alexander is interested in positive versus negative affinities. Concurrence versus conflict. Most, if not all, of the heuristics outlined above only involve positive affinity. It seems that for clustering an information architecture or model this is sufficient. However, for other aspects of information systems design, it may be necessary to consider both positive and negative.

8. Data clustering by data structure and integrity rules.

This heuristic clusters a data model by defining affinities based on the structure of the data model itself, with no reference to the activity model. This has the advantage that it can be carried out before the activity model is completely known. Furthermore, it is not dependent on the scope of the activity model.

Feldman and Miller[4] identified a method of grouping entity types into **subject areas** based around major entity types. This is a form of hub clustering sometimes known as **dominance grouping**.

In this heuristic, entity types with relationships between them are more likely to be clustered together. Mandatory relationships will have more clustering force than optional ones. Data integrity rules that refer to two or more entity types will increase the affinity between these entity types.

For some purposes, the existence of a fully mandatory relationship between two entity types may force the inclusion of both entity types in the same cluster. This is because it can be extremely difficult to manage fully mandatory relationships that span two clusters.

Data structure clustering is complete. This is because we can rank data integrity, at least in theory, as some rules will have more strategic importance than others. Thus an entity type cannot be equally pulled towards two clusters, but one pull will prove stronger, according to the precedence rules given in Box 4.5.[5]

Box 4.5
Precedence rules for
ER model clustering

> - Dominance grouping (around major entity types)
> - Abstraction grouping
> - Constraint grouping (data integrity)
> - Relationship grouping – unary
> - Relationship grouping – binary 1–1
> - Relationship grouping – binary 1–n
> - Relationship grouping – binary n–m
> - Relationship grouping – ternary and higher

9. Activity clustering by dependencies between activities

This heuristic clusters together activities that have to be synchronized with one another, or activities that are dependent upon one another. This makes it easier to design systems that manage the synchronicity and enforce the dependency rules. The heuristic is solely derived from the structure of the activity model, and is not dependent upon the existence or scope of any corresponding data model.

Some dependency rules have more strategic importance than others; thus this heuristic is complete.

10. Data clustering by data use

So far, we have considered data clustering that only considers the data structure, and activity clustering that only considers the activity structure. More interesting (and arguably more useful) heuristics emerge when we consider data and activity together.

One way of clustering a data model is to start from the usage of the data model by activities. Each activity may make use of various data objects. Data objects that are used in the same way by the same activities are likely to be clustered together.

In the simplest form, a matrix of data objects against activities is populated with Xs, to indicate usage. Usually, however, different levels of usage are indicated: for example: {read, update} or {create, read, update, delete}. The latter is often referred to by its initials (CRUD), and the matrix is popularly known as a **crud matrix**.

Multiple usage (i.e. when several occurrences of the data object are used by one execution of the activity) can be regarded as more significant than single usage (i.e. when only one occurrence of the data object is used by one execution of the activity).

For many purposes, READ is regarded as less significant than UPDATE. This may sometimes be justified by the fact that a READ does not affect data integrity. However, for some purposes READ may be as important, or even more important than UPDATE. For example, in a national telephone directory system, a telephone number may need to be retrieved frequently, from many different locations, but may keep the same data for several years without modification.

This type of clustering is highly dependent on the scope of the activity model. If, for example, the activity model concentrates on the operational processes and omits decision processing, we are likely to get clusters that are suitable for operational support systems, but are less suitable for decision-support systems. Furthermore, if we are already operating within a cluster (for example, a business area), the clustering will ignore the requirements of other business areas.

Unlike data structure clustering, this heuristic is not complete, because there is no ranking of data usage. Therefore if a data object has equal pulls towards two different clusters, this cannot be resolved by saying that one data usage is more important than another. Such open questions can only be resolved by appeal to a different clustering heuristic (or intuition).

11. Activity clustering by data used

Just as data can be clustered by analysing the similarities between usage by different activities, so activities can be clustered by analysing their similar usage of data, based on a {read, update} matrix or 'crud' matrix. The same comments as #10 apply in reverse. This clustering is dependent upon the scope of the data model, and is incomplete, for the same reasons.

12. *Derive data clustering from activity clustering*

Having produced activity clusters (e.g. using heuristics #1, #2 or #9), it is possible to derive data clusters from the activity clusters via the data-activity usage matrix.

13. *Derive activity clustering from data clustering*

Having produced data clusters (e.g. using heuristics #1, #2 or #8), it is possible to derive activity clusters from the data clusters via the data-activity usage matrix.

14. *Data/activity clustering by usage of data by activities*

Whereas #10 and #11 are affinity clusterings, producing separate (and possibly inconsistent) clusters of data and activity, we now consider an interaction clustering, producing heterogeneous combined clusters of both data and activity.

From a methodological point of view, this is the most popular clustering heuristic, producing consistent clusters of data and activity, notwithstanding the fact that many tools only contain support for affinity clustering heuristics.

In the right circumstances, this heuristic produces data clusters that are reasonably cohesive under heuristic #8 and activity clusters that are reasonably cohesive under heuristic #9. This is because if two entity types are closely related in the data model, they are likely to be used by much the same processes, and if two processes are closely dependent in the activity model, they are likely to use much the same data. However, this correspondence between the different heuristics is far from guaranteed.

A particular weakness of this heuristic is that the clustering is highly dependent upon the scope of the whole model, to a far greater extent than with any other heuristic. Thus if this heuristic is used to scope design areas within a single business area, changes to the business area boundaries could have a significant effect on the design area scopes.

15. *Choice of alternatives*

We have seen a number of different clustering heuristics in this section, useful for different purposes and situations (see Box 4.6). For most purposes, the preferred clustering is the data/activity clustering (#14). However, there will be situations where this is not possible, or where it results in trivial fragments rather than meaningful clusters.

When there is no activity model, or the confidence in the quality or completeness of the activity model is low, and a preliminary scoping is required, it may be

Box 4.6
Different heuristics
and algorithms for
different purposes

> Data clustering by data use
> Data clustering by data structure and integrity rules
> Activity clustering by data used
> Activity clustering by dependencies between activities
> Clustering by organization/management requirements
> Clustering by geographical requirements
> Clustering by existing clusters

useful to carry out a data model clustering that is not dependent on the activity model, but on the structure of the data model itself (#8), or on the mapping between the data model and some other model, such as an organizational or geographical model (e.g #1 or #2), or a breakdown of the enterprise objectives.

This will also be necessary if the purpose of a project is to design a general data repository for information retrieval, since if the activities are simply data maintenance processes (ADD, MODIFY, DELETE, VIEW, LIST), then an interaction clustering will not yield any interesting results, and a data affinity clustering will be appropriate.

With object-oriented development projects, the activities are embedded in the data objects. This again leads to uninteresting interaction clusters. A data object affinity clustering (#8) will yield better results in such situations. On the other hand, with business process reengineering projects, the data are embedded in the processes, and a process affinity clustering (#9) will be appropriate.

Hub clustering is valuable in repair projects, since it enables the extent of the changes to be reasonably predicted.

4.4.7 Alternatives to clustering

Clustering defines the scope of an area by listing the objects to be included in it. This is a complete enumeration, at least at some level of detail.

There are two main alternatives to clustering, as a technique for scoping:

1. Sometimes, an area is defined instead by a selection criterion, which is defined in advance but applied dynamically. For example, a quantified cutoff may be defined. All processes executed more than 1000 times per annum. All entity types with more than 100 occurrences. All projects with an estimated payback period of under three years. All procedures with an elapsed execution time greater than five minutes. This, which we could call **cutoff scoping**, hardly ever results in coherent or meaningful areas.
2. Intuition is frequently used, either as a technique in its own right, or as a refinement and confirmation technique.

These alternatives are not mutually exclusive. Sometimes, they may be used as supplementary techniques, to resolve issues not resolved by the chosen clustering heuristic.

4.4.8 *Use of clustering techniques*

1. Scoping

An analysis or development project is scoped by a planning study, feasibility study or similar exercise. To enable effective development coordination, this project scope needs to define:

- the objects of which this project is to be custodian;
- the objects of which this project is to be temporary custodian (until other projects start);
- the objects that this project is to use, of which some other (existing) project is custodian.

At present, we usually define project scopes in terms of high-level activities (functions or processes) and entity types (or occasionally subject areas).

2. Level of clustering and custodianship

Data models are usually clustered at the entity type level. However, it may sometimes be necessary or appropriate to cluster them at the subtype or even attribute level.

It is assumed that custodianship of entity subtypes, attributes, permitted values and identifiers belongs automatically with the custodianship of the entity type. There may be a few situations where we need to do something more complicated than this, but although we can probably cope with the odd exception, information resource administration would become impossible if everything was done at the smallest level of granularity. And in any case, relationships may need to be assigned to one or other cluster.

3. Relationship custodianship

So what about the custodianship of relationships (or associations between subject areas)?

- If two entity types have the same custodian, then any relationships between them automatically have the same custodian.
- Relationships between entity types with two different custodians will always have one of these two as custodian, never a third (i.e. you cannot be the custodian of a relationship unless you are the custodian of at least one entity type).
- Custodianship of a mutually exclusive relationship rule belongs with the entity type that is subject to this data integrity.

But these rules do not address all cases. Here are some further considerations.

- Which end is optional?
- Which end is many?

- Which end is used as an identifier?
- Which end locks the relationship?
- Which end does ASSOCIATE, DISASSOCIATE, TRANSFER?

There seems to be an implied concept, which optionality, cardinality and record-locking are all pointing towards. But what exactly is this concept?

Our aim is to make the systems (and therefore the projects developing them) as independent of one another as possible. This aim is supported by the following guidelines:

- A relationship across project/system boundaries must not be mandatory at both ends.
- A relationship across project/system boundaries should preferably be reference-only at one end (i.e. not locking).
- If a relationship is used as an identifier, it should be reference-only at the other end.
- A relationship that needs to be updated by more than one business area should be regarded with great suspicion. (From a coordination point of view, this is worse than an entity type that needs to be updated by more than one business area.)
- If a relationship across project/system boundaries is many-to-many, the custodianship of the relationship implies custodianship of any intersection entity type that may be introduced to resolve the many-to-many.
- All relationships included in a mutually exclusive rule should have the same custodian.

However, some of these guidelines may be impractical, or incompatible with the performance and data integrity aims of the reference/update concept.

If these ideas hold water, we get the following implications:

- We need to consider strategic relationships explicitly, when defining project scopes.
- Clustering algorithms should take relationships into account.
- CASE tools should provide more support (including matrix support) for the analysis of relationships.
- A clear logical concept needs to be defined, which may or may not correspond to the physical concept of record-locking, to be analysed during planning/analysis and used to support scoping decisions.
- When additional object types are introduced into the data model, we need to have custodianship guidelines for them.

4. Iteration

Clustering is carried out on a model, usually represented in the form of a matrix. This model will be imperfect. Do not expect to complete the model first, and then carry out the clustering. Instead, have a first attempt at the clustering as soon as the model is 80 per cent complete. This will highlight the areas where the model needs to be more detailed or accurate. For example, there will often be one or two objects apparently linked with all other objects. These act as 'hinges'. For example, object **D** in the following matrix (Figure 4.10).

Figure 4.10
Example of interaction matrix with hinge object

	A	B	C	D	E	F	G	H	I
Alpha				•				•	•
Beta				•			•	•	
Gamma				•				•	
Delta				•	•	•			
Epsilon				•	•				
Zeta		•	•	•					
Eta		•		•					
Theta	•			•					
Iota	•			•					

We could ignore **D**, and the remaining objects would fall naturally into clusters, but **D** would then remain as a hinge, coupling the clusters together. The alternative is to divide **D** itself into two or more objects. This would make the clustering simpler, but at the cost of destroying or at least impairing the coherence of **D**.

Hinge objects are usually highly generalized. Typical examples are such entity types as TRANSACTION or ACCOUNT, JOB or BUDGET, PERSON or LOCATION. So it is reasonable to ask what gives **D** itself its coherence.

Why is it necessary or advantageous for **D** to be integrated into a single generalized object, instead of divided into several more specific objects? There are two main arguments. First, there may be some business benefit that can only be achieved through this integration. Most writers cite the same example of such a business benefit: the bringing together of CUSTOMER across all products and services, instead of maintaining a series of separate customer files. Second, there may be an opportunity to share costs, through reusability.

Such arguments need to be spelled out. Some technologists believe that it is always necessary to integrate wherever possible, and claim that even if no specific benefits of integration have been qualitatively identified, let alone quantified, there is a 'strategic' benefit of integration. But even if there is a benefit in having such a hinge, design the hinges to fit the door, not the door to fit the hinges.

4.5 Summary of chapter

In this chapter, we have discussed the development, maintenance and use of strategic information models, known as information architectures, for the purposes of information systems planning. We have seen how the scopes of projects, systems and data stores can be derived from these architectures, using techniques such as clustering.

These techniques can be applied, although with slightly different emphasis, in the different planning approaches discussed in the previous chapter. In the hierarchical (top-down) approach, the clustering techniques are deployed on an information architecture for the entire organization, to produce a business systems architecture for the entire organization, from which detailed project plans can then be derived. In the network (organic) approach, the same techniques can be applied on a rather smaller scale, to produce coherent project scopes for individual projects and systems, each having well-structured interfaces with its neighbours.

In the following chapters, we shall see how the system development projects, scoped using these techniques, can progress in parallel with well-managed inter-project interactions, and how the systems and data stores themselves, also scoped using these techniques, can be implemented and operated as integrated yet independent modules. The better the planning and scoping, the easier will this coordination be.

Notes

1. H-J. Pels, 'Decentralized organizations versus integrated information systems', *Proceedings of International Conference on Organization and Information Systems,* Bled, September, 1989, pp. 177–90.
2. C. Alexander, *Note on the Synthesis of Form*, Cambridge, MA: MIT Press, 1964, pp. 127–8.
3. *Ibid.*, p 115.
4. P. Feldman and D. Miller, 'Entity model clustering: Structuring a data model by abstraction', *Computer Journal,* vol. 29, no. 4, 1986, pp. 348–60.
5. This table is taken from T. J. Teorey, G. Wei, D. L. Bolton and J. A. Kœnig, 'ER model clustering as an aid for user communication and documentation in database design', *Communications of the ACM*, August 1989, pp. 975–87.

5   Development

5.1 Introduction

In this chapter, we shall discuss development coordination, which is (roughly speaking) the coordination within and between information system development projects. In systems development, an information model represents the state of knowledge of a project at a given point in time. (Or perhaps we should say the collective knowledge of the project team.) A project may have several models, reflecting different historical or logical stages of the project. The perspective and scope of the model may shift during a project; the purpose of the model depends on the stage reached in the development life cycle. Furthermore, at a given time, there will usually be many projects, each at different stages of development. Development coordination will facilitate the interaction between these projects and stages, to achieve the objectives outlined in Box 5.1.

Box 5.1
Objectives of
development
coordination

To ensure systems can be integrated successfully
- set target levels of integration
- achieve these target levels

To administer sharing between projects
- data definitions
- process/procedure logic
- system components (building blocks)

To help projects work as independently as possible
- without risking integration

Coordination within a project depends on maintaining proper relationships between the several models belonging to the project. Coordination between projects depends on maintaining proper relationships between their respective models. We shall use the term **vertical coordination** to refer to coordination between two models belonging to the same project at different stages of the life cycle, or at different points in time; **horizontal coordination** to refer to coordination between models belonging to different projects at the same stage in the development life cycle, and **diagonal coordination** to refer to any other coordination. See Figure 5.1.

Note that the concepts of vertical and horizontal are relative to the chosen perspective; in this chapter our perspective is the systems development process. A business life cycle is supported by a series of systems, built by a series of projects, each following the systems development life cycle. The business life cycle is then

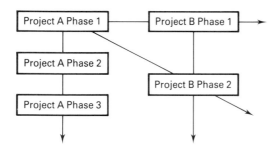

Figure 5.1
Coordination within
and between projects

regarded for systems development purposes as horizontal coordination, but in other contexts may be regarded as vertical integration.

Terminology aside then, one of the most important aspects of the coordination within and between projects, and the one on which we shall focus, is the coordination between the information models being developed and used by the project(s).

Overlaps between projects represent potential contradictions, as do gaps between projects. If an overlap results in a 'positive' contradiction, then a gap represents a 'negative' contradiction. Gaps (particularly if unrecognized and not managed) can often be worse than overlaps. But the overlaps are usually more obvious, and it often happens that coordination staff find themselves spending most of their time on overlaps.

If two or more parallel projects are building or maintaining systems that will need to coordinate, it is almost certain that some coordination will be needed between the projects. A crucial question is whether the coordination between the projects needs to be of the same kind as that between the systems. For example, if the systems are to coordinate hierarchically, does this means that the inter-project coordination needs to be hierarchically administered? Not necessarily, but it is clearly preferable to administer like structures with similar mechanisms, if possible.

5.2 Technological background

Much of the early thinking about Information Coordination dates from a period when the development and target environments were much simpler. The paradigm was a mainframe computer, running a corporate relational or prerelational database. This paradigm is rapidly shifting, thanks to new technological opportunities. In this chapter, we need to look at some of the factors affecting development; in the next chapter we shall consider some of the factors affecting production.

5.2.1 I-CASE

Integrated CASE tools allow development projects to tackle larger and more complex requirements than would otherwise be possible. These tools therefore stimulate the demand for (technical) coordination, at the same time as supporting it. Such tools use a central repository or encyclopedia, which provides a focus for coordination activity. In this chapter, and Chapters 6 and 7, we shall see some examples of the possible automation of coordination through these tools.

5.2.2 *Object-oriented technology*

In this book, we use the term **object** fairly loosely, to refer to any component of a model, whether conceptual, logical or physical. Coordination is about managing all sorts of objects, and the sharing of these objects.

We should however acknowledge a narrower usage of the term object, used in the world of **object-orientation (OO)**. In this world, an object means a specific package of data and actions (processes and services). The definitions of these objects are held in **class libraries**. The management of these class libraries raises most of the same issues as other forms of coordination: partitioning, version control, traceability. Coordination in the object-oriented world therefore inherits most of the concepts and techniques of coordination described in this book.

There is another reason for our interest in object-oriented systems. This is because object-oriented design addresses some of the difficulties of coordination by a form of modularization known as **encapsulation**. This separates the external services of an object from its internal structure, allowing for cleaner implementation and maintenance.

Superficially, there may appear to be a conflict between encapsulation and traditional information modelling, using the entity-relationship approach. This is because relationships connect, while encapsulation disconnects. But this conflict is a trap of our own making, which we can easily walk away from.

When we have a model representing a single perspective, the data and activities should all be at the same level of generality. In such a model, all objects interact in moderation: each entity type has a small number of relationships to equally generalized entity types, and a small number of CRUD interactions with equally generalized activities.

Things start to get harder when we try to combine several different perspectives into a single model. The operational specifics and the strategic generalities do not mix well. A highly generalized entity type such as PRODUCT or CUSTOMER or ACCOUNT or ORG UNIT can easily have fifty relationships to more specific entity types, and be referenced by thousands of highly specific procedures. (Easily? A single systems analyst, even brainstorming like crazy, would not have the nerve. But employ a gang of competing systems analysts to merge their requirements into a single CASE model, and the entity types and relationships sprout like tomato plants in a sewage farm.)

But if you have an entity type with fifty relationships, or a thousand procedures, the chances are extremely high that the entity type is **two-faced**[1]. In other words, it represents several different business concepts, which it is a strategic error to lump together.

Processes and services

We therefore have two ways of modelling information requirements. We can separately model the data (as entity types) and the activities (as processes). Or we can model them together (as objects in the OO sense, with external services and internal methods).

Of course processes and services are not conceptually identical. But they may be pragmatically equivalent. It is an empirically observable phenomenon that people sometimes get confused whether a generic activity operating on a generic entity type should be modelled as a process, or a subprocess, procedure step or common action block. For example, POST TRANSACTION TO GENERAL LEDGER. From an operational perspective, this is not a self-standing process. There are many operational processes (e.g. ISSUE MATERIALS FROM STORE, SETTLE PETTY CASH CLAIM, RECORD EMPLOYEE TIMESHEET, . . .) that affect the financial status of the business, and therefore must cause the general ledger to be updated, as part of the elementary process. The operational process is not complete, does not leave the business in a consistent state, until the subprocess POST TRANSACTION TO GENERAL LEDGER has been executed.

But from an accounting perspective, this usually does need to be an elementary process in its own right. Indeed, it will otherwise be almost impossible to design a coherent financial accounting system. (Although the information scientist may think that accounting data are all redundant because they are entirely derivable from operational data, it is hopelessly unrealistic to expect the accounting managers to accept a system based on such a model.)

We could resolve this confusion ideologically, by saying that an activity either is an elementary process or it is not, and therefore either the operational perspective is wrong or the accounting perspective is wrong. Or we could resolve the confusion pragmatically, by saying that both perspectives are useful, as long as we can find a way of allowing them to co-exist. OO terminology allows us to do just that. POST TRANSACTION TO GENERAL LEDGER is a service provided by the accounting model/system to the operational models/systems. These latter **use** the service as they would **use** a common action block. The interface between client and server is defined with system design constructs. (For example, in IEF they would be referred to as import and export views, commands, exit states, etc.) Within the accounting model, this activity object is modelled as an elementary process, with preconditions, postconditions, expected effects, etc. This allows it to be shown in process dependency diagrams with other accounts-related activities at the same level of generality. CASE tools already allow us to do this, but with a certain amount of manual effort in model management and integration, and with considerable risk of confusing people. (Note that Business Process Reengineering often works at the global level. It can therefore be seen as providing an efficient and effective common core for a number of local variations.)

5.2.3 *Implementing data-sharing*

Even where there is a genuine business requirement for convergence of strategic entity types such as CUSTOMER or PRODUCT, this usually means merely that there should be a common consistent core of customer or product information. It does not mean that every occurrence of the entity type should be stored on the same data store in the same format. In object-oriented (OO) terminology, it means that there is a central object called CUSTOMER, whose properties and services can (or perhaps must) be inherited by many local objects which may or may not be called XYZ-CUSTOMER. In entity-relationship (ER) terminology, this could mean that there is a strategic model containing a public entity type called CUSTOMER, which has a one-way consistency link with a local application model containing an entity type which may or may not be called XYZ-CUSTOMER.

Of course we *can* achieve enterprise-wide data sharing on CUSTOMER by having a single monolithic database, generated from a single model in which the entity type CUSTOMER has dozens of optional relationships and/or several levels of subtype. Furthermore, even though the users may have developed and agreed a small data model, this model gets merged into a large data model. With many of the user-friendly entity type names disappearing into subtypes or aliases, the user can no longer recognize her data requirements, and has to sign off the data model on trust. This is not how user-driven systems development is supposed to work.

Alternatively, we can have a central ER model, containing the global requirements, data integrity conditions and security, together with a series of local ER models, containing additional local requirements and rules. Note that we are still using ER models, and we have not broken any relationships. We have just spread the relationships across several separate (but linked) models.

Moreover, each ER model is now small enough to be meaningful. This solution does not just *preserve* the ER approach, it *rescues* it from the technicians and gives it back to the business analyst. They say a picture tells a thousand words. Let's face it, the ER diagram with hundreds of relationships only successfully communicates one thing to the user: *'Information Modelling is too difficult'*.

5.2.4 Reuse

Associated with the object-oriented approach, but independent of it, is the notion of **reuse**. Within development, the benefits of reuse are claimed to be in productivity (because objects are developed once and used many times) and in quality (because existing objects should already be debugged).

There are three approaches to promoting reuse within development:

1. **Domain analysis**. This involves a separate project to produce generic class definitions prior to starting individual development projects. (It is therefore analogous to Business Area Analysis in traditional Information Engineering projects.)
2. **Reuse evaluation**. This involves a separate reuse team, monitoring development projects, identifying opportunities for reuse, and carrying out any generalization required. (The intention of having a separate team is that this activity should not add any burden to the development project itself.)
3. **Harvesting**. This involves reviewing systems after the development is complete, to identify components that can be reused (with or without some work to generalize them).

One criticism of domain analysis is that there is a risk of 'paralysis by analysis' – spending a lot of time and effort to produce little of genuine value. Reuse is a form of technical coordination, and should therefore be justified either by specific cost-savings or by reference to enterprise coordination. Domain analysis should therefore be explicitly linked to the business strategy, perhaps via some architecture or plan as discussed in Chapter 4.

Reuse sounds good, but it does not happen unless you make it happen. This is for exactly the same reasons that make all technical coordination something of a struggle. A popular way of managing reuse is to provide a very limited amount of time and resources, both for making things reusable and for searching for reusable objects, and then to provide specific incentives for developers both to build and to use reusable objects. For example, one company pays a financial bonus, like a royalty, to the developers whenever objects they have placed in the library are reused by other developers. It also rewards developers whenever they use someone else's object, rather than developing a new one.

Cost of reuse

The costs of reuse must be reckoned across the entire life cycle of the reused object. The life cycle cost of reuse is not so much copying something, but ensuring that the copy remains identical (see Box 5.2).

> Cost of reuse
> = cost of making things reusable
> + cost of reusing things in several contexts
> + cost of maintaining reused things consistently in all contexts

Box 5.2
Life cycle costs of reuse

If the reuse costs are too high, there are two options:

- Reduce reuse costs by reducing inappropriate coordination, i.e. alter the policy.
- Or increase coordination by reducing reuse cost, i.e. alter the mechanisms.

There has been a lot of work within the software engineering community on the economics of reuse.[2] How many times must an object be reused to justify the expense of making it reusable? This work could fairly easily be generalized to other forms of technical coordination, where this coordination is for reasons of cost-saving rather than enterprise coordination. Perhaps this book will prompt further research in this area.

5.3 Coordination through project

In this section, we shall discuss some of the scenarios of the development of information systems from information models, starting from the simplest and progressing to more complex scenarios.

5.3.1 Simple development life cycle

The simplest development scenario is that we have a single model all the way through (see Figure 5.2). The development project produces an information model which completely represents the users' requirements and can be immediately transformed into a working system. The working system is put into production, and the project ends happily.

Figure 5.2
Simple development
scenario

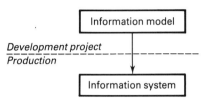

This scenario may be possible with short projects to develop small and simple systems. However, the experienced systems developer will immediately spot several things missing from this scenario, which may not matter if the project is trivial, but will certainly matter for significant projects.

5.3.2 Detailed development life cycle

Here (in Figure 5.3) is a more complex development scenario, showing different stages of development.

Figure 5.3
Detailed development
scenario

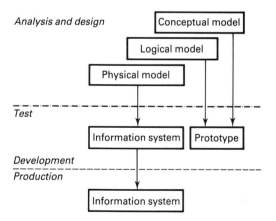

The **conceptual model** represents the business requirements of the users, the **logical model** represents the external design of the system (i.e. those features that will be visible to the users), and the **physical model** represents the internal design of the system, tuned to achieve reasonable performance on the target hardware.

Both conceptual and logical models can be expressed as entity-relationship-attribute models, or using equivalent constructs such as in object-oriented models.

Physical models are expressed in the language appropriate to the chosen DBMS. Thus if the chosen DBMS is relational (such as DB2, Oracle or Ingres), the physical model is expressed in relational data definition language (DDL), although this may also be presented diagrammatically, as a **data structure diagram**. A relational database can store formatted text and numeric data, in an integrated and non-redundant form; a post-relational database, sometimes called an information base, can store additional objects such as scanned images, audio/video and hypertext. The physical model documents the content and structure of such a database. With modern CASE tools, the database schema can be generated automatically from the physical model.

In integrated CASE tools such as IEF, a CASE model contains both an entity-relationship model and a data structure diagram. In other words, it maintains the logical and physical models together, allowing certain simple differences between them to be maintained automatically. The three levels, conceptual, logical and physical, were identified by the database community in the 1970s. At that time, there were severe technological shortcomings in database technology, making it necessary to maintain significant differences between the three levels, or incur major risks or shortcomings. Since then, much R and D effort, particularly within the CASE world, has been devoted to reducing these risks. In many projects nowadays, there may be no reason for any differences at all, or the differences may be so trivial that it is not worth maintaining three (or even two) separate models. And for most prototyping purposes, it is possible to generate test systems by assuming a physical model identical in structure to the conceptual or logical model.

If the conceptual, logical and physical models are identical in structure, or can be made identical without significant risk to the satisfaction of business require-ments or system quality, such as operational performance, this greatly simplifies the development process. A simple development process means higher produc-tivity, fewer deliverables to verify and test, fewer opportunities for error, therefore higher quality. It also reduces the effort in model management. But this is not always possible. Some valid reasons do still exist for sometimes maintain-ing significant differences between the three levels. Let us explore these reasons.

1. *Conceptual to logical*

The conceptual model represents a coherent set of business requirements. The logical model represents a computer system. Sometimes there will not be a simple one-to-one relationship between these. A single set of requirements may be satisfied by several separate systems, perhaps operating on different hardware platforms, or implemented at different times. A single system may satisfy several different sets of requirements.

Sometimes the conceptual model represents a long-term vision of what the users would like IT to do for them, and the logical model brings them down to earth. However, there may be many useful reasons to retain the long-term vision. Such a vision may influence short-term design decisions, and be fed back into long-term development plans. It may provide a context for management presentations and user training.

The logical model will contain all the short-term considerations. For example, a wholesale distribution company had a conceptual model for warehouse management in which all goods were assumed to be labelled with barcodes, and EDI links were provided to all suppliers. The practicalities of implementation in the short-term were that there were still many goods without barcode labels, and many suppliers without EDI links. This in turn meant that the computer application systems still had to allow for manual data entry and data correction. There were some messy interfaces to other systems, requiring translation tables to convert old product codes to new product codes, and suchlike. These complexities were not mere technical details, to be hidden from the business users, but needed to be visibly controlled by the warehouse manager. These differences are summarized in Box 5.3.

Box 5.3
Reasons for differences between conceptual and logical models

- Conceptual model represents 'problem'
  Logical model represents 'solution'
- Conceptual model covers broader scope

  - human activity system as well as computer application
  - several computer applications (different platforms)

- Conceptual model covers long-term vision
- Logical model may describe system linking several groups of user
- Logical model may include operational complexities

  - transitional requirements and interfaces
  - practicalities of measurement, error correction and control

2. Logical to physical

Differences between the logical and physical model are primarily for reasons of technical implementation and performance. In theory, the systems developer should be able to produce a logical design without knowing what the technical platform will be, or even whether the DBMS is to be relational or non-relational. In practice, of course, it is difficult for the information engineer to be uninfluenced by knowledge of the likely target platforms; there will often be a conflict between design goals. If you use the best features of the chosen platform, you may get the best possible functionality or performance, but at the cost of making it difficult or impossible to implement on a functionally inferior, perhaps cheaper or faster, platform. Portability is seldom if ever free; great discipline is required, either by the systems developer to avoid using non-standard features, or by the manufacturer of the platform hardware and software, to avoid supplying non-standard features. These differences are summarized in Box 5.4.

- Differences in scope
- Technological independence of logical design
- Portability between hardware and DBMS platforms
- Ability to tune for performance without affecting functionality

Box 5.4
Reasons for differences
between logical and
physical models

3. Conceptual to physical

We have seen that there may be some reasons for differences between the conceptual and logical models, and other reasons for differences between the logical and physical models. With integrated CASE tools such as IEF, which maintain close correspondence between the entity-relationship model and the physical data structure, it may be more convenient to maintain two levels of CASE model instead of three (Figure 5.4).

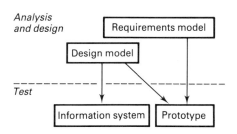

Figure 5.4
Two levels of
integrated CASE
model

With this solution, the terminology of conceptual, logical and physical becomes confusing. Practitioners with CASE tools tend to adopt the terms **requirements model** (instead of conceptual model) and **design model** (instead of logical/physical model). Both CASE models include entity-relationship models and physical data structure models; the requirements model may be only suitable for generating preliminary prototypes, but the design model will be suitable for generating fully working systems.

The design model is then tailored to the target environment. If there are several target environments, there may need to be several design models (which may be closely similar versions of one another).

4. Stages of testing

In formal system development environments, there may be several controlled stages of testing: integration testing, system testing, high-volume stress testing and user acceptance testing. Controls will often be applied to keep these stages separate. For model management, this usually implies separate CASE models for each testing stage, as shown in Figure 5.5.

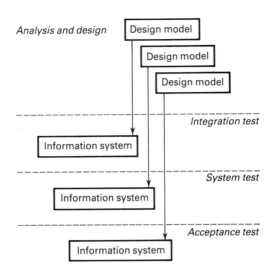

5.3.3 *Waterfall and evolution*

There are several alternative descriptions of the system development process. In the **waterfall** description, a series of specification and design documents are produced, culminating in a system. When additional requirements are discovered or negotiated, these are expected to cascade down the waterfall, through analysis and design, to system construction and test. The waterfall description separates the different elements of requirements, and assumes that one type of requirement or design can be dealt with before another type. For example, in some methodologies, it is assumed that the user information needs may be agreed before it becomes necessary to consider the screen layouts (i.e. you agree the content before discussing the format).

The waterfall is based on the premise that the development and maintenance of systems can consistently follow this flow forwards. However, some writers refer to the 'salmon effect', where there are backwards flows upwards in the waterfall. They argue, for example, that users are in practice incapable of agreeing their information needs without seeing the actual layout of proposed screens, and that separation of format from content is an abstract impracticality on real projects.

There are two ways to cope with the salmon effect. One is to allow the waterfall to have these backwards flows, which are often called 'iteration' or 'feedback'. This makes the waterfall description more complex, but still allows the developer to think of different levels of requirement, with a logical flow downwards. This is a heuristic or **backtracking** approach to problem-solving.

The other is to abandon the waterfall description, in favour of an evolutionary description. Here, we do not try to separate the levels of requirements and design, and concentrate instead on the creation of an initial version of a specification, perhaps implemented through a prototype. This is then refined by a series of small improvements or extensions. This process continues after the system is in use, to keep the system relevant to the requirements of the users, and of the business.

Some writers take the waterfall and the evolutionary descriptions to be mutually contradictory. In fact, the same development process can often be described either way. Some development methodologies primarily use one description, but this does not always mean that other descriptions are not possible. For our purposes, the difference is not in the *sequence* of analysis and design activity, but in the logical separation of different aspects of analysis and design. In a strictly disciplined waterfall methodology, development is divided into n stages, each producing a document or model whose contents and quality level will be precisely defined. Model management in this context will call for a cumulative series of models M_1 to M_n. Model M_i will then contain everything decided up to and including stage i, and nothing else. Obviously, the larger n is, the more elaborate the development process, and the more effort will be expended in model management. High values of n (> 3) will probably only be appropriate for very large development organizations, and may then perhaps be justified in terms of quality management or division of labour.

One way of getting away from the sequential aspects of the waterfall is to move towards what might be called an **estuary**. Here, the different aspects of the requirements are dealt with and represented separately, and assembled at the end. We may still have several models M_1 to M_n, but they do not overlap. It may or may not be necessary to produce a consolidated model M_0 at the end of the development process; it will certainly be necessary to provide some level of coordination between the parallel streams. These streams can effectively be managed as separate but parallel subprojects, and they can therefore be coordinated in the same way as separate but parallel projects, which we shall discuss below. A comparison between waterfalls, evolutions and estuaries is shown in Box 5.5.

5.3.4 Object transformation

1. Introduction

We are interested in managing models, and parallel models, and versions of models. Part of this management will address the content of the models. Models consist of interconnected objects. The aim of this section is to reduce model management to the (perhaps) lesser problem of object management.

This should not be read as a recommendation that the management should actually be carried out object by object. This may well be impractical, for two reasons. One is that each change affects many objects. Indeed, it can be argued that, since a model is connected, every change potentially affects every object in the model. (We shall examine this argument, and its implications, below.) The other is that there may be too many objects for individual object management to be administratively possible.

Box 5.5
Model management
implications of three
development styles

- Waterfall
  - series of requirements levels
  - separate model to represent each requirement level
  - each model contains (subsumes) its predecessors
  - new requirements are entered at the appropriate level and cascaded down

- Evolution
  - single requirement level
  - model represents complete requirements, as currently known / understood / agreed
  - each model replaces its predecessors
  - new requirements are added to the latest version, and a new version created if necessary

- Estuary
  - different aspects of requirements handled separately
  - each model represents a different aspect of the requirements / design
  - new requirements are added to the model that represents this aspect, and then analysed for any knock-on impact to any other model

However, there is some use in considering objects before we consider whole models. It is because the objectives of model management have to be stated in terms of the consistency or compatibility of model contents, which can only be defined in terms of the consistency or compatibility of objects. A change to a model can be regarded as a set of changes to objects in the model.

2. Objects and versions

If two similar (or identical) objects exist in different models, they can be regarded as being versions of each other. Thus we may have two or more versions of 'the same object'. However, this does not happen automatically, merely because the two (or more) objects are similar. It happens as the result of a deliberate decision to make the two objects the same.

In vertical coordination, two objects are made the same because of the demands of the chosen development life cycle, because of methodological principles and assumptions, or because of the needs of a particular project. (These are probably not independent reasons: the second may be inherited from the first, for example.)

In horizontal or diagonal coordination, two objects are made the same because of the need for consistency or compatibility between projects and/or systems. Models may have come from independent sources; the fact that two objects are the same (or can/should be made the same) is a discovery. (Some analysis/ coordination approaches may make such discoveries more or less likely.)

3. Managing object versions

Building models involves the naming and defining of objects. See the metamodel in Figure 5.6. As the understanding of each object develops during the analysis and model building, it may change its name and/or its definition. (For the sake of argument, let us include all properties of the object as part of the definition.)

Figure 5.6
Difficulty finding the object: many possible names, many possible definitions

At first, the definitions are likely to be ambiguous. This means that there is more than one possible interpretation. As conflicting interpretations of a definition emerge, they are resolved by clarifying the definition. This means replacing the definition by one that eliminates unwanted interpretations. Modelling forms a cycle, as shown in Figure 5.6.This presupposes that we can determine which of the conflicting interpretations is the correct one.

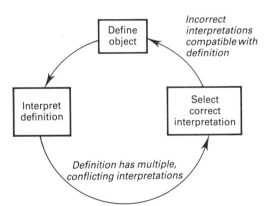

Figure 5.7
Interpretation and iteration

The longer the ambiguity persists through a project (or series of projects), the more coordination problems may be accumulated. Part of the management of development coordination is therefore to schedule the resolution of issues, perhaps using timeboxing techniques. For example, a manager may lock everybody in a room for two hours, or until specific issues are resolved. The amount of time spent resolving technical coordination issues should be geared to the degree of enterprise coordination that is involved. In other words, discussion of technical coordination issues should be severely guillotined, unless they have significant enterprise implications.

The difficulty appears to be controlling the changes of name and definition for the same objects. But we have no access to the object itself, except through its name and its definition. Thus the difficulty is controlling the many-to-many relationship between NAME and DEFINITION.

What about the identity of DEFINITION? A significant change effectively creates a new definition, whereas a trivial change does not. But what counts as a significant definition change? One that eliminates at least one incorrect interpretation. Trivial changes, such as corrections of spelling, do not do this.

There may in fact be three levels of change to definition: trivial, revising and radical. A revising change is a significant change to the definition which does not require the object to be renamed; a radical change involves a sufficiently great shift in a definition that it can no longer be considered to refer to the same object, and it would therefore be confusing to use the same name.

In classifying changes as trivial, revising and radical, we need to bear in mind the purpose of the model in question. For a planning model, the addition of an attribute may be trivial; for a systems development model, the addition of an attribute is unlikely to be trivial. Depending on the stage of systems development reached, an object should have certain properties fully defined, and changes to these properties will be regarded as non-trivial. Other properties, especially those anticipating later stages of systems development, may not yet be significant.

Some of the requirements for version management procedures are as follows:

1. Significant changes to definitions (and, of course, any name changes) need to be communicated to all analysts working on the object.
2. Changes should be discussed before they are put into effect. This implies the need for 'what if' versions of models, containing combinations of draft objects (names and definitions).
3. An analyst back from holiday needs to know what has happened to the objects he was working on before he went. This suggests the need for an audit trail, to maintain the continuity between the old name for an object and the new name. (This would also need to cover situations where two objects had been merged into one, or one object split into two.)
4. Two analysts, or teams, working on different aspects of what may turn out to be the same object, need to be able to manipulate separate definitions. Then these definitions need to be compared and either consolidated or recognized as apart. (One issue for version management is whether both teams should use the same name for the object, pending the decision whether it is the same object or not.)

4. Management of interpretation

The trouble with interpretations, like assumptions, is that it is very difficult to get people to spell them out. So how do we recognize conflicting interpretations?

1. Incompatible use of the object.
2. Incompatible business rules and integrity conditions.
3. Disputed examples.
4. Disputed cardinality or frequency. (For example, if one analyst believes there are only about a dozen products, while another believes there are thousands, the difference between them is **either** a difference in business knowledge **or** a difference in the interpretation of the object PRODUCT.)

Thus differences in the examples and use of an object, or in the rules that apply to it, allow different assumptions and interpretations to be made explicit. This is one of the reasons for including as much of this information as possible in the formal documentation of an object.

5. Model versions

The next question to determine is how these objects are assembled into models. Each name and each definition belongs within a model (see Figure 5.8).

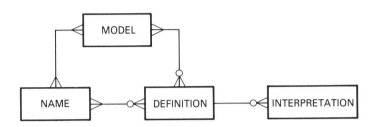

Figure 5.8
What does the OBJECT correspond to: NAME, DEFINITION or INTERPRETATION?

There is an integrity constraint, that each model can only contain one definition for a given object (i.e. for the same name) at a given time. However, a model can contain a series of different definitions for the same object at different times. The question is whether we want this, or does a significant change in one or more definitions necessitate a new model (or model version)?

6. Change

The next question to consider is why things change. In the smallest possible project, there is only one user, one analyst, and one model. The analyst produces a model as a hypothesis, and compares it with the user's perspective. Change to the model has four possible causes:

1. The user changes his/her perspective, either as a result of the modelling exercise, or for some other reason. (This is more common than you might realise.)
2. A mismatch emerges between the model and the user's perspective. (In other words, the model fails to reflect the user's world correctly.)
3. An internal problem emerges in the model. (For example, it turns out that one object clashes with another.)
4. The project changes its scope or purpose. (This itself may be initiated by the user, the analyst or some external force.)

In larger projects and coordinated programmes, there are additional reasons for change. We shall return to these reasons later.

7. Model / system variants

There is sometimes a complex structure of variations, for many different reasons, including national or regional differences, language or cultural differences, or organizational/operational differences, for example, the same processes may be carried out in house and by subcontractors.

Figure 5.9
Similar requirements, but not identical

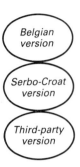

Thus some projects have to handle several parallel models, representing multiple variants of requirements (Figure 5.9).

5.3.5 *Maintenance*

Whether the development has been viewed as a waterfall or as an evolution, the same problem arises: how to manage changes to a system after it has gone live. Maintenance may be needed to reflect changes in the business users' requirements, to reflect changes in the technical or operational requirements (including interfaces with other systems), or to correct design weaknesses or other defects in the system itself.

With waterfall, new requirements are added into the appropriate level of the waterfall. In a strict waterfall, there will be a separate model for each waterfall level, as described above. Design defects and omissions will be corrected at the highest level they appear.

A unit of maintenance activity, which may be regarded as a maintenance project or merely as a maintenance task, will have a model scope, consisting of the objects that are to be changed (based perhaps on extra analysis and design), and a system scope, consisting of the system components that are to be redeveloped and retested. In some cases, the system scope will be rather broader than the model scope.

When the maintenance activity is an urgent fix to a production system, a **Production Fix Model** is created. This will contain all the objects that need to be altered. From this model, a **Production Fix System** is developed and tested, and this is then integrated back into the production environment. Such activity will need to be coordinated with any ongoing development projects affecting the same objects or subsystems (Figure 5.10).

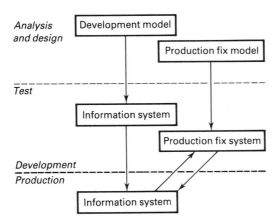

Figure 5.10
Production fix
scenario

5.3.6 *Portfolio development*

Whereas many system development projects operate in isolation, producing **single point** solutions to single point problems, a popular approach to integrated systems development, sometimes seen as the trademark of Information Engineering, is the **portfolio** approach, commonly known as **divide and conquer**, and portrayed as a kind of Christmas tree (Figure 5.11).

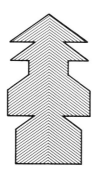

Figure 5.11
Portfolio approach –
the Christmas tree

In the portfolio approach, the development life cycle is divided into phases, and at the end of each phase, the project is divided into subprojects. Thus the scope of each project or subproject is progressively defined and redefined, using the scoping techniques described in Chapter 4. As we saw in that chapter, some form of clustering is the preferred scoping technique within many development methodologies. The essential principle of this approach is to manage and limit the amount of detail that any one project is required to handle.

The model architecture to support the portfolio approach will take a fan shape (see Figure 5.12).

Figure 5.12
Fan-shaped model
architecture
(simplified)

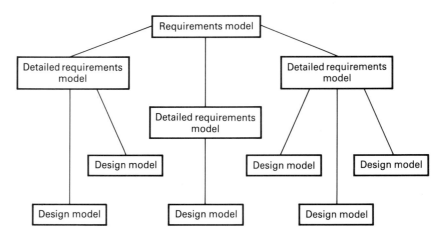

5.4 Coordination between projects

With the portfolio approach, described in the previous section, there will be parallel projects spawned from a single model. For example, several design projects spawned from a single requirements model. Or several development projects spawned from a single Information Strategy Plan (see Chapter 3).

5.4.1 Three views of model coordination

Now that we have established that we are going to have several project models in parallel, what is the relationship between them? There are three views of this.

1. Synoptic view

If you look up the word 'synoptic' in the dictionary, you will probably find a definition that refers to the three Gospels in the New Testament attributed to Saints Matthew, Mark and Luke. These three Gospels tell a common story about the life and work of Jesus. Synoptic literally means 'same eye' or 'same picture'.

A more recent usage of the word is to describe an approach to organizational planning that assumes a common and consistent view of business strategy and goals.[3] We can use the word here to denote an approach to information modelling that demands total and immediate consistency between all models. This is achieved by strictly controlled adherence to a formal top-down plan, which eliminates any possibility of surprise.

2. Adaptive view

The **adaptive view** is more pragmatic. Instead of trying to get the best possible consistency between the models, it contents itself with good enough consistency. This is what decision-theorists call **satisficing**, in other words making do with a less than perfect solution. In this case, satisficing means making do with less than total consistency between the models. This leads to an incremental approach, where inconsistency is gradually reduced, in accordance with the priorities derived from the business strategy. The top-down plan offers an 'umbrella', which covers most of the analysis activity, and allows some freedom of movement within broad constraints.

The advantage of this approach over the synoptic approach is that it allows for some degree of organizational learning. New strategies and concepts can emerge and can be encouraged to emerge. However, there is still a feeling implicit in this view that the inconsistency is a regrettable imperfection. The long-term vision is of a state of complete consistency, with full integration, which only our lack of resources and organizational inertia prevent us from eliminating quickly.

3. Interpretative view

The **interpretative view** recognizes, not only that there are different perspectives (or 'paradigms') within an organization, but that this diversity is healthy and desirable. Some writers on management have argued that it is the 'excellent' companies that are characterized by this diversity.[4] Not only is complete consistency not achievable in the short term, it is not worth trying to achieve even in the long term.

4. Summary

	Short-term behaviour	Long-term vision
Synoptic	Intolerant of diversity	Total consistency
Adaptive	Tolerant of diversity	Total consistency
Interpretative	Tolerant of diversity	Permanent diversity

Figure 5.13
Comparison of views

As we can see from the summary in Figure 5.13, there is little short-term difference between the adaptive view and the interpretative view. Both result in a concentration of effort on those areas where consistency can and should be achieved; both are tolerant of considerable inconsistency in the present. Many stimulating hours can be spent with philosophically-minded colleagues after work debating the finer points of these issues, but there is no immediate need to determine which of the two views are correct, since there is no present decision that depends upon it.

The important practical difference is between these two views and the synoptic view, since this has consequences for short-term behaviour. Those who hold the synoptic view may be more willing to consider the adaptive view than the interpretative view, because at least they can hold out hope for the long term. The discussion can then be focused on two issues: (i) What do we do right now?, and (ii) How soon will we be able to do something else?

There is also what we might regard as a compromised synoptic view. Perfect integration may not be an achievable goal, but by attempting the impossible, you may reach something worthwhile, whereas if you settle for something less, you are on a slippery slope to getting nothing worthwhile at all. Thus someone may be prepared to admit the existence of diversity, and tolerate it informally, but be unwilling to tolerate it formally. This is an extremely uncomfortable position: if the formal quality plans and standards are not achievable, they may be discredited altogether and ignored.

5.4.2 Five coordination approaches

We can identify five main approaches to the coordination between projects.

1. Separate development
2. Integrated development
3. Coordinated top-down
4. Project network
5. Divisional coordination

Let us look at the main features of each of these in turn.

1. Separate development

Some people argue that coordination is so difficult that it should not be allowed to interfere with the development projects. On this view, data sharing is an optional extra, that can be built in later if absolutely necessary. If the production systems turn out to be excessively inefficient or inconsistent, bridges may be added later. This bridge-building is managed as a maintenance project, which need not follow the systems development life cycle.

The separate development approach (see Box 5.6) allows each project to ignore all other development projects. This has advantages and disadvantages. Opportunities for synergy and reuse may be missed, but also the effort to search for synergy and reuse may be saved. It is extremely difficult to move objects, functionality or system features from one project to another. This means that any errors in the initial scoping of the projects are unlikely to be corrected later.

The productivity benefit for each project is that they can make changes within their own models without consulting any other project, and they are not required to take any notice of changes made by any other project. But this will often not be an option at all. Indeed, it is stretching terminology to the limit to refer to this approach as coordination at all. The only coordination that takes place consists in a *post hoc* reconciliation of gross coordination failures. This dooms the enterprise to a large number of stand-alone systems, as in the piecemeal approach to planning rejected in Chapter 3.

- No provision for data sharing during systems development
- Scoping is done at the beginning, for the requirements. Although a project may subdivide, no other rescoping is possible
- Changes within one area, either during initial development or as post-implementation maintenance, can be effected without impact to other areas
- Results in isolated systems

Box 5.6
Features of the
separate development
approach

2. Fully integrated development

This is the only approach that is acceptable to the synoptic view. It attempts maximum data sharing, by imposing close top-down (perhaps even synchronized) coordination between projects.

In fully integrated development (see Box 5.7), the only role for the information architecture is to provide input to the planning process of project scoping and sequencing. The information architecture does not directly influence the coordination process, because coordination needs to take place at a more detailed level than is contained in the information architecture.

- Demands full data sharing during systems development
- All objects must be identical – no variation allowed
- Prefers tight synchronization between parallel development projects

Box 5.7
Features of the
integrated
development approach

3. Coordinated top-down

In the coordinated top-down approach (see Box 5.8), strategic objects are targeted for coordination, according to coordination priorities identified in the information architecture, as described in Chapter 4. There is a top-down plan for IS development, determining which objects shall be regarded as strategic; individual projects do not have any say in this. Non-strategic objects are not coordinated. The information architecture is therefore much more influential than in the fully integrated development approach, in which everything is coordinated, whether strategic or not.

In large organizations, there may be several levels of coordination. Thus there may be large divisions or functional areas, which require greater coordination. This can be supported top-down, by having a hierarchy of strategic levels, supported by a hierarchy of common object models. This will also be controlled hierarchically, through levels of management.

Box 5.8
Features of the top-
down coordinated
development approach

- Provides for an appropriate level of data sharing
- Data sharing happens when it is chosen to happen, not as an automatic technology-driven default
- Allows for a coordination hierarchy, with similar coordination mechanisms being operated at each level

4. Project network

The network approach (see Box 5.9) corresponds to the more organic planning approach described in Chapter 3. In this approach, strategic objects are targeted for coordination, according to coordination priorities identified largely by individual projects, and negotiation between projects. Non-strategic objects are not coordinated. If there is an information architecture, this will be used as a reference, but there will be a lot of flexibility.

Instead of hierarchies of common object models, there are likely to be local and global networks of projects, sharing common object models and managing these models horizontally. Central facilities will support rather than control this coordination activity.

Box 5.9
Features of the project
network approach

- Data sharing negotiated between projects
- Responsibility for coordination lies with project managers
- Central resources available to facilitate and encourage coordination

5. Divisional coordination

The scope of integration/coordination may be the entire enterprise, or a complete operating division. If the latter, there may still need to be coordination between this division and other divisions, managed differently. For example, the coordination within a single division may be managed top-down, while the coordination across divisions may be managed via network.

Oil companies have three main stages of operations: acquisition of crude oil (by purchasing and/or drilling), refining, and marketing the refined product. This is thought of as a pipeline or stream: production (i.e. acquisition and refining) is 'upstream', marketing is 'downstream'. Some oil companies optimize upstream (production-driven), some oil companies optimize downstream (market-driven), and some attempt to optimize upstream and downstream independently. (Complete optimization of both upstream and downstream operations together is much too complex to be a practical option, at least for the major oil companies.) The choice between these three optimization strategies must be made at the highest level of management; this choice clearly affects information coordination policies and information system requirements.

Figure 5.14 shows one possible set of information coordination policies, for a typical oil company. The refinery is a complex piece of engineering, with high safety requirements, and demands high levels of integration within the information systems that support the operations. For the retail marketing operations, on the other hand, a more relaxed top-down coordination approach will be more appropriate. And as for coordination between the three main stages, this is managed ad hoc or on a network basis.

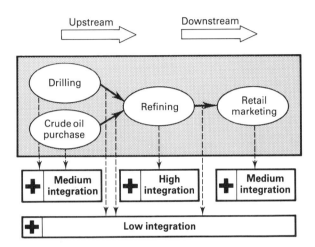

Figure 5.14
Divisional coordination policies in oil company

Whether this set of policies is chosen, or any other set, it will have very significant business implications. Such policies will therefore need to be considered at the highest possible level of management, based on clear architectures and a clear understanding of the costs and benefits of enterprise coordination.

5.4.3 Object coordination

Just as a model or project can have a life cycle, so can an individual object (within a model or project) have a life cycle in its own right. Sometimes the different life cycle of the object characterizes its participation in several different projects.

It may well be necessary to carry out (some or all) coordination activities at the object level, rather than at the model level. This provides the greatest accuracy and power, but vastly increases the number and complexity of coordination decisions and actions. It can therefore be unwieldy and impractical, whereas model level coordination is usually much easier to manage. The best approach is to coordinate at the model level as a rule, and at the object level only as an exception. For this reason, some CASE tools concentrate on providing coordination facilities at the model level. Within Oracle's CASE environment, for example, version control is managed at the application (model) level.

In the object-oriented approach, of course, the object is the main focus of attention. So we should expect to have object coordination rather than model coordination. Yet when there are thousands of objects in use across an enterprise, some grouping of objects into sets or clusters may be necessary to make the coordination manageable. (There has been surprisingly little attention given to this problem in the vast object-oriented literature, perhaps because most object-oriented development has been directed at stand-alone rather than portfolio systems.) These sets are equivalent to what we are calling models. Some writers refer to these as **frames**.

The three views of model coordination stated above (synoptic, adaptive and interpretative) apply equally to object coordination, as do the techniques. The only real difference is in the granularity of action.

5.4.4 Custodianship

One of the requirements of all the coordination approaches (except possibly the first) is to appoint a **custodian** or **steward** for each shared or common object. (This is also sometimes referred to as the **owner** of the object, but this term conflicts with the implications of shared or common ownership. And arguably all the objects ultimately belong to the enterprise, not to individual units or projects.)

The custodian of an object is (normally) the project that takes responsibility for defining and developing the object. Other projects will typically have requirements or constraints against the object and will communicate these to the custodian. The custodian then propagates (publishes) a consistent and consolidated version of the object. If requirements/constraints against the object conflict, the custodian is responsible for arriving at a workable consensus.

Sometimes the custodian is not a development project, but some other group within the IM organization. For example, certain database objects may be assigned to the database administration group. The development coordination group will act as custodian for objects where the relevant development project has not yet been started.

As we saw in Chapter 4, the assigning of custodianship to projects is a necessary part of project scoping. It may rely on clustering or other techniques.

5.4.5 Synchronous and asynchronous coordination

Migration allows correct versions of objects to be copied or propagated from one model to another. A **common objects model** (sometimes known as a **shared objects model**) allows some flexibility of the timing of migrations.

In Figure 5.15, we see schematically that the custodian project is currently working on version 4 of a particular object, but this object is not yet ready for release to other projects. The latest agreed version of the object is version 3, which is currently held in the common objects model. Of the projects that have a (non-custodial) interest in this object, one project is already using the latest agreed version of the object, while another is still using a previous version. The latter project may take version 3 from the common objects model at a time convenient

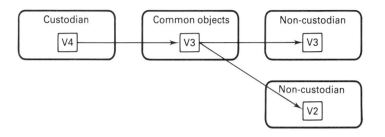

Figure 5.15
Propagation of object
versions via common
object model

to that project, or may even wait until version 4 is ready, and skip over version 3 altogether.

The three projects are therefore, quite literally, out of synch, and this reduces the need to coordinate their schedules.

5.4.6 *Version control across projects*

We need to deal with at least two situations:

1. The same analyst (or team) may have different understandings of the same object at different times (vertical coordination).
2. Two analysts (or teams) may have different understandings of the same object at the same time (horizontal coordination).

Version management at object level is about managing these differing understandings. It is often argued that development coordination has the responsibility of seeing the best understanding prevail wherever an object is shared across more than one team. But a clear precondition for this is that development coordination recognize a conflict between two teams/models.

It will be seen from Figure 5.16 that development coordination is directed by strategy, rather than technique or ideology. In other words, we do not resolve every conflicting definition merely for the sake of it, because the methodology demands it, or because of some technical principle.

Version control procedures must address the fact that the same object can be represented in more than one model. It must be possible to control the following:

1. To identify a similarity between two objects in different models (which may or may not have the same name), to compare their definitions, and to decide whether they really are the same object. (Note: this is as much a strategic decision – 'do we want them to be the same object?' – as an epistemological decision – 'can we observe them to be the same object?'.)
2. Having determined that two objects in different models are equal, to ensure that they have the same name and definition. To maintain links between the models, so that the two objects remain consistent. (Note: temporary inconsistencies can be allowed, and may indeed be desirable, as long as there is a mechanism to resolve these inconsistencies eventually.)

Figure 5.16
Contingent approach
to development
coordination

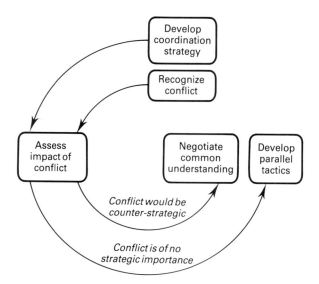

3.   Having determined that two objects in different models are not equal (either because they have observable and irreconcilable differences, or because we decide it is not worth the trouble of coordinating them), to ensure that they have different names. Once this has been settled, there should be some mechanism to prevent the same question recurring, unless there is some new evidence or insight that needs to be considered.

Remember that we do not demand that the same objects are modelled identically in all models, merely that the models be compatible. For example, the accountants' model may include an entity type PHYSICAL ASSET, while the transport model may include an entity type VEHICLE. It need not matter that the same things are included in different entity types, as long as we know how to get from one model to another. (In this case, PHYSICAL ASSET may be an aggregation of several more specific entity types in other models.) This is all right in theory, but may seem difficult (or even impossible) to implement and manage in practice, especially given the need to maintain data integrity between multiple representations of the same information. We shall return to these issues in Chapter 7.

5.4.7 *Roles and responsibilities*

In this section, we define how the development projects are typically organized to enable effective coordination, and how the responsibilities might typically be divided between the central coordination team and the projects. The usual approach is to nominate one member of each development project team, known as the project model coordinator, to liaise with the central coordination team and with other projects, and to take responsibility for managing the CASE models used by the project (see Boxes 5.10 – 5.13).

- To define scope of project model
- To act as custodian for specified objects
- To act as non-custodian user for other specified objects
- To be familiar with content and status of project model
- To adjust project schedule (in advance) to avoid model conflicts within project
- To perform model management tasks, according to agreed schedule
- To ensure changes do not exceed project budget

Box 5.10
Responsibilities of project model coordinator

- To provide initial version of object
- To propose changes to object
- To analyse and approve/refuse changes requested by other projects
- To release objects for migration into shared objects model
- To take full responsibility for the quality of the object

Box 5.11
Responsibilities of custodian

- To request changes
- To analyse and approve changes requested by other projects
- To schedule and participate in migrations from shared objects model into project model

Box 5.12
Responsibilities of non-custodian

- Create initial model for project
- Maintain custodianship matrix
- Circulate change requests/proposals between projects
- Resolve conflicts between projects
- Maintain model management schedule
- Perform/support migrations
- Assist with other model management activities
- Maintain log of issues and report to management

Box 5.13
Responsibilities of central coordination team

5.5 Diagonal coordination

5.5.1 Different development scenarios

We have seen that some projects need to maintain differences between conceptual and logical models, or between logical and physical. In some organizations, the argument will be as follows. If some projects must maintain three levels of model, then it is simpler for inter-project coordination if all projects maintain three levels, even though this places an extra administrative burden on those projects that would not otherwise need three levels of model. This makes it much simpler to compare models between projects, and to coordinate objects contained in these models, using shared object models that apply to a single level.

Other organizations will prefer a more flexible approach, where each project only maintains as many models as it needs itself. This simplifies the individual project, but complicates the inter-project coordination, since there is no longer a simple horizontal mapping from the models belonging to one project to the models belonging to another. The use and contents of shared object models becomes a little tricky, but are nonetheless still manageable.

Two or more projects following the same systems development life cycle, and reaching phase end at the same time, can be rescoped. Perhaps the boundary between the projects can be rethought, or three projects can be rearranged into four entirely different projects.

5.5.2 *Change management*

Complicated version control may be required even when projects are at different stages of the same life cycle, and becomes even more tricky when projects are following different life cycles, since a proposed change may have to be managed at several levels (conceptual, logical, physical) at the same time, or in a controlled (carefully scheduled) stagger.

1. On a small project, change management can be fairly informal, at least in the early stages of analysis – use wall charts and encourage communication between analysts, as an alternative to filling out change forms.

2. In any case, change management needs to define (or at least indicate) what counts as a change worth reporting. Does a correction to the spelling of an entity type description need reporting? What about an additional example occurrence? A new attribute? A change to an existing attribute? A new identifier? A change in the number of occurrences of an entity type? A new status value? Whether the change management system is formal (requiring the analyst to fill out forms and get sign-off from the project coordinator before making any change) or informal (requiring the analyst to mention the change at a meeting, or across the desk, or to colour in the changed object on a wall chart), it *still* needs to be understood what counts as a change.

3. Furthermore, changes need to be batched together, to make them easier to report, to manage, and to assess the impact of. Not every key stroke or mouse click counts as a change. Does a restructuring of a portion of the entity model count as one change affecting several entity types, or several changes affecting one entity type each? This may not matter so much with an informal system, but it still influences how many people need to be told about each change, and how much time they need to spend analysing the impact.

4. Also, not every change may affect the CASE model, since not every deliverable may be managed within the CASE tool.

Change management procedures have to obey three basic principles:[5]

1. 'Change serializability' – ensuring that changes are not inadvertently reversed out and lost as a result of a subsequent change.
2. Change completeness – ensuring that a change is made in its entirety, or not at all. In other words, consistency of the scope of a change. (This is sometimes called **atomicity**.)
3. Change transitiveness – ensuring that each change includes all previous changes.

5.6 Summary of chapter

This chapter has discussed what kinds of things may be desirable or possible for managing the models of one or more development project.

- Different modelling conventions

    Entity-relationship-attribute models
    Object-oriented models
    etc.

- Impossibility of working with all the enterprise concepts at once
- Need to allow people to work in parallel on different subsets of the requirements

---

Box 5.14
Reasons for multiple development start points (several conceptual models)

We have seen several reasons (see Box 5.14) why we need to manage multiple parallel streams of development, with several coordinated conceptual models, leading into a coordinated development programme (see Figure 5.17). A model is a collection of objects for the purpose of communicating a set of things to a group of people and/or machinery. Since the entire detail of the whole of a large organization cannot be communicated in one go, there is no need for a single model to contain the entire detail of the whole organization.

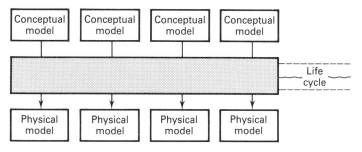

Figure 5.17
From conceptual requirements to physical implementation via one or more levels of 'logical' representation depending on the chosen life cycle

CASE tools allow information models to be represented as CASE models in an encyclopedia. The CASE tool will provide facilities for managing and manipulating CASE models, including the copying of objects and versions of objects from one CASE model to another. A development organization will need to decide its model management strategy and tactics, and develop procedures for using the facilities of the chosen CASE tool to achieve them. Sometimes, the CASE tool will not automatically do everything that is needed, and some manual effort may be required. However, CASE technology is rapidly growing in sophistication and power, and the automated support improves from one year to the next. If your strategy and tactics for development model management are sound (see Box 5.15), based on the concepts and issues of this chapter, you will be able to take advantage of this growing sophistication and power.

Box 5.15
Critical success factors for development coordination

- Clear understanding on which objects must be shared
- Clear acceptance of responsibility for shared objects
- Agreement between custodian and non-custodian
- Prompt resolution of issues
- Efficient execution of model management activities

In the next chapter, we shall turn our attention to the coordination of the physical implementation models, and the production systems that they represent.

Notes

1. For further discussion of this concept, see R. Veryard, *Information Modelling: Practical guidance*, Hemel Hempstead: Prentice Hall, 1992, pp. 32–3.
2. R. Veryard (ed.), *The Economics of Information, Systems and Software*, Oxford: Butterworth-Heinemann, 1991.
3. E. E. Chafee, 'Three models of strategy', *Academy of Management Review*, 10 , 1985, pp. 89–98. J.W. Fredrickson, 'Strategic process: Questions and recommendations', *Academy of Management Review*, 8, 1983, pp. 565–75.
4. Among those arguing for a heterogeneity of belief within an organization are T.J. Peters and R.H. Waterman Jr, *In Search of Excellence*, New York: Harper & Row, 1982, J.B. Quinn, *Strategies for Change*, Homewood, IL: Irwin, 1980, and R. M. Kanter, *The Change Masters*, New York: Basic Books, 1983.
5. Adapted from W. Harrison, H. Ossher and P. Sweeney, 'Coordinating concurrent development', *CSCW 90 Proceedings*, ACM, October 1990. See also K. Narayanaswamy and N. Goldman, '"Lazy" consistency: A basis for cooperative software development', *CSCW 92 Proceedings*, ACM, November 1992.

6 Production

6.1 Introduction

Our goal in this chapter is to implement and maintain coherent structures of information systems. This is referred to as Operations or Production. Many writers seem to regard the mere use of information systems as less interesting or important than their development. Indeed, the word 'implementation' is used by some software engineers merely to refer to the transformation of a specification into tested software, rather than the delivery of a working system into its intended business environment.

The word 'coherence' has not been used much within information systems writings. It is taken from the world of architecture, specifically from the writings of Christopher Alexander. I use the word 'coherence' rather than the word 'integration' for several reasons:

- The word 'coherence' emphasizes WHAT we want to achieve, whereas the word 'integration' seems to suggest HOW we are going to achieve it.
- The word 'integration' makes many people think of monolithic structures and close their mind against alternative ways of achieving coherence.
- The word 'coherence' emphasizes the small as well as the large. It can operate at several levels of a large and complex hierarchy.

Production Coordination comprises many linked coordination and administration activities. The most important of these are shown in Box 6.1.

Box 6.1
Tasks of production coordination

- Making changes in data structure affecting large numbers of users or applications
- Maintaining data quality and integrity within and across production databases
- Coordinating data stores and applications on different platforms
- Coordinating data stores and applications with different sources (e.g. CASE-generated versus hand-written)
- Controlling changes to the production libraries, and ensuring that the operational systems exactly match the stored source code
- Maintaining the security of production databases and applications
- Tracing and eliminating faults in complex production systems

Where does Development Coordination end and Production Coordination begin? Some experts argue that Development Coordination covers the whole field, and that Production Coordination really should be subsumed under Development Coordination. Such questions of taxonomy and labelling do not interest me very much. Release/version management and configuration management may be on the borderline. But there are some things that seem way beyond Development Coordination: for example, moving a production data store from a server machine to a client machine, which may require no development activity at all.

There are two points of similarity between Development Coordination and Production Coordination.

1. Both are to do with administering technical coordination: data-sharing, integration and reuse. The higher the degree of technical coordination required by the enterprise, the greater the coordination effort and difficulty.
2. Therefore, technical coordination needs to be justified either in terms of specific enterprise coordination, or in terms of direct technical cost-savings, or both.

However, the challenge of Production Coordination is arguably greater than Development Coordination, because it has two additional concerns:

3. In production, we are not merely concerned with the compatibility of system structures. The systems are processing real enterprise information. Whereas coordination failures in development may impact the delivery of new application systems, coordination failures in production may impact the business immediately.
4. In production, we are concerned with real software running on real hardware. This introduces practical technical issues. It may of course be desirable for development projects to anticipate these issues, but it is in production that they must be managed.

The emphasis of production is generally on stability rather than change. The critical success factor of IS production is to maintain the quality of information service for the business. Therefore for the manager responsible for production, the predominant motivating force is a fear of failure, of disruption. Only within these constraints is the manager prepared to consider opportunities for improvement.

As an analogy, we can consider the management of road traffic systems in a major city. There will often be demands by utility companies to dig up the roads for various reasons. If these demands are not coordinated, traffic may be severely disrupted. Imagine, for example, that the gas company digs up Anna Road, assuming that traffic can be diverted along Dora Avenue, and at the same time the phone company digs up Dora Avenue, assuming that traffic can be diverted along Anna Road. All roadworks temporarily reduce the capacity of the system, especially those roadworks designed to increase the capacity. This places severe limits to the amount of roadworks that can be carried out at the same time.

Similar pressures are now facing large online database systems. For many companies, in the past online processing was only required during normal office hours in one time zone. This meant that batch programs could be run overnight, routine maintenance and upgrades could be done at weekends. Apart from control applications, such as oil refineries and nuclear power plants, 24-hour non-stop operations were once a very rare requirement. It is now extremely common. Bank customers want to be able to use automated cash machines at any time of day or night. Foreign currency trading carries on around the clock. Whenever the computer is 'down', this may represent business risk or actual loss of business. One major airline estimates that if its seat reservation system is unavailable for a single minute, the business loss runs into millions.

In the light of these commercial pressures, it is understandable that the manager responsible for keeping the systems running sometimes displays an attitude bordering on paranoia, when presented with optimistically tested modifications to application systems and databases. It may sometimes seem to the developers as if these pressures prevent any changes being made to the production systems at all. It is of course frustrating for the developers to have developed systems in double-quick time, thanks to the latest CASE tools, only to have delays imposed by the requirements of production coordination. The aim of this chapter is to explore the reasons for these delays, and identify how the risks can be managed.

The structure of the chapter is as follows. First we look at the production environment created by the technological opportunities of the 1990s. Then we consider issues of coordinating changes to a single application system over time, followed by issues of coordinating changes to many application systems at the same time. Finally we show how production coordination can be made easier or harder according to how the systems have been designed and developed.

6.2 Technological background

Much of the early thinking about Information Coordination dates from a period when the development and target environments were much simpler. The paradigm was a mainframe computer, running a corporate relational or prerelational database. This paradigm is rapidly shifting, thanks to new technological opportunities. In the previous chapter, we looked at some of the factors affecting development; here we consider some of the factors affecting production.

6.2.1 Postrelational databases

During the 1980s, within commercial data processing, there was a gradual conversion of applications from prerelational systems such as IMS/DB or IDMS towards relational systems such as DB2, Oracle or Ingres.

The relational database approach has enormous advantages of simplicity over its predecessors. Now that early doubts about performance and capacity have been largely allayed, it can be regarded as a mature technology.[1]

The main limitation of the relational database approach is that it concentrates on traditional alphanumeric data types: numbers, codes, dates and character fields. The growing requirement in the 1990s is to store other forms of information: logic macros, text, image/graphics, voice/audio, video. This requirement is sometimes known as **multimedia**, but this is not always an accurate term; in principle, these forms of information can all be stored on the same storage device, and displayed on the same workstation.

6.2.2 Distributed databases

The simplest form of data storage is when all data are held in a single store, residing on a single piece of hardware and managed by a single DBMS. At the other extreme, we can imagine data being split across several continents, stored on a mixture of different hardware and software platforms, in a variety of different formats and protocols, linked by a complicated network of cables and satellite links.

The essential feature of a distributed database is that there are several data stores with some **logical distance** between them. The physical distance may be measured in kilometres or centimetres; what is probably more important is the number of steps between them, rather than the physical length of these steps. Thus logical distance is not solely a geographical concept: any translation and reformatting that may be required between two data stores increases the logical distance.

There is a greater distance between a Serb and a Croat in the same town, than between an Australian and a Canadian at opposite ends of the world.

Therefore a distributed database can in theory be contained within a small room, or even within a single box. This is certainly useful for testing purposes. However, for most practical purposes, a distributed database is likely to be spread around a building (via a LAN) or around a geographically dispersed organization (via a WAN).

Distributed data usually relies on various forms of **transparency**. The desired principle is that the user (and possibly also the application developer) should be unaware of the location of the data, and of the usage of the same data by several users at the same time, since these issues should be handled by the DBMS and/or the CASE tool. Telecommunications failure and other technical issues should also be handled outside the application.

Other forms of transparency have also been proposed, although the technology may not yet provide these forms. Migration transparency is the ability to move a database from one technical platform to another, without this being apparent to the users or affecting the applications. This is demanded by organizations seeking to provide 24-hour online service, such as the airline referred to above. Research and development in distributed processing is currently looking for reliable ways to provide such migration transparency.

6.2.3 Client-server and cooperative processing

Client/server is a form of distributed or cooperative processing, in which the **client** resides on an intelligent workstation on the user's desktop, while the **server** is a back-end computer providing such services as database access and heavy-duty processing.

The client may request services from several servers. The server may in turn request services from other servers. Complex distributed networks can be implemented, based around this simple concept.

Client/server architectures have at least three possible advantages over traditional centralized architectures, as shown in Box 6.2.

•   Enables integration across a Business Process •   Enables increased local processing independence •   Enables cost-savings through downsizing

Box 6.2
Advantages of
client/server
technology

As seen in Chapter 1, client/server can be a key enabling technology for Business Process Reengineering. Furthermore, a migration of data storage and processing from a central computer facility onto departmental minicomputers symbolizes the decentralization of power and the local responsibility for information processing. In some cases, there may even be significant cost-savings, as the better utilization of existing desktop processing power reduces the demand for processing power on the central mainframe. (This is known as **downsizing**.)

As with distributed databases, the impact on data sharing and coordination is enormous.

6.3 Coordination between system versions

6.3.1 Source management

For production coordination purposes, it is necessary to manage the source code of each application system in production. This source must be carefully protected from unauthorized alteration. When production fixes are required, the correct source must be issued to the person or team, who will make and test the necessary alteration; these changes will then be released into production. We shall consider the release management shortly, but we first have to define what exactly is meant by **source**.

Without an integrated CASE tool, there are at least three levels of coordination (see Figure 6.1). The model is used to build data definitions (DDL) and programs. A program may be handwritten in a third- or fourth-generation language, which is the final **source** of the system. This program source code is then compiled, data-bound, etc., to produce executable system components, while the DDL is used to generate databases. Maintenance may require coordinated changes to the model and to the source code, in order that the model may continue to provide an accurate description of the system.

However, if the CASE tool can generate code automatically from the data and activity specifications contained in the model, then the model itself becomes the source. Any COBOL or C programs that are generated by the CASE tool are merely intermediate products.

Many years ago, engineers argued that it was necessary, for performance or

Figure 6.1
Without I-CASE –
separate management
of source code

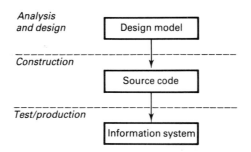

other reasons, to tinker with the executable code after compilation. This meant that you could not tell exactly what the program was doing merely by looking at the so-called source code. This practice has been all but eliminated in most computer installations.

A similar argument now occurs with CASE-generated systems. Engineers may insist that they need to tinker with the generated code. Database specialists (perhaps reluctant to see themselves becoming redundant) will argue that CASE does not always provide you with a well-tuned database, or good quality data accesses. If their arguments are accepted, this means that the generated code will have to be maintained and controlled, since there is no guarantee that the executable system matches the CASE model.

On the other hand, if an organization using CASE tools is prepared to deny itself the technical excitement of tinkering with the generated code, its controls are greatly simplified. CASE suppliers already argue that such tinkering is rarely, if ever, needed. The debate will no doubt continue for a while, but the practice of tinkering with generated code will eventually die out.

The important point here is to understand what is meant by source. For source management purposes, **source** should be defined as the last stage at which human intervention is allowed. Thus if you allow direct changes to COBOL, then COBOL is the source; but if you generate COBOL from something else, and do not allow direct changes, then COBOL is not the source, the something else is. People confuse themselves when they think that, because COBOL used to be the source, it must therefore still be.

This discussion is particularly relevant when systems are subject to external financial or quality audit, since the auditors may have fixed ideas as to what counts as source, and fixed ideas about the proper management of this source.

6.3.2 Transition and parallel running

We indicated at the start of the chapter that there is a difference in priorities between IS Development and IS Production. Whereas the former is charged with making improvements to the IS portfolio, the latter is charged with maintaining a constant and consistent quality of service to the enterprise. These two must come together in planning and executing the implementation of improvements, and effecting smooth transitions from old to new systems.

There can be a significant transition problem when implementing new versions of systems, even when these systems are similar to the previous systems already in production (see Box 6.3).

- Adding a new entity state to an entity type - e.g. to extend the life cycle forwards or backwards, or to subdivide an existing state
- Converting a process from an internal process to an external process
- Merging two operations into one

Box 6.3
Typical examples of production impact

We mentioned earlier the airline, unable to take its seat reservation system offline. Now suppose this airline has merged with a smaller airline, which also has a seat reservation system. In order to get commercial synergy between the two operations, it will be necessary to merge (or at least link) the two seat reservation systems.

The traditional view of implementation was that it was something you did so rarely that you could afford to be inefficient during the transition period from old to new, because the transition period was a trivial fraction of the total lifetime of the system. Thus parallel running was a temporary feature of systems, often inelegantly bolted on almost as an afterthought.

This always was a fantasy. We should design systems for permanent transition. This means that features for parallel running should be part of the system itself, rather than bolt-ons. But if we have some redundancy of parts and/or redundancy of function within a network of systems, then parallel running may come cheap.

With real-time systems, this is already taken for granted. You cannot close down an oil refinery in order to upgrade the software that operates it. You have to be able to have a smooth handover between the old version and the new version, similar to the handover between staff when the shift changes.

If we have an architecture that assumes the new will go in in parallel with the old, sitting side by side like pilot and copilot in an aeroplane cockpit, then we can deal with transition fairly elegantly. However, parallel running may sometimes be impossible or at least impractical. To do it properly may demand double the hardware or telecommunications capacity, or even double the clerical staff. To design systems for continuous transition, and therefore continuous parallel running, may be thought too inefficient to be seriously considered.

One proposed approach for implementing a new service, without disrupting users of the old service, is to embed the old service inside the new service. The new software module includes all the interfaces and services provided by the old software module, plus some additional ones, perhaps based on an altered internal structure. Thus other modules can interface with the new module as if they were communicating with the old. There is some merit in this idea, and it has been successfully applied in some fairly small situations. However, there are some difficulties with it as a general approach, particularly in large performance-critical systems.

- First, because unless the new service is at least as reliable as the old service, the reliability of the total system will be degraded. It may be impossible to guarantee that the new module actually provides exactly the same services as the old. (This is not just a matter of thorough testing – reliability of system components cannot be guaranteed by testing alone. Users often rightly demand parallel running.)
- Second, because it leads to an inexorable increase in the complexity of module and systems. (In practice, nobody will ever bother to go back and delete obsolete functionality, because even such deletions will need to be comprehensively tested.)
- Third, because the new system will be emulating the old system, it will often be difficult to maintain high performance for both old and new services, especially if there is a significant change in technology.

Another proposed approach is to ensure that all transition consists in the addition of new objects, rather than the amendment of existing objects. Some writers appeal to complete normalization (5th normal form, or perhaps higher) as a guarantee that new requirements can always be represented with new entity types, rather than affecting existing objects. Sadly, the guarantee is flawed. The trouble is that if the new requirements have new integrity conditions, then these must be respected by existing business activities, and obeyed by existing data occurrences.

Transition from old to new often means that data occurrences have to be upgraded, e.g. new mandatory attributes or relationships have to be set with data values. The traditional approach has been a big bang – for example, the database is unloaded and reloaded in batch, with default values added for the mandatory attributes. The new approach may be that data occurrences are upgraded when and only when they require a new service (activity) that requires the upgrade. This is known as **just-in-time upgrade**. In this case, production coordination will need to keep track of:

- Which services can only operate on upgraded data (because they assume the additional data integrity conditions).
- Which services cannot operate on upgraded data.
- Which services can operate on all data, upgraded or not.
- Which service(s) perform the upgrade.
- What proportion of data has been upgraded, so that, when (say) 95 per cent of the data have been upgraded, the old service can be scheduled for termination, and its remaining users given a deadline for conversion.

At present, there is limited technical support for just-in-time upgrade. In particular, the referential integrity (RI) provided by the DBMS is likely to cause some difficulties, since the old and new data occurrences will obey different RI rules.[2] Although in the future, it may be possible to keep such just-in-time upgrade hidden from the application, it presently requires considerable special coding, and is therefore seldom attempted.

To effect transition and bridges from legacy systems to new systems, you need to work out the implicit model(s) on which the legacy systems are based. To train users and managers to understand the new concepts, you need to work out their implicit models, and determine what needs to be done to introduce the new business concepts.

> Measurements used in reports . . . embed themselves deeply in a company's systems and communications. Changing the unit of measurement in a cost reporting system would necessitate reworking the entire accounting system from shop-floor data collection to budget reporting and then retraining all involved. In addition, the unit of measure becomes so ingrained in everyone's language and thinking [i.e. their personal mental models] that proposing to change it could appear unjustified and ill-intentioned.[3]

Thus the release of new information systems into the production environment needs to be synchronized with the release of new thinking into the business.

6.3.3 Release management

Changes to production systems have to be controlled. Changes may be released in **trickles**, where there is a constant stream of small changes, or **cloudbursts**, where the changes are batched into large groups for simultaneous release. Trickle release can be more difficult to coordinate, because you are trying to hit a moving target; cloudburst release holds the production system more stable. Cloudbursts are planned in advance, either on a regular cycle, or whenever the volume of required change reaches a certain level. The two strategies are shown in Boxes 6.4 and 6.5.

Box 6.4
Characteristics of
trickle release

- Changes can be released as soon as they are ready
- Low cost per release
- Changes can be backed out individually if they don't work
- If two changes affect the same objects, it may be necessary to release one before the other.
- Flexibility of release sequence means that the exact configuration of versions in production may not have been tested beforehand
- Possibility of 'leakage' – trickles not reaching the correct destination thanks to administrative error
- Urgent fixes can be handled as any other changes, but just more quickly

The two release strategies also entail different approaches to testing and bug-fixing. Trickle release requires very accurate tracking of object versions through testing and production environments. Most coordinators prefer cloudburst release.

The release may involve new application software alone, with new database tables, or may involve reloading existing database tables. If database unload/ reload is required, then a cloudburst release is likely to be more appropriate.

Box 6.5
Characteristics of
cloudburst release

- Release may be delayed until all the changes are fully tested
- High cost per release
- Need reasonable time to elapse between releases (often measured in months)
- It may be difficult to back-out individual changes
- Changes affecting the same object can be tested and released together
- Greater stability of test environment
- Urgent fixes need special treatment, to ensure that they are not inadvertently lost at the next cloudburst

A cloudburst release usually requires a lot of resources – both human and computer – and therefore has to be successful first time. This means planning carefully in advance. This is why cloudburst releases should be relatively infrequent. Minor imperfections may need to be tolerated until the next release, since they will not justify backing-out the entire release.

A cloudburst release can be managed by totally rebuilding and testing the application systems and databases from scratch, which provides an additional guarantee that the release will work consistently, although this may be excessively expensive. Alternatively, the production systems and databases may be analysed to determine which parts require rebuilding. (Some CASE tools provide support here.) Thus incremental rebuilding may also be an option.

Trickle release can only be managed by incremental rebuilding. Complete rebuilding every time a tiny change is made would be excessively costly. However, it may be valuable to carry out a complete rebuild once in a while, since accumulated administrative errors may cause the production systems to diverge from the correct production models.

6.3.4 Design for flexibility

Even when a systems development project is preceded by an information strategic planning exercise, there will remain some flexibility (otherwise known as uncertainty) about the scope and purpose of the project. This flexibility will be largely resolved during the requirements analysis phase of the project, although some flexibility may persist into the design phase.

Questions within the scope of the project should be resolved during the project. What about questions that go beyond the scope, perhaps referring to topics to be resolved by future projects?

There are several aspects of building flexibility into a system. The four main ones are those shown in Figure 6.2.

Let us look briefly at some examples of these four dimensions, to see how they affect production coordination.

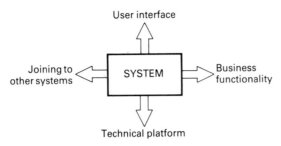

Figure 6.2
Four dimensions of
flexibility

1. Business functionality

Box 6.6 shows some examples of how systems can be built with limited functionality, and extended later.

Requirement	Stage 1	Stage 2	Stage 3
Data capture from on-line entry or feeder systems	Imperfect data will be rejected. User must resolve data errors off-line, and then resubmit.	Imperfect data will be accepted, with a status that protects the system from data integrity error. User may correct data on-line.	Imperfect data will be accepted. The system itself contains the intelligence to support data correction.
Determination of inventory levels	The inventory level is a basic attribute, obtained by a person going to the stockroom and counting.	Some of the values of inventory level will be calculated, while some will be from counting.	The inventory level is calculated for all stock items. (In other words, it is now a derived attribute.)

Box 6.6
Progressive
development of system
functionality

Sometimes business functionality can be enhanced by completing aspects of the requirements analysis previously left incomplete. In particular, some projects may leave some of the information needs unanalysed. A MISC INFO field on a screen is often an implicit acknowledgement that the analysis is not complete. (Since if all the attributes had been identified and defined during the analysis, there would arguably be no need for MISC INFO fields.)

The advantage of such fields is that they allow the user to extend the functionality of the system dynamically, without changing the data model. Information management should not discourage this, but should closely monitor the contents and usage of such fields. Often, they will identify opportunities to enhance a system by enriching the data structure, or by integrating it with other systems. Although such enhancements should be carried out reasonably quickly, before the quantity of unformatted data in the MISC INFO field causes conversion problems, the urgency is reduced as the users already have an interim solution to their new requirements.

In Chapter 3, we indicated the desirability for positive space within information systems. This can be achieved by providing such facilities as computerized scratch pads for the user to make private notes, links to desktop software such as spreadsheets, graphics and word-processing, and the ability to cut-and-paste from one application or transaction to another.

2. User interface

Flexibility in the user interface is achieved through such techniques as **screen-scraping**, which convert character-based online transactions, and provide graphical user interface (GUI) front-ends, or even visualization layers.

One issue here is how to upgrade without confusing the user. This is not primarily a coordination issue, except in so far as there are user interface standards and expectations that span many different systems. Such upgrades may need to be synchronized across all affected systems.

3. Joining to other systems

Here, the flexibility has to do with designing systems so that they will be easy to join to other, as yet unspecified, systems. Anticipating such interfaces may mean storing unprocessed data, since the processing will often be irreversible. For example, it is better to store atomic data than subtotals. Subtotals may be more efficient for the immediate set of user requirements, but may not be suitable for future requirements of these same users, let alone other users. If a future system needs the atomic data, and these are not being stored or passed through, this will necessitate considerable rework.

Another reason for storing the atomic data is to be able to produce audit trails (**traceability**). In hospital management systems, accountability of data values is an important issue.

This has always been one of the ideas behind the separation between operational data and management information. The information engineer analyses the operational requirements first, with the confidence that management information systems can be built on top, and that given a well-structured database containing high quality atomic data, users will be able to obtain and interpret for themselves whatever information they need to support business decisions. For example, in a supermarket, the short-term information needs may be directed at restocking the shelves with grocery products. For this purpose, it is enough to store the total quantities sold of each product. But next year, we may want to build a system to analyse how the purchases are being spread across the consumers: is this category of product being bought in large quantities by a few customers, or in small quantities by many customers? If our systems have been designed to store the totals, we shall have to redesign them in order to analyse individual purchases. However, if the original systems were already designed to store the atomic data, it will be much easier to build and implement a suite of analysis programs against the existing data.

Other methodologies prefer to start by analysing the management information needs, and build the interfaces top-down. Early projects may construct bridges to obtain the required information from the existing systems. Later projects will replace or enhance the existing systems in order to increase the quality (comprehensiveness, consistency, timeliness) of this information. This also obeys the principle that the bridges should serve the systems, and not the systems the bridges.

4. Technical platform

Flexibility of technical platform is known as **portability**. This means that the system should be capable of being transferred from one technical platform to another.

Portability does not come for free. Sometimes the designer of the particular system must produce designs that are less than ideal for the first platform, in order to leave the flexibility for a future move to a second platform, for example, avoiding using special features of the first platform, that are not found in other platforms. Sometimes the designers of the platforms deny themselves technical innovations, in the interests of maintaining compatibility with industry standards. In the worst case, 'open systems' can even mean technological stagnation.

6.4 Coordination between systems

6.4.1 How many production systems?

One way of managing production is to have a single system. Although each development project may have developed and tested a separate set of database tables and computer procedures, when these are put into production, they lose their separateness and become merged into a single database, with a single large library of computer procedures.

This appears to be the simplest solution. Why have many when you can have one? But there are several reasons why it is often appropriate to divide the production environment into separate (but linked) systems operating against separate (but linked) databases. These are summarized in Box 6.7.

Obviously, if data stores are being implemented on different platforms (such as with client/server), then there is a physical discontinuity between the platforms. It is desirable, although not necessary, for the physical discontinuity to correspond to a logical discontinuity. Although this discontinuity may be transparent to the

Box 6.7
Multiple physical
implementation

- Different technology
- Distributed implementation (client/server etc.)
- Manageability of operations and maintenance
- Manageability of database referential integrity
- Security and robustness (firewalls)

user (and sometimes even to the application developer), it needs to be managed as part of production coordination.

Even when systems and data are being implemented on a single physical platform, there may be a need to provide logical breaks. Large organizations in particular may be forced to divide production systems into separate parts, to make them manageable.

Release management, whether trickle or cloudburst, gets more and more difficult as the size of each production system increases. This may set a practical ceiling on the size of a production system. A particular instance of this comes with database referential integrity (RI). With some DBMSs, such as DB2, the requirements of RI may mean that changing one table forces a regeneration of hundreds of tables. This alone may mean that a single connected database is unmanageable, because database changes cannot be implemented.

Database housekeeping operations, such as back-up and recovery, also become increasingly difficult when the production database gets above a certain size. The concept of **firewalls** has been introduced to refer to the need for localization of system failure: if there is a serious problem in one part of the database, this should not be allowed to bring all operations to a standstill; the firewalls allow such problems to be contained within a single area.

In Chapter 5, we showed how object-oriented thinking leads us to separate central (public) data definitions from local (private) data definitions. This could be implemented physically with a central server, providing a user-invisible data-sharing overlay on a number of local client applications.

Of course we *can* achieve enterprise-wide data sharing on CUSTOMER by having a single monolithic database, generated from a single model in which the entity type CUSTOMER has dozens of optional relationships and/or several levels of subtype. But we should not pretend that this is the only or best solution. Apart from the production coordination problems cited above, there are serious difficulties imposing context-sensitive data integrity rules. The alternative is to adopt a client-server solution. (This may be a pseudo client-server – in some cases, both client and server may be physically implemented on the same piece of hardware.) This allows us to encapsulate the information strategy into a global structure with global integrity rules, defined within a central information model, implemented on a server. This is the 'public' side of CUSTOMER. Each client application can then access this global structure, and combine it with additional local requirements (including local data integrity rules and locally defined data security), defined within a local information model. This corresponds (roughly) to the object-oriented concept of **inheritance**.

6.4.2 *How many production models?*

If there are CASE-generated systems in production, then there must be one or more CASE models that exactly correspond to the production systems. The debate seems to be whether we can always have a single production model, describing a single integrated data store (e.g. DB2 database), regardless of the size and complexity of the enterprise, or whether there are circumstances where we should need to adopt the techniques of divide and conquer, referred to in the previous chapter as the **portfolio** approach. This would define several linked logical data stores (and therefore several linked CASE models) in order to manage this more efficiently / effectively.

But the two questions are independent. Even if you decide to have a single physical data store in production, there may still be reasons to describe this using several models rather than one. Since the purpose of the model is to aid understanding and management, there may be a limit to the size of model that will be useful. Other issues arise when there is not a one-to-one mapping between physical data store and information model, but these issues are themselves manageable.

Although there are small organizations who find a single production model manageable, it is unlikely that this will be practical for large international organizations. As the usage of I-CASE increases, and some organizations now have many systems developed using a single integrated CASE tool, there is a suspicion that the implementation of application changes becomes more and more burdensome as the production model grows. At present, there are no adequate measures of the flexibility/inertia of models. We shall return later to the possibility of defining an objective metric of model quality, that will enable production coordination to be more effectively managed.

Some writers suggest that we can break out development models from a single production model that can be re-integrated as changes are completed. The argument is that this keeps consistency automated. However, since change always means that the old and new are different, the CASE tool cannot then automatically manage the transition from old to new. So the transition still involves manual (and mental) effort. With any automated tool, having to do something manually may be a symptom of a deeper underlying problem. And as nineteenth-century hypnotists discovered, if you eliminate a symptom without understanding the underlying cause, you just get a different symptom popping up somewhere else.

6.4.3 *Assembling systems*

In this section, we shall consider the actual physical putting together of the systems or system components, and testing these assemblies. This activity is what some writers call **integration**, others call **synthesis**. However, these words are also used to refer to other parts of the development life cycle; we shall therefore use the word **assembly** as less open to misinterpretation.

1. Blackbox assembly

With blackbox assembly (see Box 6.8), we can imagine a pile of subsystems, modules, objects or whatever, which have been unit-tested. These have well-defined interfaces with the outside world. Fitting them together consists in matching interface to interface, and testing the communications between them.

Objects destined for blackbox assembly will have a public face and a private face. For traditional application modules, the public face consists in the specification of the interface, and the external behaviour of the module. (Software engineers prefer modules to have no hidden side effects.) For object-oriented design, the public face of an object consists of its services, while the private face consists of its attributes and methods.

In designing for blackbox, the public faces (i.e. the interfaces) are generally designed before the private faces. Where the design is difficult, there may be a need to iterate through the design until a simple and stable set of interface specifications is arrived at.

The fact that blackbox components are easily interchangeable is not only useful for maintenance but also for testing. Integration testing often uses the concept of the **stub**; this is a dummy component that stands in for a real component for testing purposes. The internal structure of the stub is unimportant. (In the object-oriented world, the concept of **deferred class** performs a somewhat similar role.)

Box 6.8
Characteristics of
blackbox assembly

- Consistency of interface behaviour
- Suited to object-oriented development
- Allows substitution of modules without worrying about internal structure
- Design interfaces first?
- Iterate to converge on stable interfaces?

2. Whitebox assembly

Whereas blackbox assembly resembles the symbiosis between two (or more) separate biological organisms, whitebox assembly (see Box 6.9) can be thought of in terms of cells merging to form a single indivisible organism. Instead of fixed formal walls between the components, each is capable of sharing the resources of the other. The interfaces may not need to be formally specified. This may be much more efficient than blackbox assembly, since it allows a higher degree of optimization. When developing very small systems, the development productivity may be just as high. Against these possible advantages, there is the disadvantage of complexity, and almost certainly a loss of flexibility.

3. Greybox assembly

Sometimes designers of very small systems manage to achieve some of the

Box 6.9
Characteristics of
whitebox assembly

- Identical structures or shared internal structures
- Entails blackbox integration
- Single design act, propagated into many systems (by decree)
- Danger of monolithic result
- Interface design is a trivial consequence of boundary definition and the design of the total structure

advantages of both whitebox and blackbox assembly, by defining modules and their interfaces in a semi-formal way (this can be called greybox assembly). This allows them to carry out top-down testing using stubs, for example, without committing them to all the principles of object-oriented or modular design. This should probably only be attempted for small simple systems, and should never be considered for mission-critical software, since the quality of such solutions is likely to be rather suspect.

4. Conversion

It is sometimes possible to convert a system that was originally designed for whitebox assembly into a blackbox system. This involves carefully dissecting modules, separating their public and private faces, and specifying their interfaces. This is also known as **parcelling** or **encapsulation**. This essentially converts system components, or even very large systems, into pseudo-objects. This is one of the key ideas of ODP (Open Distributed Processing).

It is also possible to do the converse: to dissolve the hard boundaries between two or more system components, in the interest of greater overall system performance, or because the interface itself has become obsolete as the system has evolved. However, at the present time, it is probably very rare that this is appropriate. Dissection is almost always more useful than dissolution.

6.4.4 Good scoping and modularization

Good scoping is essential for the coordination between systems. This has been a theme throughout the book, from planning through development to production and maintenance.

Good module structure relies on high cohesion and low coupling. These principles apply at all levels, from the smallest system components, to the structure of entire systems.

One of the main arguments for modular design is that it promotes maintenance. If a module can be replaced with a new version, without this affecting the remainder of the system, this clearly makes production coordination easier. (Of course, this does not mean that the new configuration does not need to be retested. Sometimes it will turn out that the module boundaries were not as clear cut as they were supposed to be. Such problems should not happen very often, but somehow they seem to happen much more often in those organizations that take the perfection of their module structure for granted.)

The consequences of this should be obvious. Physical breaks should correspond wherever possible to logical breaks, and the breaks between the systems and data stores should be understood in the context of a series of models, structured within an architecture. In the next chapter, we shall see how the links between these models may be described.

6.5 Summary of chapter

This chapter has discussed what kinds of things may be desirable or possible for managing the models representing production systems. These are the physical models shown at the bottom of the life-cycle diagram first seen in the previous chapter (see Figure 6.3).

Figure 6.3
From conceptual requirements to physical implementation via one or more levels of 'logical' representation depending on the chosen life cycle

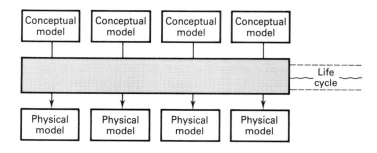

Having argued that a single development model does not make sense, we have now seen that a single production model does not make sense either (see Box 6.10).

Box 6.10
Reasons for multiple finish points (physical implementation)

- Different technology
- Distributed implementation (client/server etc.)
- Manageability of operations and maintenance
- Manageability of database referential integrity
- Security and robustness (firewalls)

Therefore, the production systems (and their underlying models) need to be coordinated in much the same way as the development projects and their models.

Finally, we should reiterate the way production coordination relies on high-quality design and development, as well as on good coordination tools. This is shown in Box 6.11.

- Good scoping and modularization
- Design for flexibility
- Design for reuse
- Design for implementation

Box 6.11
How production
coordination depends
on good planning and
development

Notes

1. R.G. Fichman and C.F. Kemerer, 'Adoption of software engineering process innovations: The case of object-orientation', *Sloan Management Review*, Winter 1993, pp. 7–22.
2. P. Voke, 'Practical ways of introducing referential integrity into databases', Unpublished paper, 1993.
3. R.S. Kaufman, 'Why operations improvement programs fail: Four management contradictions', *Sloan Management Review*, Fall 1992, pp. 83–93.

7   Model management techniques

7.1   Introduction

This chapter describes tools and techniques for model management, which will support the coordination requirements described in Chapters 5 and 6. This is a fairly technical chapter, which the non-technical reader may prefer to skip.

7.2   Models and CASE

Models can be expressed on paper or whiteboards, especially in the early stages of development, but most projects today use some form of Computer Aided Software Engineering (CASE) tool to support the modelling activity, to store the resulting models, and allow them to be viewed and maintained.

For the purposes of our discussion, we do not have to be very concerned about the technical facilities of these CASE tools, nor the physical storage of the models (usually in a special database known as a **repository** or **encyclopedia**). This is a rapidly developing technological area, and we do not intend to provide technical descriptions of particular products in this book. (The Information Engineering Facility (IEF™), which is the Texas Instruments I-CASE tool, is occasionally mentioned for illustrative purposes, because this happens to be the one with which the author is most familiar.)

There is one point we do need to clarify, however. In our discussion of information models, we have said that a model has a single purpose, scope and perspective. Such a model may be represented by a connected set of objects, stored in an encyclopedia. CASE tools such as IEF refer to this as a model. However, what such CASE tools refer to as a model may contain many other things as well, such as the process details from which the operational code may be automatically generated. Where it is important to distinguish between the model itself, and its physical representation in a CASE encyclopedia, we shall refer to the latter as a **CASE model**.

A further complication is that, depending on the technology and in certain limited situations, a single CASE model may represent more than one perspective. For example, IEF allows both the 'logical' and the 'physical' perspective to be combined in a single CASE model.

7.2.1   Models and model families

An information model is a consistent set of objects, and has a specific scope, purpose and perspective. As indicated in the previous paragraph, a CASE model may sometimes contain more than one purpose or perspective, but must still be consistent. In this chapter, we are mainly talking about the management of CASE models, although of course managing the CASE models necessarily entails also managing the information models that the CASE models contain.

A set of related CASE models, containing different versions of objects, is known as a **model family**. A family *can* be structured hierarchically. This is the traditional top-down approach, as practised by many information engineers. However, there is a school of thought that prefers network or horizontal transactions, and this school of thought dominates the emerging standards on Open Distributed Processing. If this trend continues, CASE tools such as IEF will need to support both hierarchical and network coordination.

In order to understand model families as a network, we need to start from the models, and work out different ways to link them together usefully into a family; whereas to understand model families as a hierarchy, we need to start from the model family itself, and work out different ways to contain temporary or permanent inconsistency within it.

7.3 Links between models

7.3.1 *Dilemma*

Either one large and unmanageable model (see Figure 7.1):

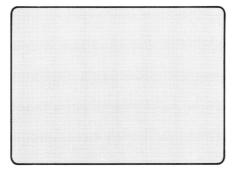

Figure 7.1
Single monolithic model

Or a family of separate models (see Figure 7.2):

7.3.2 *Solution*

The solution to this dilemma is a family of connected models (see Figure 7.3):

As indicated in Figure 7.3, we shall try to restrict ourselves to horizontal and vertical links between models. Diagonal links shall be defined as combinations of horizontal and vertical. The aim shall be to connect the family properly, with as few links as possible, since each link entails coordination effort, both to define and to maintain.

Figure 7.2
Unconnected family of
models

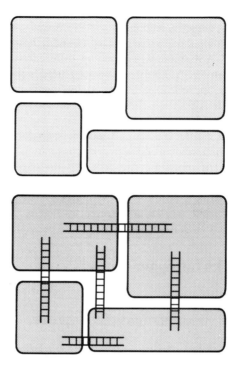

Figure 7.3
Linked family of
models

7.3.3 Type of link

There are three types of link we could define between models (or objects in separate models):

- **Identical structure**   This is where the structures in the two models are supposed to be (and remain) identical.
- **Equivalent structure**   This is where the structures in the two models are supposed to represent exactly the same things, but for different purposes.
- **Alternative structure**   This is where the structures in the two models are supposed to represent similar things in different contexts (which may be parallel or completely different purposes).

Each link has an **extent** (sometimes known as an **aggregate object**). For example, two alternative structures may be centred around different versions of a particular entity type, but may include differences in relationships, attributes, identifiers, data integrity rules, process logic. In the object-oriented world, there may be differences in services or methods.

Two models may have several such links between them. Suppose we have two models A and B, containing aggregate objects $\{a_1, \ldots, a_n\}$ and $\{b_1, \ldots, b_m\}$ respectively. Then we could conceivably declare that we want a_1, a_2 and a_3 to be identical to b_1, b_2 and b_3; a_4 is to be equivalent to b_4, and a_5 is to be an alternative to b_5. This example is shown in Figure 7.4.

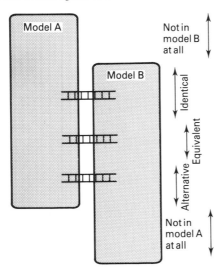

Figure 7.4
Several links between
two models

Two models are **consistent** if there are no alternative structures. In other words, all structures are identical or equivalent.

1. Identical structures

For structures to be identical, they must not only have the same syntactical structure (relationship cardinality etc.) but the same semantic structure (meaning). In other words, the occurrences of the entity types should be identical.

The converse of this is that the object descriptions must be semantically sufficiently precise as to prevent different structures masquerading as identical. (If Sandy thinks we have thousands of occurrences of PRODUCT, and Jo thinks we only have one, then they are not operating with the same concept of PRODUCT.)

In database design circles, it is often supposed that this is a necessary condition for integration. It turns out that this is too strong a requirement.[1] Integration can be based on weaker conditions of compatibility or equivalence.

2. Equivalent structures

There are two main reasons why the information engineer may be interested in equivalent structures.

1. Different user/application views of the same data.

    Example: the model for Accounting will be at a different level of aggregation to the model(s) for Operations. The former may have a single entity type FIXED ASSET, which acts as a supertype for

2.	Different development views of the same data requirements (conceptual/ logical/ physical)	several separate entity types in the latter model(s) (e.g. BUILDING, VEHICLE, MACHINE TOOL). Example: the Design model for Operations divides the data into geographical partitions, whereas the Requirements model ignores this division.

The crucial point about equivalent structures is that there is an exactly specified transformation from one to the other. (One possible way of specifying these links is through an SQL-like language, similar to the way relational views are specified. Alternatively, some diagrammatic specification may be possible.) Typical transformations are:

(i)   Aggregating several entity types in one model to a single entity type in the other model.
(ii)   Various forms of normalization and denormalization, such as collapsing a relationship with another entity type in one model to a simple attribute in the other model.
(iii) Objects that are derived in one model may become basic in the other model (because the objects they are derived from are absent from the second model).

Depending on how the link is going to be used, it may be necessary to be able to specify the transformation in both directions, or only in one direction. For example, it may only be necessary to specify a one-way transformation from logical to physical, without specifying the reverse transformation from physical to logical.

3. Alternative structures

There are five main reasons why the systems developer may be interested in alternative structures:

1.	Local variants in requirements	Example: European address formats versus US address formats. Different local algorithms for calculation of sales tax or value-added tax.
2.	Local variants in implementation/ technology	Example: physical models tuned for different technical platforms, or for different volumes/ usage patterns.
3.	Replacement of old versions with new versions	Example: the business intends to replace historical costing algorithms with standard costing algorithms. This change will need to be rolled out systematically, but not necessarily simultaneously in all areas.
4.	Alternative structures already exist for historical reasons	Example: an organization with 30 existing integrated CASE-developed systems merges with another organization with 20 existing

integrated CASE-developed systems. Both organizations have a CASE-generated invoicing system, representing overlapping but different requirements. (Assume for the sake of this example that the two organizations have either used the same CASE tool, or two compatible CASE tools.)

5. Deliberate diversity   Example: in analysing business planning concept such as COMPETITOR or OPPORTUNITY, it may be dangerous if everyone in the organization adopts an identical viewpoint.

7.3.4 Illustrations

These concepts can be applied to the model coordination needs described in the previous two chapters. This section explores three: (1) database design (variations between conceptual, logical and physical), (2) multiple (business) requirements, and (3) multiple (overlapping) data stores (production models).

1. Vertical development coordination

In database design, technical experts define differences between the conceptual, logical and physical models to enable successful technical implementation on the chosen DBMS, and to optimize performance. The simplest way of managing this is through two CASE models: the Requirements Model unmodified by the database designers, and the Design Model with any necessary modifications.

There are eight possible mappings from the Requirements Model to the Design Model:

1. One-one mapping (same object type)   This is the normal case. A data object in the Requirements Model corresponds exactly to a data object in the Design Model.
In favourable circumstances, at least 95 per cent of the data model can be mapped one-to-one.

2. One-one mapping (different object type)   A data object in the Design Model corresponds to a single data object in the Requirements Model, but with a different object type. For example, an entity subtype in the Requirements Model is promoted to an entity type in the Design Model. Or a relationship in the Requirements Model is converted to a foreign key attribute in the Design Model (thus preventing the CASE tool from automatically preserving data integrity).

3. One-many mapping (same data store)   A data object in the Requirements Model corresponds to more than one data object in the

Design Model. This is usually when an entity type is split into two or more entity types. Either vertically (selection by attribute) or horizontally (selection by occurrence) or both. For example, to simplify processing of current transactions, historical data may be represented in separate tables. (This is an example of **horizontal partitioning**.) For another example, to enable security software to control data security on database tables, divide entity type PERSON into confidential and non-confidential attributes. (This is an example of **vertical partitioning**.)

4. One-many mapping (different data store)

A data object in the Requirements Model corresponds to data objects in more than one Design Model, which will result in duplicate implementation in more than one data store.

This will be required when several separate data stores are to be implemented, since some cross-reference tables will be needed to link the data together.

Another common example is the implementation of separate (parallel) data stores for transaction processing and for *ad hoc* enquiry.

5. One-zero mapping

A data object in the Requirements Model is not included in the Design Model, because it is not planned to implement this object in the current release.

6. Zero-one mapping

A data object is introduced in the Design Model that does not correspond to anything in the Requirements Model. This may be a design entity type or attribute, or a redundant relationship. For example, date-stamp attributes. For another example, tables of next identifiers.

7. Many-one mapping

One data object in the Design Model corresponds to more than one data object in the Requirements Model. For example, several trivial entity types are merged into a single entity type, to simplify access or prevent wastage of disk space.

8. Many-many mapping

Complex combinations of the above.

2. Horizontal development coordination

Two projects are exploring and developing requirements for similar or overlapping concepts, which we can think of as multiple requirements on what might appear to be the same entity type. For example, two projects are developing systems for departments which have different concepts of GEOGRAPHICAL AREA (see Figure 7.5).

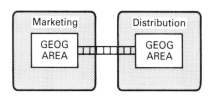

Figure 7.5
Is this the same entity type?

Although the attributes and relationships are similar, the occurrences are different. Marketing divides the United States into ten areas, while Distribution divides the United States into three areas. We may assume this is for excellent business reasons: Marketing would lose focus if it had fewer areas, and Distribution would lose efficiency if it had more areas. Therefore the two projects cannot just get together and unilaterally impose a single concept of GEOGRAPHICAL AREA on both departments.

The required approach is more subtle:

1.   Declare the two versions of GEOG AREA as *variant alternatives*. This means analysing exactly how far the variation extends.
2.   Analyse the consequences of the variation. Does it matter? Would there be any benefit in reducing the extent of the variation, or eliminating it altogether?
Either 3(a). Define new versions of each variant that will be closer together. (In other words, with smaller variation extent.)
or 3(b).   Define a consolidated version that will replace both. (This might be identical to the present version of one or other variant, but usually will not be.)
Either 4(a). Migrate to the new version(s).
or 4(b).   Declare equivalence between the old version(s) and the new consolidated version.

3. Production coordination – multiple data stores

A system is a set of procedures (automated and manual) with access to one or more public data stores. In Information Engineering and similar data-sharing methodologies, a system does not normally have its own private data stores.

A data store is a collection of data that must be implemented together, on a single machine. In planning we define a logical data store in terms of subject areas and/or entity types. During the requirements definition phase, we refine the scopes of the logical data stores, whose contents are now defined down to the attribute level. In some projects, we may carry out distribution analysis during the detailed analysis phase, to define vertical data partitions, based on geographical or organizational divisions.

During the construction phase of the project, physical data stores are defined from the logical data stores, consisting of tables and indexes. It is usually advisable to manage the data as several physical data stores, for housekeeping and security purposes. (Metaphorically, these are firewalls, designed so that one data integrity problem does not bring the whole company to its knees.) There may be a one-to-one mapping from logical data store to physical data store, or then again there may not.

With client/server, different data stores may be implemented on different platforms. However, currently available DBMSs do not support a single data store being divided across platforms.

All data stores should normally be accessible by all systems, unless there are specific operational requirements (such as security or performance) that demand more complicated structures. Such structures will usually be more expensive to build and maintain.

At a given time, there may be three types of data store:

1.   Data stores generated by the CASE tool, and maintained using CASE-generated code.
2.   Data stores not generated by the CASE tool, but in a form that is accessible by the CASE tool. For example, if the CASE tool can generate relational database tables, it may also be able to access relational database tables created and populated before the acquisition of the CASE tool. (To achieve this, it may be necessary to create CASE models by reverse engineering, which then enables CASE-generated code to access these data stores.)
3.   Data stores that are not implemented in a form that is directly accessible by CASE-generated code. (For example, some CASE tools can only access data in relational databases, and have no automatic interface to prerelational databases such as IMS/DB.) However, these data stores may be accessed using handwritten code called as a subroutine by CASE-generated programs.

Inevitably, there will be relationships between entity types in one data store and entity types in another data store. To implement these relationships, there will have to be some duplicate data somewhere, either a table of record identifiers in one or both of the data stores, or a cross-reference table in a third (link) data store, as shown in Figure 7.6.

In some cases, the desired sequence in which the data stores will be implemented forces the decision about the location of these duplicate data, since it is often impractical to alter the data structure of an existing data store.

Data integrity between the data stores must (at present) be maintained by handwritten code. There are several design alternatives:

1.   Real-time update and integrity check
2.   Real-time update, off-line integrity check and clean-up
3.   Off-line update and integrity check

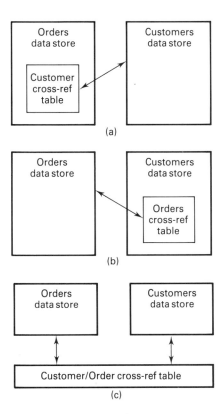

Figure 7.6
Relationship between
data stores – three
possible structures

Obviously alternative 1 is the best, but may be impractical for performance or network reasons. In the past, batch processing has often been necessitated by such reasons. Among designers habit dies hard, and even now some systems are designed for batch operation, when real-time update may be perfectly feasible.

7.3.5 Possible structure

Figure 7.7 shows a possible structure for the horizontal and vertical links between models.

Vertical links must be identical or equivalent structures. Horizontal links may be alternative structures.

If we have hundreds of working models, there will be thousands of links. To reduce the number of links, we can introduce local hubs and define links via these hubs rather than directly between working models. We call these hubs **common object models**.

(We have already seen the benefit of common object models to development coordination, in allowing asynchronous coordination between projects in parallel. Now we see an additional benefit: reducing the complexity of the model network itself.)

Figure 7.7
Possible structure for
links between models

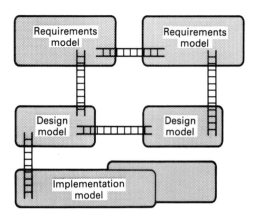

7.3.6 *Mechanisms*

The following rules need to be implemented, either in procedures or in automated tools, or a combination of both.

1.	Identical structure	Particular objects must remain identical across the two models. One model is defined to be the master source model for these objects. Any changes to the objects must be migrated to the other model. Changes to the other model are prohibited.
2.	Equivalent structure	The extent of the equivalence should be clearly scoped. The equivalence must be precisely specified. The custodian for the equivalence link will usually be the custodian of one of the models. The reason for the difference should be recorded.
3.	Alternative structure	The extent of the alternative should be clearly scoped. The reason for the difference should be recorded. Each model will usually have a separate custodian.

7.3.7 *Manageability*

There are practical limits to the number and complexity of different links that can be managed between models. Therefore, there will be some advantage in converting alternative links into equivalence links, and equivalence links into identical links, wherever possible.

However, the provision of automated support for these links should increase the number and complexity that can be managed. The main complication is probably the overlapping of extents.

7.3.8 Maintaining data integrity

1. Introduction

This section returns to the concept of consistency and compatibility between models. If two objects (or two object versions) are not identical, then in order for them to be compatible, there must be a logical transformation from one object/version to the other. The same transformation must then be obeyed by the respective systems.

2. Linked models

The alternative to packing all the analysis into a single model is to spread it across several models. This then raises the question: How do you tie the models back together?

The usual situation is that different areas of the business need to perceive things at different levels of generalization. There is a difference in perspective between the **lumpers,** who concentrate on the similarities, and the **splitters** who concentrate on the differences. When considering assets, for examples, accountants are lumpers ('treat all assets the same'), while production engineers may be splitters ('treat a furnace differently from a numerically controlled cutting tool').

Consider a fictional oil company. Transport strategists (producing long-term plans) regard oil pipelines and oil tankers as interchangeable, while transport schedulers (concerned with day-to-day logistics) regard them as entirely different. Thus we want two models: a 'lumper' model in which pipelines and tankers are occurrences of the same entity type, and a 'splitter' model in which they are occurrences of different entity types.

In my previous book it is explained how to establish a compromise between the lumper and the splitter, by using entity subtypes.[2] Thus if it is absolutely necessary (or strategically appropriate) for the transport strategists and the transport schedulers to share the same model, this can be done by defining an entity type TRANSPORT MEDIUM with two subtypes: VEHICLE and FIXED CHANNEL. Then the strategists can work with the supertype, while the schedulers work with the subtypes.

However, every time this is done, it makes the data model more complicated. We can consolidate two or three sets of requirements in a single model, but if we try to consolidate dozens of different requirements, at different levels of generalization, a single model becomes incomprehensible.

So what are the alternatives? If we have a 'lumper' model **L** and a 'splitter' model **S**, how are the two linked together? There are five possibilities:

1. **Linking by partition** – occurrences are added into the model **L** and are instantly available to model **S**.
2. **Linking by aggregation** – occurrences are added into the model **S** and are instantly available to model **L**.

3. **Linking by process (downwards)** – occurrences are added into the model **L** and are subsequently available to model **S**.
4. **Linking by process (upwards)** – occurrences are added into the model **S** and are subsequently available to model **L**.
5. **Complex linking** – some combination of the other four.,

3. Linking by partition

The two entity types VEHICLE and FIXED CHANNEL in **S** are defined through a partition of the entity type TRANSPORT MEDIUM in **L**. All occurrences of TRANSPORT MEDIUM in **L** (i.e. all occurrences relevant to **S**) automatically become occurrences either of VEHICLE or of FIXED CHANNEL in **S**.

In some cases, the occurrences of the entity type in the 'lumper' model **L** may be distributed among entity types in several 'splitter' models **S^i**, and control of the entity type is therefore via the 'lumper' model **L**, and the entity types in **S** are derived from **L**.

4. Linking by aggregation

The entity type TRANSPORT MEDIUM in **L** is defined as the aggregation of the two entity types VEHICLE and FIXED CHANNEL in **S**. All occurrences of VEHICLE and all occurrences FIXED CHANNEL in **S** automatically become occurrences of TRANSPORT MEDIUM in **L**.

In this case, control lies with the 'splitter' model **S**, and the entity type in **L** is derived from **S**.

This structure is often useful for modelling accounting and finance, where ledgers contain financial aggregations of non-financial transactions.

5. Linking by process

A process is defined to bridge between **L** and **S**. There will be some event causing the release of a given occurrence from one model to the other. This is appropriate where one model needs a longer life cycle than the other, or when some business control is required. For example, 'what if' products, subjects of research and development projects, may be of interest to the product planning and control function, but should be invisible to the product support function, and therefore absent from the product support model, not only to avoid confusion and clutter, but to prevent products being sold to customers prematurely (see Figure 7.8).

It may be that nobody is interested in the entire life cycle of an entity type. Each model may only contain a portion – these portions may or may not overlap, as required. Thus for most purposes, the personnel function does not want to be bothered with candidates or pensioners (see Figure 7.9).

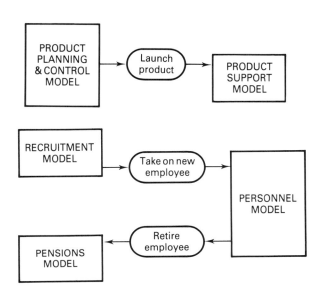

Figure 7.8
One model contains
more of the entity life
cycle of PRODUCT than
the other

Figure 7.9
Each model only
contains part of the
full entity life cycle of
EMPLOYEE

7.4 Model security

7.4.1 Shared object management

Project team A is given a model to work with, containing objects that are currently being modified by project team B. There is a plan to merge the two models at a future date, which means either that the versions of the objects may not be allowed to diverge, or that any divergence will have to be reconciled before the merge can be successful. Assuming that team B has the custodianship of the object, we need **locking protocols**, to define what team A may do with the object, and **refreshing protocols**, to define how team B's work is communicated to team A.

7.4.2 Locking protocols

There are three main possibilities:

1.	Strict (hard) locking	Team A cannot make any changes to the object in model A, although they can look at it, and possibly link other objects to it (i.e. create references to it). If team A requires any changes to the object, these must be carried out on its behalf by team B.	*Synchronous*
2.	Lenient (soft) locking	Team A can make changes to the object in model A, but is warned beforehand, and the change is notified to team B. Team A's changes are temporary and provisional, and must be ratified or authorized by team B, before they can become permanent.	*Asynchronous*
3.	Zero locking	Team A can make changes to the object in model A, which must be reconciled with team B's version, by negotiation between team A and team B.	

Hard locking means that if team A wants a change, not only the content but also the timing of the change have to be negotiated with team B. Team A's productivity may be affected, if team B cannot effect the change immediately. On the other hand, if team B must respond immediately to requests from team A, this affects team B's productivity.

Soft locking allows team A to go ahead with its own changes, as does zero locking. There is of course always a risk that the changes will not be ratified by team B, and the project manager of project A must decide whether this risk is acceptable.

7.4.3 Refreshing protocols

There are three main possibilities:

Synchronous

1. Instant refresh   When team B makes a change to the object in model B, this change is instantly transmitted to model A, thus becoming available to team A. If team A has made any changes to the object, team A's version will be archived, and team B's version put in its place. Team B can access model A, in order to view any links that team A has created to the object. Team B can delete the object from model B, and it will instantly and automatically disappear from model A.

Asynchronous

2. Delayed refresh   If team B makes changes to the object in model B, these changes are transmitted from model B to model A at a time convenient to both teams. Thus at any given time, team A may be working on an out-of-date version of the object.

3. Zero refresh   Changes are not transmitted from model B to model A. Differences are reconciled when models A and B are merged.

The 'instant refresh' protocol makes project A highly vulnerable to instability in model B. It forces team A to work with versions of objects that have not yet been properly analysed or tested by team B. Model A may suddenly and unexpectedly become incoherent as a result of changes from team B, making it impossible for team A to achieve its project deadlines. No project manager would accept responsibility for project A, without having either the ability to deny or delay changes from model B, or some influence over team B.

The 'delayed refresh' protocol allows team A to postpone receiving changes from model B. This protects team A's ability to meet short-term deadlines, such as important project checkpoints or implementation of subsystems. Of course, there is a risk that work done on out-of-date versions of objects will have to be revised or thrown away later. To reduce this risk, the project manager of project A will prefer, wherever possible, to accept changes from model B as soon as the changes have reached an adequate level of quality and stability. But this should be a decision for the project manager, whose judgement may be backed up by impact analysis and risk analysis.

The 'zero refresh' protocol has the advantage that the teams can (at least in theory) ignore one another during the parallel working stage. The reconciliation is carried out as a single task at the end. If the possible clashes between the two teams are trivial, this may be the most efficient option; however, this option carries the risk that the two models cannot be reconciled without substantial rework, which could then make it the most expensive option.

7.4.4 Implementing the protocols

The leading I-CASE tools, such as the IEF, provide partial support for these locking and refreshing protocols. (It is not the purpose of this book to describe the current facilities of such tools.) The facilities of these tools will need to be supplemented by team procedures, including liaison meetings. These procedures will usually need to be administered by a central development coordination group, which will (among other things) monitor the status and consistency of all models, administer the refresh schedule (if a delayed refresh protocol is adopted), carry out impact analysis, and help resolve clashes between teams.

7.4.5 Political pressures

There are many political strategies or 'games' available to the project manager, to increase the changes of project success. For example, some project managers abuse the soft locking or zero locking protocols, by deliberately building so much work on top of a provisional change to an object, that the team with nominal responsibility for the object will have no choice but to accept the change, since the overall cost of rejecting the change would be unacceptable. One of the main arguments for the hard locking protocol is that it eliminates such political strategies. Another political strategy is to bargain between project managers, to trade favours.

To be effective, a development coordination group needs to have enough political influence and skill to play the same games. We shall return to these political issues in the final chapter.

7.5 Administration

The management of coordination, whether done by central specialists or by projects themselves, requires a fair amount of accurate information. Who is currently doing what to which objects? Where is the latest version of that?, and so on. Many administrators are still trying to manage this information through complex paper systems, with form-based change control. Such paper systems quickly become unmanageable, and have to be at least semi-automated. In some technical environments, the necessary functionality may be provided by IPSE-like facilities, integrated (or at least interfaced) with the encyclopedia itself. Otherwise, stand-alone systems will have to be acquired or developed, preferably accessing a shared database of project and control information.

Some situations may demand fairly sophisticated audit trails, to track exactly what changes have been made to objects within the encyclopedia by different projects, and to verify that proper management procedures have been followed.

This whole area is one where the reader is entitled to expect fairly hot competition between the CASE and ISPE vendors over the next few years. It is not possible here to provide an accurate forecast of these technical developments; details of the current state-of-the-art should be sought directly from these vendors.

7.6 Summary of chapter

In this chapter, we have looked at the kinds of link that can be established between models. The management of these links in the models, and in the systems built from the models, provides the technical basis for the coordination of both development and production.

Notes

1.   H-J. Pels, 'Decentralized organizations versus integrated information systems', *Proceedings of International Conference on Organization and Information Systems,* Bled, September, 1989, pp. 177–90.

2.   R. Veryard, *Information Modelling: Practical guidance,* Hemel Hempstead: Prentice Hall, 1992, p. 170.

8 Management

8.1 Introduction

This final chapter is about the management and administration of coordination. It includes some guidelines on suitable coordination mechanisms, and the implementation of organizational and technical support for coordination. It also covers such related issues as quality management.

8.2 Increasing formalization

In this book, we have looked at the problems of coordinating and integrating information models resulting from the analysis of several business areas within the same organization.

As an organization grows older, larger and more complex, it tends to become more formal. 'Growth tends to generate a reduction in the frequency and comprehensiveness of personal contacts among the key members of the original core group and between the original and new people in the system. This condition tends to result from the physical distance and organizational subdivisions which usually accompany increases in size.'[1] The first sign of this is often a formalization of information systems.[2]

This is confirmed by Mintzberg,[3] whose model we shall examine in more detail later in this chapter. He argues that an organization tends to require different coordinating mechanisms as the environment's demands on the organization change. These assertions seem also to apply to subsystems within an organization, both activity systems and departments. (In this case we can regard the enterprise itself as a major component of the environment in which such a subsystem operates.)

Information management (IM) may be viewed either functionally or by department; in an abstract functional view, information management includes all activities supporting the enterprise, which need not be carried out by full-time members of an IM department. (Thus the steering committee for an information systems development project is included or excluded, depending on which view we take.)

Thus the Mintzberg model predicts increasing formalization within information management, as the use of computer systems spreads within an enterprise, and as the average age of the software in use increases.

This increasing formalization is also predicted by a well-known and simple model of the evolution of information management within an organization. According to Nolan,[4] information management passes through six stages of growth; as an organization grows more mature, its information systems become more integrated and better managed.

This is also a feature of various generic and specific maturity models. Increasing attention in software quality circles is being paid to the process maturity model emanating from the Software Engineering Institute (SEI, see Box 8.1), based on generic work by Philip Crosby[5] and specific work by Watts Humphrey.[6] Parallel models have been developed by Bill Curtis[7] and Gerry Weinberg.[8]

Box 8.1
Levels of maturity

Model Level	Management Attitudes	Software Process	How we treat people	Congruence between what is said and done	
1	Uncertainty	Initial	Herded	Variable:	'We do whatever we feel like at the moment.'
2	Awakening	Repeatable	Managed	Routine:	'We follow our routines, except when we panic.'
3	Enlighten-ment	Defined	Tailored	Steering:	'We choose among our routines by the results they produce.'
4	Wisdom	Managed	Institution-alized	Anticip-ating:	'We establish routines based on our past experience with them.'
5	Certainty	Optimizing	Optimized	Congruent:	'Everyone is involved in improving everything all the time.'
Author:	Crosby	Humphrey	Curtis	Weinberg	

In general, these models can be used in three ways:

1. To provide a vision of excellence, towards which organizations may be motivated to progress.
2. To provide a yardstick, to enable organizations to measure their current level of maturity.

3. To provide the basis for short-term action planning, to identify improvement actions needed by a given organization at a given time.

In addition to attempting to increase their level of maturity, many IM organizations are starting to implement formal quality systems. There has been much talk recently about quality standards; these include generic standards such as the ISO 9000 family, as well as software-specific standards such as the TickIT scheme originated in the United Kingdom.

8.3 Culture and mechanism

8.3.1 Introduction

What organization structure, policies and procedures are appropriate for achieving an appropriate level of coordination? How does the Information Coordinator deal with the variety of expectations (often unrealistic) about coordination, encountered from different stakeholders?

Different organizations have different structures and cultures, and this has an important impact on IS coordination. An approach that would work well in a highly centralized organization may have no chance of success in a decentralized organization. Small organizations may coordinate by direct personal contact; large organizations may coordinate through full-time internal liaison officers, or through elaborate networks of middle managers.

This section discusses alternative approaches to coordination in organizations, and shows how the IS coordination function should be designed to match the coordination style of the organization as a whole.

8.3.2 Eight mechanisms

The following table (Box 8.2) shows eight possible coordination mechanisms, each appropriate to organizations facing different situations: the third column states the most appropriate coordination mechanism for an organization facing such a task in such an environment, and the fourth column provides a convenient label for an organization thus coordinated. All but two of these coordination mechanisms are taken from Mintzberg's book on organization structure.[9]

This table can be used in several ways.

1. To choose the best coordination mechanism to control a given task in a given environment.
2. To identify a need to stabilize the environment or simplify the task, in order that a given coordination mechanism has a chance of working.
3. To predict or explain a failure of coordination, in the event of a severe mismatch.
4. In complex situations requiring a combination of mechanisms, to identify which mechanism should be dominant.

The table shows us that different coordination mechanisms will be appropriate for

Box 8.2
Alternative
coordination
mechanisms

Environment	Task	Coordination Mechanism	Organization can be characterized as:
Stable and predictable	Complex	Standardize skills	Professional bureaucracy
	Simple Diverse	Standardize procedures	Machine bureaucracy
		Standardize norms (indoctrination)	Missionary
Moderately dynamic	Complex	Standardize inputs (common components)	Engineering culture
		Standardize through tools	
Dynamic or unpredictable	Complex	Mutual adjustment (collaboration)	Adhocracy
	Simple	Direct supervision (centralization)	Simple structure
Multiple	Diverse	Standardize outputs (divisionalization)	Divisional form

organizations of different types. In fact, managers responsible for these matters have not always chosen the most suitable mechanism for their own situation.

A variety of expectations (often unrealistic) abound about coordination. Some people seem to think that an integrated CASE tool guarantees integration and consistency, as if the standardization of procedures or outputs resulted automatically from using the CASE tool. In other IS development organizations, a standards manual, enforced through quality inspections, is expected to achieve standardization of outputs, and possibly standardization of procedures as well.

Although some CASE tools may be designed to support particular coordination mechanisms, there is usually considerable flexibility in the use of the CASE tool within the organization. Different mechanisms will be appropriate for organizations of different types.

The key question raised by Mintzberg's model is how stable or dynamic information management is within the organization. The table can be used here in two ways.

1. To examine the present situation of information management within the organization, choose the development coordination mechanism (or combination) that best fits this situation, and devote our energies to implementing this mechanism.
2. To strategically alter the situation of information management, by changing its

relationship to the enterprise in which it is embedded (environment), and/or by changing its development programme (task), so that a different coordination mechanism can be implemented. This could take place when an Information Strategy Plan (ISP) is created, since it predicts the demands on information management from the rest of the enterprise. By increasing stability, we enable coordination by standardization of skills and/or procedures. (Some ISPs have achieved this, although it is certainly not their prime purpose.) However, even a good ISP cannot reduce all uncertainty (either business-driven or technological), especially where the intention is to develop strategic information systems.

8.3.3 IS coordination styles

1. Standardization of skills

Standardization of knowledge and skills is achieved through training, sometimes supplemented by formal qualifications. Professionals are capable of handling fairly complex situations in a reasonably predictable way – predictable to other professionals, that is. Well-established professions maintain national or international consistency, and have elaborate procedures to adjust their skills as the world changes. Software engineering cannot yet claim this, but can attempt consistency of skills within a single IS department.

Communication channels are important – one of the reasons why liaison between professionals may sometimes be a more effective coordination mechanism than liaison between line managers is that professionals have a common skills base and terminology, perhaps even a common culture, which improves communication between them. However, this advantage is often outweighed by the greater communication distance which professionals may have to the key decision-makers within the organization. Therefore, for professionals to be effective in such situations, they need good channels of communication with client decisions-makers.

2. Standardization of procedures

If a procedure is mechanical, leaving no room for human discretion, then it might as well be carried out by a machine. There is nothing further to coordinate, until and unless the procedure itself needs to change.

What is more interesting is where the procedure needs to be intelligently interpreted and applied. The procedure should increase the likelihood of similarity between similar things, but will not guarantee this.

3. Standardization of norms (indoctrination)

Common values promote homogeneity. Some consultancy companies elevate certain design or organizational principles to the status of ideological or quasi-religious credos. Thus if everyone believes fervently in a particular form of normalization, or a particular form of user participation, this itself will cause convergence on the orthodox form.

Some areas are more susceptible to this approach than others. People can have passionate arguments about normalization, or the need for a definition of PERSON to extend from cradle to grave. Fewer people can get very excited about the 'right' sequence of options on a menu, or whether 20 characters will be sufficient length for a given attribute. They may be more or less enthusiastic about the need for agreement, but the agreement itself is arbitrary.

Indoctrination is very useful for things that are not going to change, but can be disastrous where evolution may be needed.

4. *Standardization of inputs*

A library is provided of standard building blocks. These may be templates, that are to be taken and modified, or fixed components that are to be used without local modification.

If a fixed component is made compulsory, there is no further design decision to make. There is nothing to coordinate, because the machine can automatically include the component in a standard way. What is more interesting is where there is intelligent selection and adaption of the component in question.

The pattern approach recommended by the architectural theorist Christopher Alexander for designing buildings can also be regarded as somewhere between the standardization of inputs and the standardization of procedures. A pattern is a template rule, that solves a design problem in a standard yet flexible way. For example, he describes patterns that define the preferred ways that natural light should enter a room. He deliberately stops short of dictating the shape and size of the window, but he provides a rule-of-thumb that prevents the designer producing something inappropriate or incoherent. For another example, he describes a pattern called ENTRANCE TRANSITION, which defines the characteristics of a good doorway, without dictating what the designer has to do in order to produce a doorway with these characteristics.

In information systems likewise, we could define a set of patterns that would create a common look-and-feel for the user interface. Each screen would be different, and yet there would be a coherence about the system, because the patterns would inform the designer what properties each screen should have. By following the set patterns, every update transaction would give the user the confidence that the correct updates had been made to the database. (Some of this is provided by CUA standards, but local patterns will often need to be added to this.)

5. *Standardization through tools*

To the man with a hammer, everything looks like a nail.

At the very least, some homogeneity of appearance will be promoted by the use of a given tool. However, as stated above, there is usually considerable flexibility in the use of the CASE tool. This is therefore not likely to be an adequate mechanism on its own.

6. Mutual adjustment (collaboration)

This is the core of the informal network approach to development coordination. Direct liaison between project managers results in an appropriate level of consistency, at least in the strategic areas.

Some IS development organizations start out with external consultants directly supervising one or more systems development project. Coordination between projects is assumed to result from mutual adjustment by the consultants themselves, together with the supposition that the consultants all have identical knowledge and skills. There are three problems with this approach. First, it relies on the consultants having enough time and proximity for real coordination to take place. Second, it raises concerns about the authority exercised by the consultant, since these coordination decisions often have major business implications. Third, there is often no sensible migration path away from reliance on the consultants, since internal staff may not be capable of mutual adjustment, and management may not be capable of the same quality of supervision.

7. Direct supervision (centralization)

A single architect makes all important design decisions. Various approaches have been suggested to enable one person to perform this function, going back to the idea of the Chief Programmer Team in the 1970s.

The great weakness of this approach is the reliance on one person. As problems increase in scale and complexity, the number of people capable of properly fulfilling this role dwindles.

8. Standardization of outputs (divisionalization)

If the products of systems development are specified sufficiently precisely, in terms of their forms, formats and other qualities, then the methods of arriving at these products can vary from one part of the organization (division) to another, without this actually mattering very much. The definition of standard interfaces between systems also fits this category.

8.4 Politics of coordination

Why does coordination occur? It may be demanded top-down, or it may result from bottom-up action. Top-down demands alone will probably not achieve true coordination, if there is no motivation from below. Neither will bottom-up action alone achieve true coordination, if there is no senior management commitment. (The literature of management science contains both assertions and denials of the need for senior management commitment, for the implementation of all kinds of strategies. However, these often derive from one-sided research. Many technocrats, such as Owen,[10] expect top management to provide the commitment for change. In contrast, Alexander[11] interviewed top management, who opined that their own support and backing were a less critical success factor than the commitment and involvement of their employees.)

So what is the situation with regard to Information Coordination? Senior management often want coordination more than middle or junior management do. This may be for three reasons:

1. They are the ones that reap the direct benefits.
2. They perceive an issue as settled as soon as they have agreed a strategic direction, whereas lower management does not perceive an issue as settled until the details are sorted out. People are often more motivated to avoid loss than to achieve gain.

    This explains the usually negative reaction from senior managers when they are told that their strategies cannot be fully achieved, thanks to some technical difficulties at the lower levels. It is because they have already counted their chickens as hatched.
3. Senior management does not directly experience the pain of coordinating.

However, senior management may take coordination for granted, and thus be less worried about it than lower management. Since motivation (to any action) requires both a desire for the ends and an understanding of the means, then true organizational motivation will only result from a meeting of minds between those that want and those that understand.

1. Coalition theory

There are two puzzles associated with coordination. One is why everyone pays lip service to it, and the other is why it does not happen.

We start with four propositions about change in social situations, offered by Jon Elster.[12]

1. *If the actors in a situation perceive that they are behaving in a contradictory manner, they will try to organize themselves for the purpose of overcoming the contradiction.* In other words, people value consistency, and will be motivated to achieve it (although not necessarily above all other goals).
2. *The probability of success in the attempt at organization varies inversely with the communicational distance between the members.* Because contradictions are resolved by communication, the closer the people the better the liaison. Note that 'distance' is not merely a geographical concept: cultural barriers may increase distance, while good and well-implemented technology can reduce it.
3. *The probability of success in the attempt at organization varies inversely with the rate of turnover in group membership.* Both the awareness of contradictions, and the ability to do something about them, grow over time. New individuals or teams are less likely to have the insights, and the personal contacts, to resolve contradictions. However, this is not a linear calculation. 'The existence of a hard-core minority of permanent members may do more for solidarity than a larger mean duration with a small dispersion about the mean.'[13]

4.   *The probability of success in the attempt at organization varies inversely with the irreversibility of the contradictions.* This simply means that when the actors finally agree on a cooperative strategy, it may already be too late.

The obvious conclusion from this is that communication channels are important. This is a major focus of organizational change for the coordinator.

2. Coalition tactics

One way to achieve multiple changes is to establish a coalition between the groups favouring each change. Then the forces for change can be added together. What are the circumstances that favour such coalitions?

1.   One possibility is that the changes are entirely independent (orthogonal) of one another. The coalition is an entirely political entity, formed to exchange support. Each group is disinterested in the changes supported by the other groups, but exchanges supporting these changes for being supported in turn to carry out its own favoured change. This is known as **log-rolling**.
2.   More frequently, the changes are somehow linked. Then some coordination is required. The changes must be more or less compatible. Sometimes this leads to compromise, to water down or amend a change in order to gain the support of another group.

We can speak of coalitions as if they were represented by distinct groups of people. However, in the modern organization, the groups may overlap. Indeed, changes may be carried out by the same person, wearing different hats. However, it suits us to speak as if each set of (abstract) forces were represented by an army unit or SWAT team.

It is a useful metaphor for complex change, to regard the forces for change as if they were all interested parties or stakeholders. We can then look for positive-sum negotiations between the coalescing forces. An abstract model of such negoti-ations is provided by mathematical game theory,[14] which considers the commun-ications between players, both to establish coalitions and to establish shares of costs and benefits between players. We saw in Chapter 3 how coalitions can form for planning purposes; here we are interested in coalitions for implementing coordination policies. Similar issues arise in both cases.

Game theory offers some insights on the optimal size of a coalition, which can be applied to the resolution of two contradictory desires: for consensus and effectiveness. Some sociologists have argued that the ideal coalition should be as small as possible (measured either as its number of members or as its access to resources), consistent with achieving power.[15] We can express this in party political terms as follows: a coalition with 55 per cent of the seats in parliament will tend to have greater internal coherence – and therefore be more effective – than a coalition with 85 per cent of the seats. For organizational politics, the key message is **just enough consensus**. In other words, if you have to convince **every** member of the organization, before you can start changing **anything**, this may inhibit all coordinated action.

Both in party politics and within an organization, coalitions are essentially unstable. Thus they may be suitable as (tactical) transitional devices, to obtain momentum, but they are not reliable as long-term (strategic) supports for irreversible changes. The manager using coalition tactics must have a clear view on the length of time, and at what cost, the coalition can be held together. The Information Coordinator must attempt to build permanent coordination structures; coalitions may be used as scaffolding during the building process, but should perhaps then be dismantled.

3. Promoting cooperation

Mathematical game theory can be used not only to analyse coalition politics but other phenomena also. The political scientist Robert Axelrod demonstrates that frequent interactions between people help to promote stable cooperation. He argues that this is found in hierarchical bureaucracies.

> Hierarchy and organization are especially effective at concentrating the interactions between specific individuals. A bureaucracy is structured so that people specialize, and so that people working on related tasks are grouped together. This organizational practice increases the frequency of interactions, making it easier for workers to develop stable cooperative relationships. Moreover, when an issue requires coordination between different branches of the organization, the hierarchical structure allows the issue to be referred to policy makers at higher levels who frequently deal with each other on just such issues. By binding people together in a long-term multilevel game, organizations increase the number and importance of future interactions, and thereby promote the emergence of cooperation among groups too large to interact individually. This in turn leads to the evolution of organizations for the handling of larger and more complex issues.[16]

However, similar levels of familiarity and cooperation may also emerge in other forms of organization, including matrixes and informal networks.

8.5 Measuring and controlling coordination

8.5.1 Introduction

To manage coordination, it would be useful to be able to measure coordination activity, not merely by the amount of time and effort that it consumes, but also by the quantity and quality of what it achieves (see Box 8.3).

Box 8.3
Why measure?

* Track/reward achievement
* Produce resourced plans
* Set/achieve business goals

With such measures, it becomes possible to measure the productivity or efficiency of coordination activity, to compare different approaches, and to make improvements to the coordination function, including investment in tools or additional staff. Without such measures, planning becomes subjective or arbitrary.

However, there are no commonly accepted measures of coordination. Each organization has to develop its own. This section discusses some of the possibilities.

8.5.2 Development productivity

There are now some commonly accepted measures of the productivity of systems development, so let us look briefly at these before attempting to define coordination measures.

The concern about development productivity can be addressed by function points.[17] Development activity is measured by the number of function points contained in the developed system. If the number of function points can be estimated in advance, the total development effort can be estimated by multiplying by a standard productivity factor. When the project is completed, the actual effort can be compared with the estimated effort; any variance can be divided into a functionality variance (i.e. producing more/fewer function points than originally estimated) and a productivity variance. Alternatively, a development project can be function-boxed (i.e. constrained to developing a pre-agreed number of function points) or time-boxed (i.e. constrained to consuming a pre-agreed amount of resource-time). The productivity of such function-boxed or time-boxed projects can also be estimated in advance, and measured in arrears.

8.5.3 Complexity measures

One possible measure for coordination effort already exists in the McCabe Complexity measures, formulated by Thomas McCabe.[18] This measures the internal complexity of a module, or the collective complexity of a module hierarchy. It is used to estimate (among other things) the expected effort for testing and maintenance of software components.[19] It therefore seems possible to formulate a version of the McCabe Complexity measure to assess the amount of hierarchical complexity between systems, and therefore (implicitly) between the projects developing these systems.

However, the McCabe Complexity measure ignores other dimensions of complexity, such as data structure and physical distribution.[20] We therefore also need a measure of the complexity of a network diagram, such as an entity-relationship diagram, and of physical network structures such as a database or LAN.

8.5.4 Coordination productivity

To measure the efficiency of technical coordination, we need to be able to quantify the achievements of coordination activity in a reasonably standard way. This measure is defined similarly to function points, and is called **coordination points**. It suffers from most of the imperfections of the function point measuring system (which we do not need to spell out here), plus some additional issues. It is therefore a very crude measure. However, any measure is better than none.

Coordination points is a composite measure derived from quantitative measures of the following:

1.   Amount of object reuse – i.e. number of objects shared between systems/projects, number of times each object shared. The higher these numbers, the greater the coordination achieved.
2.   Amount of system reuse – i.e. number of users and/or organization units and/or locations using the same versions of the same systems. The higher these numbers, the greater the coordination achieved.
3.   Stability of reused and shared objects – i.e. number of times each shared object is altered, and the size of impact of any changes. The lower these numbers, the greater the coordination achieved.
4.   Number of times a given item of information is transformed or re-keyed during the business process chain. The lower these numbers, the greater the coordination.

As yet, unfortunately, no useful standard has been defined for comparison of coordination points between different organizations. This awaits further definition and calibration.

8.5.5 *Controlling coordination activity*

Perhaps you want to keep bureaucracy and rigid uniformity in check. So you have to consider the control of the coordination function itself. How much diversity do you want, and how much are you getting? Is the degree of uniformity healthy, or do we want more/less? Is coordination achieving its mission? Are people made more or less productive by it? If so, by how much, and is it worth it? Is the technical coordination achieving visible enterprise coordination?

8.5.6 *Summary*

In this section, we have sketched the possible ways that the success or failure of coordination activities can be measured and controlled. This is an area where further research is needed. In the meantime, some provisional measures, even if subjective, must be formulated.

8.6 Implementing coordination

Information coordination tends to be a very difficult topic to present to the key decision-makers, especially at the early stages of projects or development programmes. The need for coordination becomes more visible during the typical project, but so does the cost, especially once things have started to go astray.

Managers are strongly tempted to say 'yes, we should have had coordination at the start, but it's too late now.'

When there is one (albeit large) project that is pioneering the use of Information Coordination within an organization, then the implementation of coordination mechanisms and tools is usually included in the budget for this project. This simplifies the coordination, but raises the danger that the coordination mechanisms will be skimped or slanted to the interests of the one project. Managers are not usually much motivated to make things easier for their successors.

A reduced communication distance between users and the information management organization appears to be a critical success factor. In the short term, we may prefer to exploit existing communication channels: in other words, we work around the mutual incomprehension of IM organization and user departments. In the longer term, we ought to develop new channels: in other words, break down the cultural barriers.

Both the communication distance and the staff turnover rate are significantly affected by the use of external consultants or contractors on development projects. This can be expected to affect the rate at which the organization can assimilate the new concepts and techniques. There may be a trade-off between using outsiders (to acquire knowledge and skills instantly but locally) and relying on insiders (thus acquiring knowledge and skills more slowly but more broadly).

Meanwhile, there is a perceived contradiction between two important principles of systems development. On the one hand, systems development should be under the control of the users, rather than controlled on their behalf by a disinterested (or even uninterested) IM department. There is therefore a deliberate shift in the power structure of the whole organization. But supporters of the IM department argue that it has (or ought to have) a greater incentive or ability than the user departments to make coordination work. They therefore oppose the power shift because it would reduce the success of development coordination.

Whether or not this contradiction is genuine, it raises serious issues for the implementation of Information Coordination. If it really is impossible to satisfy both principles at once, then you may have to make a choice, which one you prefer. If it is possible under certain conditions, then some effort may be required to create these conditions. And some effort may also be required to overcome the arguments of those who are convinced it will not work (or act as if they were so convinced).

One factor is the relative rate of turnover among users compared to IM staff. (In other words, who has to live with the consequences?) Is the IM organization in a stronger or weaker position to guarantee information coordination than the user departments?

The need for coordination becomes more visible as the problems increase. This raises a contradiction for technical experts: if we wait until management demands coordination, it will be more successful since the organization will be more motivated. But our professional responsibilities may be to introduce these ideas proactively. This may need much persuasion and mutual trust.

Implementing coordination requires five management steps:

1. Define situation and strategy.
2. Select mechanism(s) and policies.
3. Define procedures and metrics.
4. Acquire knowledge and skills.
5. Introduce progressively.

8.6.1 *Define situation and strategy*

As we established in Chapter 2, technical coordination should be subordinate to enterprise coordination. Therefore, before establishing specific coordination mechanisms and policies for the enterprise, we need to analyse the situation in which the enterprise finds itself, and the strategic drivers, which will in turn influence the appropriate level of coordination to be implemented (see Box 8.4).

Box 8.4
Key questions for determining strategic drivers

* Why is the organization this large?
* What are the strategic economies of scale/scope?
* What synergies does the organization rely upon?
* What opportunities for synergy (if any) are currently being missed?
* How does/should the organization maximize the experience curve advantages of its market share?

8.6.2 *Select mechanism(s) and policies*

The goal may well be to establish one or more organization units devoted to coordination, with defined scope, charter and powers.

If the charter of Information Coordination is solely to coordinate the Information systems and projects with one another, who will plan/coordinate/ synchronize the IS projects with the non-IS projects? Some coordination will usually be required outside Information Management, to liaise with corporate Human Resources, Quality Management, Procurement and other functions.

The coordination function(s) will of course need meaningful and measurable objectives. This is extremely important, not only for the sake of effective management , but also for the job satisfaction of the coordination staff. Systems developers and project managers are accustomed to delivering systems; this gives them something specific to be proud of at the end of the project. Moving into development coordination roles, the personal achievement is much less clear cut. I have often heard the complaint from such people, that they no longer had specific achievements to point to or look forward to. Sometimes their former colleagues in systems development projects now see them as more hindrance than help. All the more reason for those managing the coordination activity to ensure that the achievements of all coordination staff are planned in advance, and clearly visible afterwards, both· within the coordination team (direct feedback) and elsewhere in the IM organization.

Who are the 'customers' of the coordination function? Perhaps current systems development projects, perhaps future systems development projects (as laid out in the IS development plan). Certainly the coordination team needs to support these projects. But if the point of technical coordination is to achieve enterprise coordination, then the 'customer' of this activity is probably outside the IM function, and may even be the Chief Executive of the organization. The coordination policies need to be focused on defining and delivering benefits to the enterprise as a whole.

8.6.3 Define procedures and metrics

We have talked in earlier chapters about the techniques of Development Coordination and Production Coordination. These need to be defined and embedded into a set of methods. Some organizations will seek to formalize these methods, while others will seek to avoid bureaucracy as far as possible.

It is possible to swamp the coordination function with paper, possible to convert all coordination into a bottleneck, and possible to add administrative controls upon controls. No reader will expect me to recommend such an approach. However, it is useful to be clear not only what coordination activities will be carried out, but how they will be carried out, and how their success will be measured. Metrics (as discussed in the previous section) need to be selected and calibrated.

It is also useful to implement automated support for these coordination activities, either through the I-CASE tool or through stand-alone administration software.

8.6.4 Acquire knowledge and skills

There is a wide set of knowledge and skills required by the coordination team (see Box 8.5):

• Technical
• Negotiation/political/management
• Strategic/organizational development/change
• Business/commercial

Box 8.5
Knowledge and skills required for effective coordination

These are challenging requirements, and many IM organizations choose to place their best people into managing the architectures, and coordinating development and production. (Having read this far into the book, you deserve a little flattery!) It is sometimes possible to fill such positions by external recruitment, but the required combination of knowledge and skills is rare. It will often be necessary to put together a team of different talents and experience, mostly from within the organization, and provide training and/or consultancy to build up the team's collective expertise.

8.6.5 Introduce progressively

There are basic principles of organizational change, which apply here. Managers who expect overnight results are likely to be disappointed. Build capability gradually, don't run before you can walk, try out new procedures before imposing them across the board, allow staff to participate in planning the changes.

8.7 Summary of chapter

1. Whoever is responsible for Information Coordination must have good communication channels (direct or indirect) with the senior management of the business.
2. The perceived need for Information Coordination increases over time. But delay introducing it may incur costs and other risks.
3. In the short term, Information Coordination may need to be controlled by the existing IM organization. The ideal organization structure and responsibilities will depend on the situation, which may develop over time.
4. Because Information Coordination is aimed at achieving lasting consensus within an organization, and because coalitions are unstable, political coalition tactics are not usually appropriate.
5. The Mintzberg model can be used to design or select the appropriate coordination mechanism(s) for a given situation.
6. Coordination should be introduced step-by-step into an organization. Do not expect too much too quickly.

8.8 Summary of book

The traditional approach to computer systems development is less than ideal, because each system is designed and implemented as an isolated application. This tends to result in large inconsistencies or overlaps between systems, and unworkable interfaces between systems.

This is a collective failure, not an individual failure. An individual manager may well recognize the imperfection of his own systems, yet not have the resources to overcome this.

Methodologies such as Information Engineering are intended to remove this imperfection. Among other things, they offer a number of coordination mechanisms, including standardization of skills, work processes and outputs, as well as mutual adjustment processes. These coordination mechanisms (which are partially automated through the use of a good integrated CASE software tool), enable decentralization and professionalization of information management, thus helping an organization achieve integration of systems and technology without excessive centralization.[21]

The popular view of information coordination, as described in many standard textbooks on information systems planning and data administration, is that it is a central function, promoting homogeneity of data structures, data occurrences and data processing throughout an organization. Many organizations contain data administration groups, fighting fairly and sincerely for an increase in data sharing, under the stirring banner: *Information = Corporate Resource.*

But in many organizations, these worthy individuals seem to be fighting a losing battle. Despite hearing the slogan repeated by managers at all levels of the organization, and despite acquiring advanced tools supposed to facilitate coordination, they often feel their efforts as ineffectual as those of Sisyphus, whose punishment (for unspecified crimes) was to roll a heavy stone uphill, which would constantly roll back.

As we have seen in this book, the mission of centrally coordinated information systems, based on a single corporate data model, is not appropriate for all organizations. For decentralized organizations, and across networks of separate organizations, different styles of coordination are needed. Some of the concepts, tools and techniques are the same or similar, although some styles (especially open distributed processing) demand additional ones.

Consistency is contrary to nature, contrary to life. The only completely consistent people are the dead. (Aldous Huxley)

The important thing is to fit the style of information coordination to the requirements of the enterprise, and not to a fixed ideology. Sensitivity and flexibility are crucial. Coordination may be complex and difficult to achieve, but it is not necessarily made easier by being made over-simple.

Notes

1. R.E. Quinn and D.F. Andersen, 'Formalization as crisis: Transition planning for a young organization', in J.R. Kimberly and R.E. Quinn (eds.), *New Futures: The challenge of managing corporate transitions,* Homewood, IL: Dow-Jones-Irwin, 1984.
2. D. Miller and P. Friesen, 'Archetypes of organizational transition', *Administrative Science Quarterly,* 25, 1980, pp. 268–99.
3. H. Mintzberg, *The Structuring of Organizations,* Englewood Cliffs, NJ: Prentice Hall, 1979.
4. R. Nolan, 'Managing the crises in data processing', *Harvard Business Review,* March–April, 1979.
5. P.B. Crosby, *Quality is Free,* New York: McGraw-Hill, 1979.
6. W.S. Humphrey, *Managing the Software Process,* Reading, MA: Addison-Wesley, 1989.
7. B. Curtis, 'The human element in software quality', *Proceedings of the Monterey Conference on Software Quality,* Cambridge, MA: Software Productivity Research, 1990.
8. G.M. Weinberg, *Quality Software Management Vol 1: Systems thinking,* New York: Dorset House, 1992.
9. H. Mintzberg, *The Structuring of Organizations,* Englewood Cliffs, NJ: Prentice Hall, 1979.
10. A.A. Owen, 'How to implement strategy', *Management Today,* July 1982, pp. 51–3.
11. L.D. Alexander, 'Successfully implementing strategic decisions', *Long-Range Planning,* vol. 18, no. 3, 1985, pp. 91–7.
12. J. Elster, *Logic and Society,* Chichester: John Wiley, 1978, Chapter 5.
13. J. Elster, *op. cit.,* 1978, p. 146.

14. A useful introduction is H. Hamburger, *Games as Models of Social Phenomena,* San Francisco: W.H. Freeman & Co, 1979. The classic text is J. von Neumann and O. Morganstern, *Theory of Games and Economic Behavior,* Princeton, NJ: Princeton University Press, 1944.

15. See W.H Riker, *The Theory of Political Coalitions,* New Haven: Yale University Press, 1962, and W.A. Gamson, 'A theory of coalition formation', *American Sociological Review,* 26, 1961, pp. 373–82.

16. R. Axelrod, *The Evolution of Cooperation,* New York: Basic Books, 1984, Penguin edition, pp. 130–1.

17. A.J. Albrecht, 'Measuring application development productivity', *Proceedings of the IBM Application Development Joint SHARE/GUIDE Symposium,* Monterey CA, 1979, pp. 83–92.

18. T.J. McCabe, 'A complexity measure', *I.E.E.E. Transactions on Software Engineering,* vol. SE-2, no. 4, December 1976.

19. P. Mannino, B. Stoddard and T. Sudduth, 'The McCabe software complexity analysis as a design and test tool', *Texas Instruments Technical Journal,* March–April 1990, pp. 41–54.

20. N.E. Fenton, *Software Metrics: A rigorous approach,* London: Chapman & Hall, 1991.

21. C. Finkelstein, *An Introduction to Information Engineering,* Sidney: Addison-Wesley, 1989.

Index

accounting, 66
activities, key, in Information Architecture, 82
activity clustering, 98–100
adaptive view, 124–5
adhocracy, 5–6, 176
adjustment, mutual, 179
ADS, *see* Astrophysics Data System
Advanced Network Systems Architecture
 (ANSA), 45, 46, 65
affinity clustering, 93
agency costs, 26
aggregate objects, 158
Alexander, Christopher, 64, 89, 178
algorithms, 93
analysis, 13
ANSA, *see* Advanced Network Systems
 Architecture
application modules, 94
application templates, 55
assembly, of systems, 151–3
Astrophysics Data System (ADS), 45
asynchronous coordination, 130–1, 165, 169–70
attributes, 14, 83
Axelrod, Robert, quoted, 182

behaviour, consistency, 36
Berlin, Isaiah, 29–31
blackbox assembly, 152, 153
blackbox integration, 12
bonding costs, and agency costs, 26
bureaucracy, 3–5, 32, 176, 184
business functionality, as dimension of
 flexibility, 147–8
Business Process Reengineering (BPR), 8–11,
 60, 62, 141
Business Systems Architecture (BSA), 56, 58–9
 example, 57
business thinking, and alteration of business
 concepts, 145

cartels, 36
CASE, *see* computer assisted software
 engineering
central coordination team, 133
centralization
 and funding infrastructure, 67, 68–9
 and standardization, 179
change management, 134–5
chaos, and non-linearity, 33
chief programmer team, 179

class libraries, and object-orientation, 108
client-server technology, 10, 140–1, 150
cloudburst release, *see* release management
clustering, 89, 90–1, 101, 102–4
 alternative heuristics, 96–100, 101
 geo-political uses, 95–6
 and gravitational rule, 93
 and portfolio approach, 123
clusters, 91–3, 94–5
coalitions, 67, 68, 69, 180–2
coherence, 49, 90, 137
coherent structures, 56–7
common object models, and linkage between
 hubs, 127, 128, 130–1, 165
communication, 23
communication distance, 185
 see also logical distance
companies, 78–9, 81–2
complex systems development, uses, 14–19
computer assisted software engineering (CASE),
 115–16, 129, 134, 142
 models, 151, 156–7, 161–2
 two-level, 115
 technology, 54, 55
 tools, 14, 93, 113, 140, 141, 164
 and standardization, 178
 use, 136, 176
 see also integrated computer assisted software
 engineering
conceptual model, 112–14, 115, 135, 154
conflict, between users, and information
 coordination, 13
consensus, and cooperation, 33
consistency, 33, 35–6
constituencies, as clusters, 95–6
contradiction, as lack of coordination, 22
control, of information coordination, 182–4
cooperation, 33, 182
cooperative processing, uses, 140–1
coordination, 21–2, 24–6, 28–34, 41–2, 107
 management and administration, 173–88
 within/between projects, 16, 45–6
coordination, biological, 22–4
coordination, diagonal, 133–5
coordination loop, illustrated, 19
coordination, near, 28, 44
coordination points, 183–4
coordination, synchronous and asynchronous,
 130–1, 169–70
costing, standard, 7–8